HARLEM: THE MAKING OF A GHETTO

An honest question merits an honest answer. . . . The answer is, directly and bluntly: American whites and blacks both possess deep-seated resistances against the Negro problem being presented even verbally, in all of its hideous fullness, in all of the totality of its meaning. The many and various groups, commissions, councils, leagues, committees, and organizations of an interracial nature have consistently diluted the problem, blurred it, injected foggy moral or sentimental notions into it. This fact is as true of the churches as of the trade unions; as true of Negro organizations as of white; as true of the political Left as of the political Right; as true of white individuals as of black.

RICHARD WRIGHT, 1945

Harlem: The Making of a Ghetto

NEGRO NEW YORK, 1890–1930

By Gilbert Osofsky

Second Edition

ELEPHANT PAPERBACKS
Ivan R. Dee, Publisher, Chicago

HARLEM: THE MAKING OF A GHETTO. Copyright © 1963, 1965, 1966 by Gilbert Osofsky. This book was first published in 1966 and is here reprinted by arrangement with HarperCollins Publishers.

First ELEPHANT PAPERBACK edition published 1996 by Ivan R. Dee, Inc., 1332 North Halsted Street, Chicago 60622. Manufactured in the United States of America and printed on acid-free paper.

Library of Congress Cataloging-in-Publication Data:
Osofsky, Gilbert, 1935–
    Harlem, the making of a ghetto : Negro New York, 1890–1930 / Gilbert Osofsky. — 2nd ed., 1st Elephant paperback ed.
        p.   cm.
    Originally published: 2nd ed. New York : Harper & Row, 1971.
    "Elephant paperbacks."
    Includes bibliographical references and index.
    ISBN 1-56663-104-1
    1. Harlem (New York, N.Y.)—History. 2. Afro-Americans—New York (N.Y.)—History. 3. New York (N.Y.)—History—1898–1951.
    I. Title.
F128.68.H3086   1996
305.896'07307471—dc20   95-26633

TO MOM AND POP,
THE REAL SCHOLARS

Contents

Preface

The following pages will explore the history of the Negro community of New York City in the late nineteenth and early twentieth centuries. As the major development of these years was the emergence of Harlem as a Negro ghetto, I have entitled this study *Harlem: The Making of a Ghetto.*

In order to fully understand the importance of the creation of this ghetto its history must be set against the background of pre-Harlem Negro life in New York City. This in turn must be related to the radical changes in patterns of race relations that were taking place throughout America in the late nineteenth and early twentieth centuries. The rapid growth of Negro New York in these years created social problems and racial tensions unequaled since slavery days. The poverty, violence and segregation of these years were typical of the difficulties Negroes confronted in every major northern urban area in the twentieth century. Part One will describe these developments and place them within the framework of our national history, Part Two will explain how and why a white upper-middle-class genteel community became the largest segregated neighborhood in America, and Part Three will show how the ghetto became the slum it remains today.

I have also attempted to re-examine some major themes of American Negro history and urban history. It has been customary, for example, to begin discussions of northern Negro life with the Great Migration of World War I. Although this was certainly dramatic and important, significant Negro migration to northern cities began in the 1890's. Harlem was an important area of Negro settlement *prior* to the war. The Negro ghettos of Philadelphia and Chicago were also founded before World War I.

Accompanying the increase in Negro population was an intensification of discrimination and racial hatred. Negroes never had full equality in northern life, but there were a few periods of relatively decent race relations in our history. One such period occurred between 1870 and 1890. What made the racial antagonisms of the years after 1890 especially tragic is that they followed a time which seemed to promise improvement in the position of the Negro in northern cities. The hopeful signs of the earlier years, however, were replaced by myriad examples of racial alienation. The most glaring symbol of the changed racial relationships of these years was the development, for the first time in American history, of the large Negro ghetto—the Harlem. "Cities within the city" was what contemporaries aptly called them.

The early twentieth century was also a period of significant reform in all areas of American life—one of the major periods of reform in our history. It has been customary for historians to argue that the Negro was the one blind spot of the Progressive movement. In fact, some have written, Progressivism contained significant overtones of racism. Whatever the truth of the statement for the rest of the country, it certainly was not the whole truth for New York City. The fourth chapter will describe the very significant positive and hopeful response of this generation of municipal reformers and social workers to the problems created by rapid Negro urbanization.

The book ends with the Great Depression. This is a natural historical breaking point. Not only had most Negroes and Negro institutions come to Harlem then, but the entire country was made aware of the existence of this ghetto. Slumming parties visited Harlem cabarets to share its supposedly gay life. Intellectuals gloried in the imagined exotic and erotic lives that Harlem Negroes lived. "White folks," a Negro writer said, "discovered black magic there." And, while intellectuals and bohemians created an image of a semimythical dreamland north of Central Park, Negro Harlem became the most appalling slum in the entire city; the slum that has not changed significantly since the 1920's.

Three outstanding teachers and scholars have helped ease my way into the complexities of historical scholarship: Robert D. Cross, John Higham and Eric L. McKitrick. Professor Higham opened my eyes to the subtleties and beauties of American history and Professor Mc-

Kitrick helped keep them open. My greatest debt is to Professor Cross, an amazingly warm, sympathetic and gifted person, who advised, cajoled and directed me throughout the writing of this book. I hope his demands for intellectual independence are somewhat met in the pages that follow.

Ernest Kaiser and Jean Blackwell Hutson introduced me to the treasures of the Schomburg Collection, and dozens of other librarians went out of their way and occasionally stretched regulations to assist me in my research. I would like to thank the staffs of Columbia University's Oral History Research Office, the New York City Municipal Archives, the Archives of the New York City Hall of Records, the New-York Historical Society, the New York Public Library, Yale University's James Weldon Johnson Memorial Collection and the Manuscript Division of the Library of Congress. Some of the chapters in this book have been published in different form in *American Quarterly, Journal of Negro Education, Freedomways* and *New York History;* they appear here with the permission of the editors of these journals. A University of Illinois Faculty Fellowship and grants from the University's Graduate Research Board permitted me to complete my research. Folkways Records made a generous gift of Negro folk songs, excerpts of which appear throughout the book. Whatever the value of this book, its style and content have been considerably enhanced by the interest and effort of Jeannette Hopkins of Harper & Row. Mrs. Ida Cullen Cooper, Langston Hughes, Mrs. Gerri Major of Johnson Publishing Company and Joan Meinhardt of Harper & Row aided in the securing of illustrations. Marcia, Lisa Kate and Judith Aileen, my swinging family, helped make the work enjoyable and worthwhile.

GILBERT OSOFSKY

Preface to the Second Edition

When *Harlem: The Making of a Ghetto* was first published in 1966 it received as wide attention as any "scholarly" book could expect. Some one hundred reviews appeared in newspapers and journals throughout the country; my mail box was stuffed with letters from people who remembered this or that incident, person, or block; one correspondent even spotted his father among the marvelous faces that appear in the photograph of the Harlem Board of Commerce dinner in 1913. It was an engaging experience.

And lots of other folks had (and still have) advice to offer; a shade of interpretation here, some more comparative illustrations there, I was told, were just what the historian ordered. It was fascinating to meet people who wanted *my* book to be created in *their* image.

Some suggested *Harlem* failed to recognize fully the ethnic diversity of American life. As a professor who partially earns his keep by studying and teaching about immigration and race and cities, as one who grew up on the streets of a polyglot neighborhood in New York City, as someone whose father got off the boat to enter a garment industry sweat shop (and now lies buried with his fellow townsmen of Diveen), I never fully sympathized with that critique. My objection is not to a pluralist vision of American life—what rational human, what son of an immigrant, can deny that?—but to the way pluralism is sometimes used as a cloak for a *conservative* ideology.

No perception of the American past is accurate which insists on underemphasizing the special factors of color consciousness, color caste and racism. To insist that blacks are simply the most recent "ethnics" in the city is deficient history and deficient social commentary. It is deficient history because it ignores the fact that migrations to the North began in the first half of the nineteenth century; it is deficient history because it shunts aside institutional racism—such as the denial of suffrage to most native born Northern blacks in the 1840's and 1850's at the very moment the great masses of Irish and German immigrants were using political clout as a principal weapon of advancement and acculturation; it is deficient history because it depreciates the psychological implications of generations of color restrictions on the labor market; it is deficient history because it fails to analyze adequately the underpinings and implications of American racial values and mores. We are certainly "a nation of immigrants," but much else besides. And it is deficient social commentary because it doesn't explain why our cities are burning.

Of all the other comments that came down the pike at the time, the one that seemed most compelling dealt with the possibility of my writing a second volume. I had no intention of doing so and yet I wanted to make more explicit than I already had my *sense* of what an overview of the two centuries might look like. I decided that an interpretive and impressionistic essay was the form that best fit my needs and the logic of the questions at issue and so "The Enduring Ghetto" was written in the winter of 1966–67; and appeared in the *Journal of American History* in September 1968. It was part of the same conceptual vision that created *Harlem* and is now placed where it belongs in this second edition. That is the only important creative difference between this edition and the first. Books must have an integrity of their own and shouldn't be patched over each year with plaster of Paris intellectuality.

GILBERT OSOFSKY

September 1970

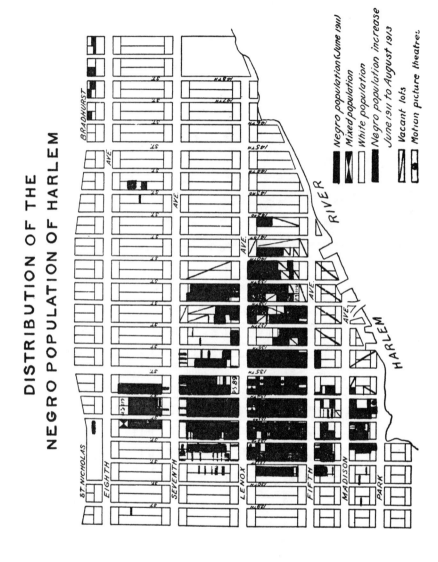

1. Black Harlem, 1911-1913. *New York City census.*

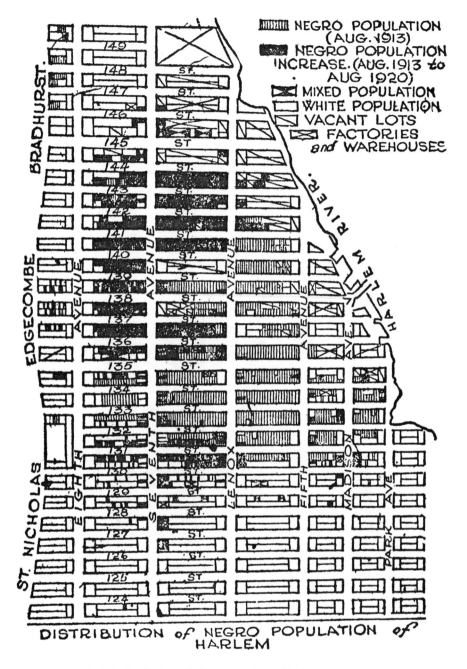

2. Black Harlem, 1913-1920. *New York City census.*

PRINCIPAL NEGRO AREA OF MANHATTAN, 1930

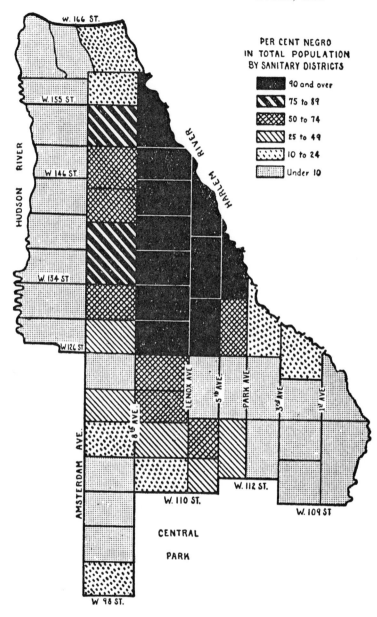

3. Black Harlem, 1930. *New York City census.*

PART ONE

The Negro and the City

CHAPTER 1

"No Crystal Stair": Negro New York, the 1890's

"Life for me ain't been no crystal stair."
—LANGSTON HUGHES, *Mother to Son*

I

In the early twentieth century Booker T. Washington made a tour of eastern and western Europe to study working-class life. He wanted to find "The Man Farthest Down," he said, to gauge the relative position of American Negroes with poor people elsewhere. Washington doggedly avoided museums, art galleries, cathedrals and palaces to mingle with the peasantry, urban industrial workers and miners. When he completed his journey he believed that American Negroes were much like "men at the bottom" throughout the world, and that the future seemed promising for all. "To the man in the tower the world below is likely to look very small," wrote Washington characteristically. However, he concluded, he never found "things as bad as they were advertised." Had Washington made an intensive survey of Negro New York in the late nineteenth and early twentieth centuries, he most certainly would have judged the colored man "The Man Farthest Down" in America's largest metropolis.[1] To have concluded that the situation contained significant signs of improvement would have been utopian. Negro life in New York City was certainly "no crystal stair" in the 1890's; nor had it ever been.

The 60,666 Negroes of New York City at the turn of the century were widely scattered throughout the five boroughs, but most heavily concentrated in Manhattan. Some 5,000 were foreign-born, from many islands in the Caribbean, but primarily from the British West Indies. Although they represented an exceedingly small portion of the general population, there were more foreign-born Negroes in New York City than in any other city in America. Approximately two-thirds of all the Negroes in New York State lived in the city, and of

3

these, more than half resided in Manhattan. There were considerably more Negro women in the population than men: "The excess of negro females," wrote Howard University professor Kelly Miller, "is a most striking feature of the Negro population in most of the large cities." In 1890 there were 810 Negro men for every thousand Negro women in New York City; in 1900, 809 for each thousand; in 1910, 850.[2]

This disproportionate number of women in the general Negro population, a reflection of the greater economic opportunities for Negro women in cities, created social problems of importance. Most Negro women in New York City were young and of marriageable age, but there were simply not enough men to go around: "In their hours of leisure," social worker Mary White Ovington recorded, "the surplus women are known to play havoc with their neighbors' sons, even with their neighbors' husbands, for since lack of men makes marriage impossible for about a fifth of New York's colored girls, social disorder results."[3] Nor did the typical married man earn enough money to support a family without the assistance of his wife. These conditions largely account for the fact that more than twice as many Negro women (59 per cent) in the city had to work to support themselves than did foreign-born (27.2 per cent) and native-born (24.6 per cent) white women. There was also, as W. E. B. DuBois noted in 1901, a high rate of illegitimacy among them.[4]

The greater financial stability of Negro women created serious social and psychological difficulties for Negro men. Forced reliance on female economic power minimized the sense of control and responsibility that Negro men had for their families, and often (more often than for other ethnic groups) led to disrupted or broken homes. This economic situation deprived Negro males of an essential symbol of full manhood. Family instability became a dominant characteristic of Negro urban life in the twentieth century.

Most of the Negro population in the 1890's worked at varieties of unskilled and low-paid jobs. The Negro middle class was quite small. The largest number, some 450, were clerks, followed, in descending order, by actors and actresses, musicians and music teachers, and small businessmen. A population of about 60,000 was serviced by only forty-two Negro physicians and twenty-six Negro lawyers. More than 90 per cent of the community, male and female, were employed as menials or laborers: servants, porters, waiters, waitresses, teamsters, dressmakers, laundresses, janitors and "laborers not specified" (as the census-takers termed it).[5]

Many members of the Negro community in the late nineteenth century believed that economic conditions had deteriorated since the Civil War. Samuel R. Scottron, an aged Brooklynite in the 1890's, a well-known inventor of household appliances, and a member of Brooklyn's Board of Education, spent a good part of his old age writing about the displacement of Negroes from occupations they supposedly dominated previously. "The ancient colored New Yorker didn't wait for some one to hire him," wrote Scottron, "he went at it alone and made a place for himself." "Think of our city's most famous caterers of forty or fifty years ago," he continued. "They were Downings, Watsons, Van Dykes, Ten Eycks, Drys, Greens and others, all colored. Their names were . . . representative of high class work. . . ." "In fact," Scottron concluded, "it would be quite difficult to name a livelihood in which [Negroes] had no representation." This, he and others bemoaned, was all gone now—"superseded by foreign white help"; "gone out of fashion."[6]

There was some truth in Scottron's observations. One of the key sources of wealth among New York Negroes in the nineteenth century was the catering business. Some caterers began as janitors in banking and business houses. At first they sold sandwiches and snacks to employees and eventually expanded their services to full-scale businesses. William H. Smith, for example, began as a janitor in the Bank of New York and died a comparatively wealthy owner of New York real estate. There were a handful of others with similar careers: Peter Van Dyke, Thomas Downing, Charles G. Bowser, David Roselle. Many of these people, and other members of the Negro middle class—small merchants, clergymen, journalists—lived in comfortable homes in Brooklyn, owned summer houses, and left substantial estates at their deaths. Their children often became lawyers, teachers, physicians, businessmen. "Had they been white," wrote Mary White Ovington, "they would have slipped into the population and been lost. . . ."[7]

These careers were far from typical of the general Negro population, however. They were the elite of the race, lived apart from the masses, and objected to being lumped together in the public image with lower-class Negroes. The small Negro middle class continually bemoaned the fact that white America refused to distinguish between different Negro social classes, and equated them with the "worst class [of the] great stream of rural immigrants from the South simply because they happen to be of the same race." "All Negroes are not alike," said one wealthy Negro in 1895. "There are various grades of colored people. . . . We are not to be judged by the street loungers and drunkards of our race."[8]

Scottron's memories, blurred by the passing of time, tended to overlook the poverty of the race as a whole in the nineteenth century. Many of the jobs he and others remembered as part of the glories of the past ("occupied almost exclusively by Negroes") were in domestic service: coachmen, chambermaids, waiters, chefs, footmen, valets. To employ Negro servants was a mark of stature among upper-class white families in the city in the nineteenth century. This was clearly a heritage of slavery when ownership of Negro slaves was a sign of social distinction. "The Nineties," records one New York historian, "saw about the last of the old family servants that were part of every well regulated menage among the elite of the city . . . as much fixtures to a house as the very walls themselves."[9] The passing of this slave tradition was then not an unmixed blessing. Nor, given the relatively small numbers of Negroes in New York City in the early nineteenth century, is it conceivable that they dominated even the service positions then: "Did the colored man have all this fifty years ago when they were only one and a half per cent of the population?" wrote a student of Negro life in the early twentieth century. "If so, there were giants in those days. . . ."[10] It was historically true that a disproportionate number of Negroes were employed as domestics in the city in the mid-nineteenth century but, in numbers, they ranked a far third behind Irish and German servants.[11]

Complaints of limited economic opportunities for Negroes, similar to Scottron's, were often made in the age he characterized as a period of prosperity. There was very little upward mobility among the majority of Negro New Yorkers in the nineteenth century: "The Negro American found it extremely difficult to rise above manual labor and domestic service," concludes one historian of New York City in the early nineteenth century.[12] When J. W. C. Pennington escaped slavery in Maryland and arrived in New York City in 1829, he was so shocked with the "misery, ignorance, and wretchedness of the free colored people" that he, the slave, devoted his life to "*their* elevation. . . ." (Pennington became a leading Negro clergyman and militant abolitionist.)[13] A teacher at a Negro school in 1830, Charles C. Andrews, wrote that the Negro student graduated "with every avenue closed against him which is open to the white boy . . . [he is] doomed to encounter prejudice and contempt because he is black."[14] Negro newspapers published articles on the low-paid jobs that racial prejudice forced Negroes to accept in Jacksonian America; complained that "colored youths" were barred from "workshops and offices" in the 1830's.[15] Negroes "are sunken much lower than they were a few years ago and are compelled to pursue none but the meanest avocations," concluded an observer in 1846.[16] In the 1850's the perceptive Frederick Douglass complained that Negroes "were shut from all lucrative employments and compelled to be merely barbers, waiters, workmen and the like at wages so low that they could lay up little or nothing."[17] Charles L. Reason, a prominent nineteenth-century Negro educator, echoed Douglass's views in 1854. As the Civil War began, abolitionist Henry Ward Beecher commented that the "only chance for a colored man North nowadays is to wait and shave and they are being driven from these as fast as possible."[18] Only a very small number of New York City Negroes could meet the qualification of a $250 freehold for voting established by the state constitution of 1821. In 1865, for example, 44 Negroes in a population of 9,943 owned enough property to vote.[19] "The Black man goes to the wall," was the *New York Tribune*'s summary of the economic status of Negro New Yorkers in the nineteenth century.[20]

II

And similar generalizations can be made about practically every other aspect of Negro life in the metropolis. The Negro population of New York City remained relatively stable and small throughout most of the nineteenth century, for example, primarily because of an exceedingly high death rate. Between 1800 and 1865 the numbers of Negroes living in Manhattan wavered between 9,000 and 15,000—about one per cent of the city's population on the eve of the "Rebellion." In each of the three decades preceding the Civil War the Negro population actually declined. By 1865, in fact, there were fewer Negroes in Manhattan (9,943) than there had been in 1820 (10,368).

It was not until southern and West Indian migrants came to New York City (in small numbers between 1865 and 1890, and in much larger numbers after that) that the Negro population actually expanded. By 1900, for the first time in New York history, more than half the Negro population (53 per cent) was born outside the state.[21]

An exceptionally high death rate had been a major fact of Negro life in slavery; it continued to be so after emancipation: "And Death heard the summons/And he leaped on his fastest horse," wrote poet James Weldon Johnson. Of all the peoples in New York City, foreign-born as well as native, Negroes had, proportionally, the highest mortality rates. In 1890, for example, 37.5 Negroes in every thousand died, contrasted with 28.5 deaths in the white population. Between 1895 and 1915, in fact, the Negro death rate in New York State exceeded the birth rate by some 400 annually. And what was true of the state was also true for the city.[22]

Death took a tragic toll of very young Negro children either through stillbirths or other causes in the first year of life. Consumption (the "Plague of the Cities"), and pneumonia, however, were the great adult killers. From 1884 to 1890 the Bureau of the Census conducted an intensive study of New York City and found that more Negroes died of these illnesses than of all others. Almost one-fourth of Negro deaths then were caused by tuberculosis, and the general rate of death among Negroes from this disease was twice that of the white population. "Tuberculosis in all its forms is met with everywhere," wrote a social worker active in the Negro districts.[23] Ironically, the Great White Plague took, and would continue to take, its highest toll among black New Yorkers.[24]

This "frightful mortality rate from lung and bronchial diseases" offered great opportunities to local quacks whose private and ingenious home remedies were reputed to cure everything from a broken heart and overly curly hair to the most lethal ailments. They exploited a real need of the Negro community—the desire for answers to medical problems which science itself had not yet found. ("If you want to prevent the contraction of tuberculosis," preached one Negro clergyman, "you must lead moral lives.")[25] One man who regularly advertised in the Negro press sold "Hale's Honey of Horehound and Tar" guaranteed to purge the recipient of every imaginable ailment.[26] Another, Dr. T. A. Slocum, was so sure that his formula cured tuberculosis that he gave free samples away.[27]

CONSUMPTION

I have a positive remedy for the above
disease. . . . Indeed, so strong is
my faith in its efficacy, that I will
send TWO BOTTLES FREE. . . .

The continual presence of sickness and death in the Negro community permitted other bogus healers, Negro and white, to enrich themselves in similar fashion for generations. Reliance on quackery and medical superstition played a more harmful role in Negro social life than it did for any other minority group.

III

Throughout the nineteenth century most Negroes lived in the poorest working-class sections of the city. Negro neighborhoods were traditionally located in the less attractive residential areas on the outskirts of Manhattan Island, or along the east and west sides near the waterfronts—the sections doomed to become slums by the unimaginative grid pattern of urban planning instituted in 1811. Here Negroes lived apart in generally rundown quarters because of their poverty and were further separated from other working-class families in these neighborhoods on the basis of color. Within this pattern, however, was a built-in source of instability. New York was a rapidly expanding city throughout the nineteenth century and, as its population grew, new neighborhoods came into existence. What was the periphery of town or a slum for one generation was not necessarily the same for the next. As the city moved northward, so did the principal places of Negro residence.[28]

In the early nineteenth century New York Negroes generally lived in the Five Points district, on the site of the present City Hall and in the blocks surrounding it, which were then considered "well uptown." The Sixth Ward, which encompassed most of Five Points, was a heavily populated working-class neighborhood; the Negro section within it was popularly called "Stagg Town" or "Negro Plantations." This was the first place of major settlement of New York's freed slaves. The gradual abolition of slavery in New York began in 1799 and was finally completed on July 4, 1827. The Five Points, parts of which were grazing land, housed the freedmen.[29]

Descriptions of life in this section repeatedly emphasized its dire poverty, its squalor, its vice. It was known as a "notorious center of crime." Charles Dickens visited some of the local Negro homes in 1842 and described them as places where "dogs would howl to lie." Here, he wrote, "women and men . . . slink off to sleep, forcing the dislodged rats to move away. . . ."[30] A teacher in the area found that Negro children failed to come to school because they lacked proper clothing. "A large number of our colored people are very poor," he observed, "and [are] unable to provide for their children suitable clothing to attend school. . . ."[31] When a missionary came to comfort a dying "Poor Black Man," he found him lying on a homemade bed of straw surrounded by a ragged family.[32] Negroes lived in the rickety frame houses of this shantytown, and in unpaved cellars known as the "Dens of Death."[33] Others were housed in the "Old Brewery," an early-nineteenth-century beer factory turned into a tenement. Drunkenness and prostitution were commonly found in the neighborhood.[34] In response to these conditions of poverty and degradation, the Association for the Improvement of the Condition of the Poor built the Workingmen's Home in 1855. This first model tenement for the city's poor was constructed for Negroes at Elizabeth and Mott Streets.[35]

But poverty alone did not fully define Negro life in the Five Points. What the occasional visitor like Dickens failed to see were the solid institutions of the neighborhood and the more hopeful side of life there. The African Society of Mutual Relief, a Negro beneficial organization, was founded in 1808 and continued its existence into the twentieth century. There was a Negro theater, the African Grove, on Mercer Street in the 1820's.[36] Abyssinian Baptist Church, founded in 1808, was on present-day Worth Street. St. Philip's Protestant Episcopal Church (1809) was located on what is now Centre Street; Bethel African Methodist Episcopal Church (1819) was on Mott Street; and there were a few other churches as well spread across the Lower East and West sides.[37] At Leonard and Church Streets stood the queen of Negro religious institutions, "Mother Zion" Church (African Methodist Episcopal Zion), founded in 1796. In 1800 a frame building replaced the stable in which its founders worshiped; in 1820 a stone structure replaced the frame; in 1840 a solid brick building took the place of the stone.[38]

The outstanding nonreligious institution of the neighborhood was African Free School Number 2, founded by the New York Manumission Society on Mulberry near Grand Street in 1820.[39] Many of

the most prominent Negroes of the city and the North in the
nineteenth century were educated there. Charles L. Reason, teacher;
Patrick Reason, engraver; J. McCune Smith, physician; Ira Aldridge,
actor; Samuel Ringgold Ward, abolitionist; Henry Highland Garnet
and Alexander Crummell, clergymen; and Thomas Downing, caterer,
to mention a few of the outstanding, were all students at the school.[40]
The "Old Mulberry Street School" was remembered with pride by
its graduates. The Reverend Dr. Crummell delivered eulogies on John
Peterson, a Negro teacher there for half a century.[41] Former students
of "Number 2" gathered together in the John Peterson Association in
the 1880's to preserve its memory and keep bright some outstanding
aspects of Negro life in New York City in the nineteenth century.[42]

IV

By the 1830's the Negro population of Five Points began to decline.
Some Negroes continued to live there until the end of the century, but
it essentially became a backwash community as the majority of
people moved north and west into Greenwich Village. A survey made
of Five Points in 1860 found it to be an overwhelmingly Irish district.
There were only a few hundred Negroes left there.[43] By the 1880's
only a handful of Negroes remained: "In a few years there will not be
a family living on the East Side of our city, that part known as Stagg
Town, where the colored people lived years ago," an editorial in a
Negro journal said in 1887.[44]

"Little Africa" replaced "Stagg Town"—Bleecker, Sullivan,
Thompson, MacDougal and Carmine Streets took the place of their
counterparts to the south and east. The public reputation of the
Negro community in Greenwich Village was simply an adaptation of
the previous general impressions of Five Points. By those who were
attracted vicariously or directly to fast living, it was called "the
notorious district,"[45] "Coontown,"[46] "Nigger Alley."[47] In it were
"black and tan saloons" where all kinds of underworld and salacious
activities could supposedly be bought for the right price.[48]

The general Negro population of the Village, those who worked
regularly at hundreds of different menial jobs and were members of
the many Negro fraternal orders, were unnoticed by the creators of
such stereotypes. These Negroes, whose contributions built the fine
churches which followed them into the new neighborhood, constituted the majority of the population. Between 1880 and 1890,

however, their numbers began to decline. At the turn of the century they had dwindled to 1,900. In 1920, the few hundred Negroes of Greenwich Village were janitors living in basements of tenements that housed whites, or tenants in the very few houses still occupied by colored people.[49] "Look at West Broadway . . . Thompson Street, Sullivan Street, Bleecker Street and think of those streets . . . years ago," wrote Samuel R. Scottron in 1905. "Think of our people . . . and look upon the present occupants, all [Italians]."[50] The "Old Africa," Jacob Riis observed in 1890, "is now becoming a modern Italy."[51] As "Little Africa" had replaced "Stagg Town" a generation or so before, now the Tenderloin and San Juan Hill continued the "steady procession passing up the West Side."[52]

V

At the turn of the century most Negroes lived in what would be the present-day midtown area, on a wide range of blocks between Twentieth and Sixty-third Streets. Although there were sections of Negro concentration within this area, no single large neighborhood was an all-Negro community. Handfuls of small and densely populated ghettos, usually a block or two in length, were found throughout Manhattan Island, on the east and west sides, from Greenwich Village to Harlem and even further north. Thirty-seventh and Fifty-eighth Streets, between Eighth and Ninth Avenues, for example, were Negro blocks. They were surrounded by white people, the majority of whom were first- and second-generation Irish and German immigrants. There were six wards in Manhattan in 1890, the twelfth, fifteenth, sixteenth, nineteenth, twentieth and twenty-second, in which 2,000 to 4,000 Negroes lived.[53]

Of these sections the Tenderloin and San Juan Hill were the most heavily populated in the 1890's. They were areas "thickly studded with black and colored faces," recalled Negro journalist John Edward Bruce.[54] As the "Tenderloin" was a folk designation, its boundaries are nowhere clearly defined. Contemporaries sometimes spoke of an "Old Tenderloin" which perhaps ended near Forty-second Street, and a "New Tenderloin" which extended north from there through the upper Fifties.[55] The Negro sections scattered within this general area began at approximately Twentieth Street and ended at Fifty-third. The boundaries of San Juan Hill, on the other hand, are easily delineated. They stretched from Sixtieth to Sixty-fourth Streets, Tenth and

Eleventh Avenues. San Juan Hill was one of the most congested areas in America's most populated city—3,580 people, more than a town in itself, lived on just one of its streets.[56] The western boundary of this Negro neighborhood was the open railroad tracks that ran along Eleventh Avenue. (Because of the number of accidents involving children who played along the tracks, contemporaries called this street "Death Avenue.") San Juan Hill received its name after the Spanish-American War as a parody on the neighborhood interracial battles that took place on the steep upgrade leading to Sixtieth Street.[57]

Between 1890 and 1900 the Negro population of the city expanded by 25,000 people and both these new neighborhoods were a response to the demand for more Negro living space. As Negroes moved in whites moved to more desirable residences in upper Manhattan. When New York City built its elevated lines on the West Side in the late nineteenth century another stimulant for movement was created. The clatter and noise of the new trains made for less than pleasant living, and those who could afford it moved out. Apartments were taken over by Negroes ("The Choicest Apartments in the City for Select Colored Families"), many recent southern migrants, who were forced to accept second-class accommodations at first-class prices. Of the twenty-seven ethnic groups in the neighborhood, Negroes paid the highest rents—generally two to five dollars per month more than others. "A colored man in this city . . . pays higher rental and gets far less for his money than does the white man," a group of housing reformers recorded at the turn of the century. "The colored people of New York City suffer more injustice in the matter of rental than any other class of citizens," agreed the Negro journal, *New York Freeman,* in 1885. "The present housing conditions of the vast majority of colored families in New York," another man wrote, "can only be characterized as disgraceful."[58]

New institutions as well as new neighborhoods were called for to meet the needs of an expanding population. For the first time in decades new Negro churches were founded in the city. In the last thirty years of the nineteenth century six new Negro churches were opened in the Tenderloin and San Juan alone.[59] Some, like Union Baptist Church, were housed in storefronts and catered to the needs of recently arrived southern migrants. The Reverend Dr. George H. Sims, pastor of Union Baptist and a Virginian himself, gathered the "very recent residents of this new, disturbing city" and made Christianity come "alive Sunday morning," a contemporary remembered. Union Baptist was known as a "shouting church."[60] Others, like St. Cyprian's Episcopal Church, offered somewhat more reserved services. By 1900 the majority of religious institutions formerly established in Greenwich Village had moved to the Tenderloin and San Juan Hill.

The reputation of the new sections was as unsavory as that of any former Negro neighborhood. The Tenderloin, for example, housed New York's red-light district and was generally known as the roost of underworld characters. Preachers called it "The Terrible Tenderloin." The Reverend Dr. Charles H. Parkhurst, always in the forefront of some antivice crusade, attempted to clean up the area in 1892–1895, but business was being carried on as usual in 1900.[61] Negroes and whites owned saloons, cafés and gambling houses that were scattered throughout the neighborhood.[62] "These dens of infamy . . . are little less than a corner of hell," warned a Negro clergyman. "Fathers and mothers, away down south, or far off in the West Indies, little know of the shame and degradation that have overtaken many of their sons and daughters who have come to the city. . . ."[63] The Reverend Dr. Adam Clayton Powell, Sr., of Abyssinian Baptist Church lived in a coldwater flat "with prostitutes living over me and all around me." He preached what he called "gospel bombardments" to the "pimps, prostitutes, keepers of dives and gambling dens," who sometimes attended his prayer meetings. They seemed to shout the loudest for the Lord's forgiveness. Others never came to church. Some "harlots would stand across the street on Sunday evenings in unbuttoned Mother Hubbards soliciting men as they left our service," Powell recalled.[64] The Tenderloin was also a plum for corrupt and grafting municipal officials. Policemen preferred to work there, it was said, to get their share of underworld graft. A means of reprimanding a disobedient officer was to move his beat from the vice areas. "Anyone who was captain of that district a year," said one man, "could live on tenderloin steaks the rest of his life."[65] Local police inspectors were known as "Czars of the Tenderloin."[66]

There was also a vital and hopeful aspect about life in this Negro community. It centered around West Fifty-third Street between Sixth and Seventh Avenues—the Main Street for respectable folk of Negro Tenderloin. "West Fifty-third Street," the pastor of Bethel African

Methodist Episcopal Church remembered, "was the principal place of resort for *our* group."[67] On this street could be found, in 1900 or shortly thereafter, many of the major institutions of Negro New York: Negro political clubs, Mount Olivet Baptist Church, St. Mark's Methodist Episcopal Church, St. Benedict the Moor Roman Catholic Church,[68] offices of the major Negro fraternal societies, two Negro hotels, varieties of small businesses and the Negro YMCA.

The YMCA was the center of intellectual and social life of New York Negroes in the first decade of the twentieth century. Lectures were given, plays and music performed, classes in liberal arts as well as industrial skills were offered to the public. The Y was originally founded in 1899 at Mount Olivet Baptist Church by its pastor, the Reverend Dr. Charles T. Walker. Walker, a clergyman of national reputation, appealed to his church members and to the Negro community for financial assistance. He wanted to establish a home in the metropolis for southern migrants: "So much trouble is made by the poor fellows having no place to go when they come here. What we need is a place that shall be known to every young man in the South as a home where he can come and find friends. . . ."[69] Walker raised enough money to lease a building on West Fifty-third Street for one year and applied to the general New York YMCA for membership in 1900. His appeal was accepted and the "Colored Men's YMCA" became one of the first of many all-Negro Y's established in northern cities in the early twentieth century.[70]

The Tenderloin was also known as the gathering place of "Negro Bohemia." New York City was the center of Negro vaudeville at the turn of the century and James Weldon Johnson has described the active and productive lives of Negro show people in these years. Bert Williams, George Walker, Aida Overton Walker, Will Marion Cook, Theodore Drury, Rosamond Johnson, Bob Cole, Harry T. Burleigh, Johnson himself—outstanding artists, actors, vaudevillians, songwriters—lived on West Fifty-third Street and met at Jimmie Marshall's Hotel to trade stories and discuss race problems: "Our room, particularly of nights, was the scene of many discussions; the main question talked about and wrangled over being always the status of the Negro as a writer, composer and performer in the New York theater and world of music," Johnson recalled. "It was an alluring world, a tempting world."[71]

Most of the performers earned money that would have staggered the imaginations of the majority of Negroes of San Juan Hill and the Tenderloin. The royalties that Johnson earned for a few songs were equal to twice his annual salary as principal of a Negro secondary school in Florida. The typical Negro of the neighborhood, and of the city as a whole, was employed as a laborer or servant and earned four to six dollars a week at the turn of the century. The average combined incomes of all the working members of a Negro family was twelve to fifteen dollars a week.[72] A greater proportion of this income than that of any other ethnic group in the area had to be expended for the necessities of life. Houses in which Negroes lived were reputed to be the worst of the district, often ill-ventilated and located in the rear portions of dumbbell-shaped tenements so that they could be reached only by passing through a long and often dingy alleyway: "from 61st Street to 62nd Street [Negroes] occupy 400 rooms that have no access to the outer air," concluded a study of a group of church reformers in the 1890's. To make ends meet more Negro women had to be employed ("the laundress is the economic supplement of the porter"), more lodgers taken in, and more children kept out of school than in any other minority group. The average Negro wage earner, male or female, had to work more hours to earn less money than anyone else.[73]

"Now I started at the bottom, and I stays right there, don't seem like I'm gonna get nowhere," runs a line from the Blues. "The rise of a nation, the pressing forward of a social class," wrote W. E. B. DuBois, "means a bitter struggle, a hard and soul-sickening battle with the world such as few of the more favored classes know or appreciate."[74]

CHAPTER 2

"Come Out from Among Them": Negro Migration and Settlement, 1890 – 1914

"There can be no doubt of the drift of
the black South northward."
—W. E. B. DuBois, 1901

"The Afro-American population of the large
cities of the North and West is being
constantly fed by a steady stream of new
people from the Southern States."
—*The New York Age*, 1907

I

The most important factor underlying the establishment of Harlem as a Negro community was the substantial increase of Negro population in New York City in the years 1890–1914. That Harlem became the specific center of Negro settlement was the result of circumstance; that *some* section of the city was destined to become a Negro ghetto was the inevitable consequence of the Negro's migration from the South. This pre-World War I population movement, the advance guard of the Great Migration (as the movement of Negroes during the First World War is generally called), laid the foundations for present-day Negro communities in Chicago and Philadelphia as well. These were the formative years for the development of Negro communities throughout the North.

In spite of the high Negro death rate, the colored population increased by "leaps and bounds"[1] in New York City in the early twentieth century. By 1910 there were 91,709 Negroes in the metropolis,[2] the majority southern-born: "A Census of the Negroes in any city of the North," said a speaker at the first organizational meeting of the NAACP in 1909, "would show that the majority of . . . them . . . were more or less recent arrivals from the South."[3] Mary White Ovington, in her excellent study *Half A Man: The Status of the Negro in New York,* found that most of the Negro neighborhoods were populated by southerners.[4] Only 14,309 of the 60,534 Negroes in Manhattan in 1910 were born in New York State. The majority of the others (61 per cent) came from other states, practically all in the South. Virginia, North Carolina, South Carolina, Georgia and Florida, in perfect geographical order, were the major southern sources of New York's migrant population.[5]

Contemporaries in both the North and South, Negro and white, were aware of this movement. Unable to foresee that the First World War would bring even larger numbers of Negroes northward, they were staggered by the myriad problems this migration created for them: "There are more Southern Negroes in the North and West than original Northern ones, and they are coming all . . . the time," wrote a Negro journalist in 1913. "What to do with the needy and those who fall by the wayside is becoming a problem of the greatest magnitude. . . ."[6] Historians, impressed by the enormity of changes that occurred at the time of the "Great War," have tended to overlook or underestimate the significance of the pre-World War I migration of Negroes to northern cities.

II

Since the end of the Civil War there was a steady but small movement of Negroes northward. It averaged 41,378 persons for each decade between 1870 and 1890. In the following ten years, however, the migration more than doubled as at least 107,796 southern Negroes moved north and west. The Negro populations of the states of New Jersey, Pennsylvania and Illinois increased some two and a half times between 1890 and 1910 and that of New York almost tripled.[7] In 1910, New York City was the second largest Negro urban center in America (just behind Washington, D.C.); Philadelphia was fifth; and Chicago eighth. By 1920, they were ranked first, second and fourth respectively. A total of some 200,000 Negroes migrated from the South and to the North and West, primarily to cities, between 1890 and 1910.[8] In the decade 1900–1910, for the first time since their establishments as states in the early nineteenth century, Mississippi and Louisiana lost Negro population through emigration.[9] Practically every southern state showed the first significant deficit in its Negro birth-residence index (the index that measures population increase and decrease through migration) for the decade 1890–1900. "Prior to 1890," observes one student of population movement, "the migration of Negroes was not great and seems to have been local, from state to state, and only to a slight extent out of the South. But after 1890, the northward direction of the movement has been steadfastly maintained and has increased in amount decade after decade."[10] The number of Negroes migrating to the principal southern cities declined significantly in the years 1890–1900. The Negro population in these cities increased 38.7 per cent between 1880 and 1890, but the growth amounted to only 20.6 per cent in the next ten years.[11] Northern cities were draining off the residents of, and prospective migrants to, the larger southern cities at the turn of the century.

A few discerning analysts were aware of this new shift in Negro migration in the 1890's. Working with census data, Frederick J. Brown pointed to the new northward migration from the Border States in 1897.[12] In 1898, W. E. B. DuBois noted the decline of Negro population in Farmville, Virginia, and explained it as "a fact due doubtless to the large emigration to Northern cities."[13] In his pioneering study of Philadelphia Negroes (1899), DuBois showed a significant increase in southern immigration since 1887,[14] and later depicted the "typical colored man" of Philadelphia as a young person "from the South, from twenty to forty years of age. . . ."[15] Similar conclusions were made by a student of New York City's Negro community in 1898,[16] and the United States Department of Labor undertook a detailed analysis of the movement of Negroes to urban areas in these same years.[17]

By the first decade of the twentieth century the migration was well recognized: "It needs no long argument to prove the existence of a large movement of Negroes northward," a social scientist recorded in 1905.[18] An entire issue of the social service magazine *Charities* was devoted to a survey of the migration and the problems that arose from it in the first decade of the twentieth century.[19] New York's leading Negro journal, *The New York Age,* carried innumerable articles in the early 1900's on the "marvelous increase of Afro-American population," "the enormous and steady growth in the Negro population," "the young people in New York City from our

Southern States who are constantly coming,"[20] and so on. In 1901 a Negro minister delivered a public lecture on what seemed to him to be "The Wholesale Exodus of the Negro from the South."[21]

This pre-World War I exodus has sometimes been characterized as the "Migration of the Talented Tenth." Politicians, businessmen, the educated, and especially skilled workmen, are supposed to have constituted the majority of people who left the South in these years. Southern Negroes, it has been said, were robbed of their leadership as the talented fled north.[22]

It is undoubtedly true that many educated and gifted Negroes did come north then. William Lewis Bulkley, for example, a South Carolinian born a slave, became a principal in the New York school system and a leader of the Negro community during these years. P. B. S. Pinchback, for a time Reconstruction governor of Louisiana and thereafter an active Republican politician, worked in the New York City Custom House a short while. He used the influence of Booker T. Washington and the Negro Republican leader of New York City, Charles W. Anderson, to get the position.[23] Pinchback's friend, J. Ross Stewart, a former member of the Louisiana legislature, worked there too.[24] North Carolinian George Henry White, member of Congress 1897–1901, practiced law and became a banker in Philadelphia when Negroes were disfranchised in his state. White later established an all-Negro communiy in New Jersey.[25] T. Thomas Fortune, editor of *The New York Age,* was a Floridian by birth. There were, in fact, *very few* prominent Negroes in New York City in the early twentieth century—lawyers, physicians, businessmen, clergymen, politicians—who were not born in the South.

These people were not typical urban Negro migrants, however. The majority, like all migrant populations, were young people, generally unskilled and unmarried, the earliest Negro generations born in freedom. W. E. B. DuBois described them as "the Southern freedman's sons and daughters," "untrained and poorly educated countrymen, rushing from the hovels of the country or the cottages of the country towns. . . ."[26] Most contemporaries spoke of them as such.[27]

In one group of 240 Negroes interviewed in New York City in 1907, for example, only eighteen were born in New York, and just three of the 222 others were over forty when they migrated. The vast majority were between the ages of fifteen and thirty, and 96 per cent had arrived in New York City after 1887.[28] Another survey of 365 workers found that 68 per cent were born in the South, the largest number single young men and women.[29]

III

There were as many individual and varied reasons for migration as there were people who moved. The less respectable as well as the educated came north. Negroes themselves characterized some as a "hoodlum element," "rovers," "wanderers," "vagrants," "criminals in search of a sporting life."[30] "Many of the worthless people of the race are making their way northward," said *The New York Age* in an editorial.[31] Some wayward husbands—the "travelin' men" of Negro folk songs—abandoned their families and responsibilities and sought the anonymity of a city: "I was raised in the country, I been there all my life/Lord I had to run off and leave my children and my wife."[32]

Others came north on excursion trains to get a look at the big city and never returned.[33] One man "heard so much of this town," he said, "that he decided to look it over." Another stated that he "didn't want to remain in one little place all my days. I wanted to get out and see something of the world."[34] Migratory laborers found work on New Jersey, Pennsylvania and New York farms every spring and summer. Some traveled back and forth each year; others simply went to the nearest city when winter came.[35] "Tired of the South," "Wanted to make a change," "Ran away from home," were some of the reasons advanced by Negroes for coming north.[36] All received nominally higher wages in the North, and this was certainly a great attraction. One woman who came to New York City from Virginia, for example, said she was "willing to live anywhere, if the wages were good."[37]

There were also those who fled social proscription and violence in the South. C. Vann Woodward has described the "Capitulation to Racism" that characterized the southern attitude toward the Negro from the late 1880's through the early twentieth century. Vast numbers of Jim Crow laws were passed in these years as the forces which held virulent southern racism in check suddenly crumbled. The conservative, *noblesse oblige* attitude of former Whig leaders ("it is a mark of breeding to treat Negroes with courtesy") was replaced by a violently racist white supremacy movement; the paternalism of a

Wade Hampton was followed by the viciousness of a Ben Tillman (whose racist tirades even embarrassed his southern colleagues). Free rein was given to mass aggressions as all forces joined together in an active program of "keeping the Negro down." The great heresy that proclaimed the Negro capable of attaining equality with the white had to be rooted out at all costs, it was argued. There were more Negroes lynched, burned, tortured and disfranchised in the late eighties, nineties and first decade of the twentieth century than at any other time in our history. The militant Negro Ida B. Wells graphically and sadly described this *Red Record* in 1895.[38] It was not surprising to find that the American Colonization Society, organized in 1817, experienced a long-hoped-for revival in the 1890's,[39] and various other plans to colonize Negroes in Africa were rekindled in these years. "I used to love what I thought was the grand old flag, and sing with ecstasy about the stars and stripes," wrote Negro Bishop Henry McNeal Turner of Georgia, "but to the Negro in this country today the American flag is a dirty contemptible rag. . . . Hell is an improvement upon the United States when the Negro is involved." "No man hates this Nation more than I do," Turner said on another occasion. He looked longingly to Africa as the only possible place of Negro freedom.[40]

Negro leaders and the Negro press continually stressed their belief that migration was primarily a movement away from racism: "The large cities of the North and West have had a marvelous increase of Afro-American population in the last ten years, and the increase is growing . . . because of the conditions in the Southern States which make for unrest"; "the terrors of mob wrath."[41] When T. Thomas Fortune, William Lewis Bulkley, and North Carolina educator and politician Edward A. Johnson came north, each emphasized he could no longer live under Jim Crow and racial violence.[42] George Henry White said he left North Carolina because he "couldn't live there and be a man and be treated like a man." He believed that thousands of others would follow him.[43] Booker T. Washington told the Board of Trustees of Tuskegee, in 1903, that "for every lynching that takes place . . . a score of colored people leave . . . for the city."[44]

In general, however, the migration could best be considered not so much a flight from racial violence, as it was a desire for expanded opportunity. This is best summarized in a phrase commonly used by the migrants themselves—the attempt "to better my condition."[45]

People moved away from the South in search of a better and more fulfilling life. A Negro shoemaker came north, for example, because he felt "choked" by the "narrow and petty life" he was forced to lead in a small Virginia town. To him, the great attraction of New York City was the "wider scope allowed the Negro."[46] One woman who "never could work . . . in a menial way" was proud that she could earn a living as an independent seamstress in New York.[47] Moving north, wrote DuBois in 1907, offered "the possibility of escaping caste at least in its most aggravating personal features. . . . A certain sort of soul, a certain kind of spirit, finds the narrow repression and provincialism of the South simply unbearable."[48]

> Where I come from
> folks work hard
> all their lives
> until they die
> and never own no part
> of earth nor sky.[49]

The *possibilities* for such movement resulted from two basic changes in American life. One was the overwhelming industrial expansion of the late nineteenth century. The Industrial Revolution created economic opportunities for rural people, Negro and white, and both migrated to industrial and urban centers in the North. For the Negro, hedged about by union restrictions and racial antagonism, employment was usually found in the fringe jobs that an industrial and commercial society creates—as janitors, elevator operators, general laborers of all kinds, longshoremen, servants. Negro women almost always worked as domestics. During periods of labor disputes, Negroes were commonly found among the strikebreakers.[50]

There was, however, an added factor that influenced Negro migration and distinguished it from the general rural migration to cities. Why, it might be asked, had Negroes not moved in similar numbers in response to industrializaton in the 1870's—the period of great social upheaval and dislocation that followed the destruction of slavery? The answer undoubtedly lies in an understanding of the differences between the slave and post-slave generations. The Negroes who came north now were the first descendants of former slaves. They had listened to tales of slavery, gentle and harsh, but had not experienced and lived its blight—the denial of full manhood.[51] To them, *"War, Hell, and Slavery were but childhood tales. . . ."*[52] Their parents and grandparents, psychologically and economically unprepared to enter what contemporaries called the "competition for life," tended to remain as tenants, sharecroppers or laborers on their former plantations or on places similar to them. They continued in freedom to live the only life they had knowledge of. "There were great upheavals in political and labor conditions at the time of emancipation, but there was little shifting in the populations. For the most part, the freedmen stayed on in the states and counties where they had formerly existed as slaves," writes one historian of Negro life.[53] In 1900, practically all southern Negroes continued to work on the land and some 75 per cent remained sharecroppers, tenants and laborers.[54] On one Georgia plantation in 1901, as on others, lived many Negroes who had been slaves there: "I have men," the white owner testified, "who were slaves on the place. . . . They have always lived there and will probably die there, right on the plantation where they were born." "It was predicted [during the Civil War] that the Negroes would leave the . . . fields and fill the towns in case of emancipation," said a southern planter at the turn of the century. "That prediction has not been realized suddenly as we anticipated it would be, but it seems to be approaching."[55]

Those who migrated to the North in the 1890's were a new generation. Many Negroes no longer felt any strong attachment to the soil. They could at least *conceive* of life in a new and different way. For some, the discontented and restless, there was now both the ability and willingness to move. They left a South in which their futures were sealed: "There is absolutely nothing before them on the farm. . . . Working year in and year out with . . . no prospect . . . but to continue until they die."[56] In many rural communities of the South, it was reported in 1907, a "number of youths have expressed their conviction that since their fathers and mothers have accumulated nothing after years on the land, they did not intend to stay on the plantation to repeat the process."[57] A leading Republican politician and defender of Negro civil rights, James S. Clarkson, took a trip to the South in the 1890's and "saw many a grey head . . . talking to the young people . . . encouraging the young people to become content," he wrote a Negro confidant.[58] The migrants who came north were aptly described by George Edmund Haynes as "groping seekers for something better. . . ."[59]

IV

To southerners this seemed to be a different and puzzling kind of Negro—not a people especially educated or skilled, but a group willing to make some change in the traditional patterns of its life. To the stereotype of the docile, irresponsible, immoral, dishonest Negro was now added a new "racial" characteristic—"a migratory disposition."[60] Philip A. Bruce, Virginia historian, called the "new generations" worthless. They "rarely remain long enough under the supervision of any planter to allow him sufficient time to teach them," he wrote.[61] "Habits of diligence, order, faithfulness"—all the qualities of a good slave—were absent in the "new generation," said another. There exists "a certain unrest and discontent," a white planter commented.[62] "Under its influence the boys and girls are beginning to drift to the cities." To contrast the supposedly "faithful old darkies" with "the new generation, which has become restless, dissatisfied, and worthless" (and "migrated from the plantations to the cities") was a standard and hackneyed statement found throughout the racial literature of the time.[63]

This attitude toward the Negro was accepted in popular thought as well: "The superiority of the older farm-hands to the younger generation is so universally asserted throughout the South," wrote Thomas Nelson Page in 1904, "that it must be given some of the validity of general reputation. The Negro has retrograded as a workman," he concluded.[64] There existed, said a Georgia Negro minister, "among a large number of older people, both white and black, the definite conviction that the present generation of Negroes is hopelessly degenerate. . . ."[65]

Most southern farmers who testified before the United States Industrial Commission in 1899–1901 expressed similar opinions. They spoke of the differences in attitudes between the freed slave and his children. The "good old negroes, as we call them . . . negroes about grown before the war," "old-time negroes" ("before-the-war negroes," they were sometimes called), were touted as the best farm workers and tenants. "The younger ones" are "discontented and want to be roaming." "The older class of colored labor," repeated a West Virginia farmer, "men that are pretty well up in years—are a first rate class of labor. The younger class . . . are . . . very trifling.

. . ." The Negro "is not as steady as he was," thought another. "The South laments to-day the slow, steady disappearance of a certain type of Negro—the faithful, courteous slave of other days, with his dignified . . . humility," W. E. B. DuBois commented at the turn of the century.[66] "He is passing away just as surely as the old type of Southern gentleman is passing. . . ."

Related to the belief of the emergence of a new and different Negro generation was the revival of scientific attempts to prove the Negro a degraded being. During this same period Darwinism invaded the South (as well as the North) to revive the debate over the place of the Negro in the human community. Arguments strikingly similar to the old proslavery diatribes of natural Negro inferiority were dressed up in the new scientific garb and presented to the public by "objective social scientists" who claimed to be uninfluenced by "preconceived ideas."[67] The improvident, dishonest, immoral, lazy, lascivious Negro was shown to be incapable of education: "he is a fungus growth that the white man will totally destroy. . . . The only race that has never made any progress in any respect," more similar in mind to the chimpanzee than to man.[68] The greatest menace and curse to our Anglo-Saxon civilization, some thought, was its pollution with the blood of the "depraved Ethiopian." Aryan supremacy could only be achieved, it was argued, after total separation, by colonization or extermination, of the entire Negro race.[69]

This ideology combined with the reality of Negro migration and encouraged southerners to attempt to replace Negro laborers with European immigrants. The substitution of immigrants for Negroes was an integral part of the philosophy that preached southern progress through industrialization—the New South. It was in these very years that the South attempted to rejuvenate its efforts, first begun in Reconstruction, to attract European immigrants.[70] State immigration bureaus were created and offices established in the principal port cities to direct the newest arrivals to southern farms. Southern emigration agents were even sent abroad.[71] There was more myth than reality in the conception of a New South—a South where factories were to spring up "like stars after twilight."[72] The movement to encourage settlement of immigrants to replace Negro labor was an almost total failure.[73]

This reality presented southerners with a major paradox. The new generation of Negroes seemed unreliable (even inhuman) and yet, at the same time, it was also clearly recognized that the southern economy was largely dependent upon them: "I think the Negro is a necessity in the South as a farm laborer," stated a South Carolinian. *"We have no other. . . ."* "I do not know how the South could live without negro labor," a Georgia plantation owner said. "It is the life of the South; it is the foundation of its prosperity. . . . God pity the day when the negro leaves the South. . . ."[74] "Think twice, before committing the State to a policy which may strip the land of its best . . . laborers," editorialized a North Carolina newspaper opposed to European immigration.[75] In the minds of most southerners, Negroes seemed racially adapted to agricultural life, permanently tied to the soil. To forsake farm life would necessarily lead to their degradation. This was their only "proper calling," their "proper place."[76]

Negro farmers in the South cultivated twice as much acreage as did all the farmers in New England combined. Nearly one-half of all farms under fifty acres in the South Atlantic states and one-fourth of those between fifty and one hundred were operated by Negroes. Negroes were also the most important farm laborers throughout the South.[77]

If Negroes began leaving the South in great numbers, Senator George F. Hoar of Massachusetts predicted, "there would be a general alarm on the part of the men who now depend on their labor, and they would find themselves pretty earnestly solicited to change their minds."[78] It was the reality of this practical dependence on Negro farm labor that produced a series of laws limiting the free movement of Negro workers and tenants and heavily taxing all labor agents sent south to "entice" them away. From the late 1880's through the first decade of the twentieth century such legislation was passed in Alabama, Arkansas, Florida, Georgia, Kentucky, Mississippi, North Carolina, South Carolina, Louisiana, Tennessee and Virginia.[79] Southern courts generally interpreted these laws for the benefit of the white farm owner, forcing Negro workers to remain on the land. The Department of Justice in 1907, for example, received eighty-three complaints from Negroes protesting what they considered to be their practical peonage.[80] Although the Supreme Court outlawed peonage in 1911, the practice continued through subterfuge for decades. (As late as 1947 the President's Committee on Civil Rights documented a case of forced labor.)[81]

Exaggerated accounts of the destitute conditions of migrants were commonly published in the press and every hint of failure was described as destitution. The high Negro mortality rate in northern cities was presented as absolute proof that the Negro could not live in cold climates: "they will take colds and develop pneumonia and consumption . . . and will die there."[82] The Southern Negro Anti-Exodus Association was founded in Virginia in 1905 to "preach the gospel of contentment to the colored people South of Mason and Dixon's line. . . ." When a labor agent was arrested in Georgia, an editorial in the *Age* said: "If there is one thing the Southern man preaches all the time it is that the young Negro is worthless and is not to be mentioned in the same breath with the older. . . . The young Negro is pictured as worthless and a general nuisance that has been tolerated too long. . . . But as yet no one can be found to deny the cold fact that this agent was arrested to put a stop to the exodus. . . . In spite of all this talk, there is a desire to keep the Negro help in the South."[83]

These reactions were a reflection of a basic dichotomy in southern thought. On the one hand, it was believed that the Negro was worthless, inefficient, untrustworthy, less faithful than the slave. The failure to use improved agricultural machinery and in industrialization in general was often blamed on his ignorance.[84] On the other hand, the Negro was encouraged to remain in the South (and sometimes forced to do so) as the only source of labor available— "the backbone of the South when it comes to labor"; "the best labor we could have in the South."[85] With the failure of attempts to attract European immigrants the reliance of the South on Negro farmers and laborers became even more evident. In reality, Southern society fundamentally distrusted the very people it seemed most hopelessly dependent upon. It was caught in a vise of restricting the migration of Negroes who, at the same time, were looked upon with the utmost disdain, even denied fully human qualities. This paradox in southern thought provided a seedbed for bitter racial antagonism. It added an emotionalism to the racial hatreds of these years that make them stand out, above all others, as a period of great violence.

V

Most of the Negro migrants who came to New York City prior to the 1930's settled in Manhattan. The Negro population of that borough increased by 24,288 between 1900 and 1910, whereas that of

Brooklyn expanded by 4,341. Seventy-eight per cent of the city's industry was located in Manhattan in the early twentieth century and the migrants filled many of the unskilled jobs that these factories created.[86]

The typical Negro migrant to the metropolis originally came from some rural area in the South. Most grew up on farms or in small southern towns. In 1913 a study was made of thirty-five Negroes in Harlem. Thirty-four came from the rural South, and only one grew up in a town whose population exceeded 10,000. Of the twenty-one born on farms, only three were children of parents who owned their land outright. The others were sons and daughters of sharecroppers and farm laborers. The majority of Negroes in this group were indirect migrants—they had lived in some large town or city for a time before coming to New York. All but four were presently employed as domestics, servants or laborers.[87] Similar findings were made in other surveys of northern cities.[88]

Among the immigrants who settled in New York City were young women who came north on what were sometimes called "Justice's Tickets."[89] These were tickets supplied to them by employment and labor agents. In exchange for transportation and the guarantee of a job on arrival, the women signed contracts to work where the agent placed them and swore to pay a fee usually equal to one or two months' wages. These employment agents thus collected money from both employers and workers. The following is a typical labor contract:

> In consideration of my expenses being paid
> from Richmond to _____ and a situation
> provided for me, I agree to give _____
> services after arrival as _____ to party
> or persons paying my expenses. And I further agree
> that all my personal effects may be subject to their
> order until I have fulfilled that contract, forfeiting
> all claims to said personal effects after sixty days
> after this date should I fail to comply with agreement.[90]

Social service organizations founded to assist Negroes in the city were vitally interested in protecting these girls from "the agents with oily tongues [who] come about and offer flattering inducements. . . ."[91] "Many of them," concluded one report, "are brought from the South, consigned like merchandise to Northern agents." Trunks, "slender satchels," clothing, trinkets—personal possessions of all kinds—were often kept as security until fees were paid.[92] Migrants commonly complained of extortionate charges and generally shoddy treatment.[93]

These women who worked as domestics and most of the Negroes who came to the city prior to World War I made the trip on boats that ran along the Atlantic Coast. "Negroes," observed one man in 1898, "are coming on every boat from southern waters." "Nobody knows how it happened," an old resident of the Tenderloin recalled, "but [on] every old Dominion Steamship that docked there [were] from two to three hundred negroes landed in New York."[94] This was the cheapest means of transportation from the South, and New York's migrant population was, and would continue to be, primarily composed of Virginians or people from states bordering the Atlantic. Steerage fare, with meals, from Norfolk or Richmond cost $5.50 or $6.00—the approximate equivalent of a week's wages in New York City. Cabin fares were $9.00. The Old Dominion Steamship Company (migrants called it the "O.D. Line") had a bi-weekly service between Virginia and New York. The Baltimore, Chesapeake and Atlantic Railway ran steamers from Washington and Baltimore, and others went as far south as Florida. Many of the waiters and seamen on these ships were Negroes, some of whom lived in New York City.[95] Negroes were generally berthed in separate quarters, ate at separate tables, and were served food inferior to that given white passengers. Some migrants complained that, besides these indignities, the Negro sections of the boats were also reserved for the dogs and pets of other travelers.[96]

It was common practice for migrants, who lived within a day's journey of their former homes, to shuttle back and forth for regular visits. If European immigrants found the Atlantic no great barrier to such journeys (as evidenced by what contemporaries called the "birds of passage"), the Negro migrant was even less restricted by distance and cost. Practically every issue of The New York Age carried some report of such movement: "R. C. Turner the barber, is back in the city after two months' vacation to his old home, Hillsboro, North Carolina"; "Mrs. Mary E. Swan . . . has gone to Virginia to bury her niece. . . . She will soon return."[97] Many migrants wrote home of their supposedly glowing successes in the North. Some returned to their birthplaces dressed in the latest fashion, pockets full of cash, to tell the rural folk of their exploits. George Edmund Haynes described "the exaggerated stories of prosperity which relatives and friends in these cities write to friends at home and the prosperity shown by those returning home in their display of clothes and cash."[98] Negro students and teachers from the South regularly came to study in New York City during their summer vacations. Some attended the summer session at Columbia University and lived in segregated quarters in Hartley Hall. Others came in search of summer jobs, lived at the Negro YMCA and YWCA, saved their money and returned south when school began: "New York is . . . crowded with a host of young men and women students from . . . southern schools. . . . These young [people] come North every season and work. . . ."[99]

For those who remained permanently, the city was a strange and often hostile place—it was so noisy and unfriendly, so cold, so full of "temptations and moral perils," a "pernicious influence," a "fast and wicked place." "Many of those who have come North complain of cold and chills from the like of which they had not previously suffered," wrote one scholar.[100] The oft-told tale of the sale of the Brooklyn Bridge to the rural hayseed had a basis in fact. One naive migrant wanted to know how it was done: "I heard about 'selling the Brooklyn Bridge,'" he said, "and I wondered how it was sold, and asked questions about it."[101] In 1902 Paul Laurence Dunbar published a novel, *The Sport of the Gods*, which described the dissolution and eventual destruction of a southern Negro family in the "fast life" of the "great alleys of New York."[102] Southern Negroes were commonly subject to intraracial as well as interracial prejudice.

Confronted with this estrangement and antagonism many migrants banded together to try to retain as much contact with the patterns of their former lives as possible:

> I'm a poor boy and I'm a stranger blowed in your town,
>   Yes I am,
> I'm a poor boy and I'm a stranger blowed in your town,
> I'm a poor boy and I'm a stranger blowed in your town,
> I'm goin' where a friend can be found.[103]

Negroes, foreign-born and native, established benevolent, fraternal and protective societies to keep up old friendships and provide insurance for themselves and families in sickness and death. The vast majority of New York's Negro population belonged to insurance and fraternal societies. The largest Negro insurance company of Virginia, the True Reformers, had a branch office in the city.[104] Prior to

World War I, New York City had its Sons and Daughters of South Carolina, Sons of North Carolina, Sons of Virginia, Sons of the South, Southern Beneficial League. When one North Carolinian was appointed Assistant District Attorney of New York County a celebration was given for him "in the fullness of the North Carolinian pride."[105] Storefront churches revived the spirit of southern preaching. These and other churches held special services and celebrations in honor of communicants from individual southern states. There were regular South Carolina days, Virginia days, and so on.[106] When the World War drew migrants in greater numbers from the Deep South and the West Indies, new societies were founded by Floridians, Georgians and the varieties of West Indians.

The entire Negro community of New York City took on a southern flavor. Businesses expanded to service the wants of a growing population: "The great influx of Afro-Americans into New York City within recent years from all parts of the South has made . . . possible a great number and variety of business enterprises," editorialized *The New York Age* in 1907.[107] Negro restaurants, undertaking establishments, saloons, barbershops—the plethora of small businesses necessary to satisfy a community's needs—catered to the newcomers. Restaurants advertised special "southern-style" breakfasts and dinners. Negro grocers specialized in Virginia fruits, vegetables and chickens. Migrants asked friends to send them special southern delicacies.[108]

New York was also the center of Negro philanthropy.[109] The offices of the Armstrong Association which supported Hampton Institute, the Board of Trustees of Tuskegee, Rockefeller's General Education Board, the Phelps-Stokes Foundation and the John F. Slater Fund were all located in the city. Many wealthy New Yorkers contributed individually to the support of southern Negro schools. Southern ministers and educators arrived in town regularly in search of financial assistance. Many of the clergymen preached "southern-style" sermons in local Negro churches that were "not soon forgotten." Southern Negro school principals, including Booker T. Washington in the 1890's, held mass meetings "to request race support." Fisk University Jubilee Singers and the Hampton Quartet came north to give concerts. "As the recently arrived Richmonder meanders along," commented one man, he "recognizes so many familiar faces [that] he readily concludes there is some . . . relationship between his city and this."[110]

Migration to the city created possibilities for economic mobility that were largely absent from southern life. Many of the businesses which provided services for Negroes were owned by migrants themselves. Some recent arrivals began as small entrepreneurs but made modest fortunes in a relatively short time.

Perhaps the most interesting and among the most successful was Lillian Harris, born in a shanty on the Mississippi Delta in 1870. She came north as a teenager and, in 1901, after having knocked around many northern cities for a decade, hitched her way from Boston to New York City on hay, milk and vegetable wagons. Miss Harris had $5.00, and with this capital went into business. She spent $3.00 for an old baby carriage and boiler and $2.00 for pigs' feet. This was the beginning of her career as New York's most widely known Negro peddler. Her converted buggy became a "traveling restaurant."

Hawking her wares in Negro sections, specializing in southern cooking (hog-maws, chitterlings), Lillian Harris was popularly called "Pig Foot Mary." She lived in a tiny room and scrimped and saved for years: "Saving for a respectable old age," she always said. When Negroes began moving to Harlem this astute street-corner saleswoman grasped at opportunity and invested her savings in Harlem property. By the First World War "Pig Foot Mary" (now Mrs. Lillian H. Dean) was a wealthy landlord—"one of the wealthiest women in Harlem"; "one of the most successful colored business women in New York." "Send it and send it damn quick," she wrote tenants who fell behind in their rent. "Pig Foot Mary" spent her "respectable old age" in retirement in California, where she died in 1929.[111]

William Mack Felton was another southern Negro who made good in New York. He arrived in the city in 1898 with a dollar tucked away in his shoe: "Heeding the call to the Big City," he said. Felton grew up on a small farm in Georgia with little opportunity for formal education. He was naturally bright, however, and gifted with mechanical ability. When he came to New York he worked as a longshoreman long enough to save some money to open a repair shop. The first big job that came his way called for the repair of dozens of clocks left in a Manhattan pawnshop. Most of them had simply stopped running because they had picked up dust and dirt lying around the shelves. Felton realized this, bought a large washtub, filled it with gallons of kerosene and oil and cleaned all the stripped-down clocks in one day. He used this same ingenuity to fix watches, pistols, bicycles—anything that needed repairing. In 1901, when wealthy New Yorkers began to buy the new automobile, Felton opened an auto school and garage. He later invented a device that washed cars automatically. By 1913 his Auto Transportation and Sales Company employed fifteen people and was housed in a seven-story building which he owned. Felton rode back to Georgia in his new car to visit his family and old friends and tell them of life in the "Big City."[112]

Success came to other southern migrants who arrived in New York City in these years. Madame C. J. Walker, born in Louisiana in 1867, was a laundress before she discovered a hair-straightening process (the "Walker System") which brought her great fortune. In 1913 she built a mansion for herself on West One Hundred and Thirty-sixth Street and four years later built a magnificent country estate, Villa Lewaro, in exclusive Irvington-on-the-Hudson.[113] H. C. Haynes, formerly a southern barber, founded a company which manufactured razor strops; Edward E. Lee, a Virginian, was Negro Democratic leader of New York County for fifteen years; J. Franklin Smallwood became chief collector of the State Bank of New York; J. S. Montague ran a mortgage and loan company on Wall Street; Ferdinand Q. Morton, of Macon, Mississippi, was prominent in Democratic politics and ruled "Black Tammany" from the First World War through the Great Depression.[114]

Practically all of these migrants were born in the direst southern poverty and achieved their positions, as the Reverend Dr. Adam Clayton Powell, Sr., later wrote, "Against the Tide."[115] Very few southern Negroes had such fortune, however. The majority of those who came to New York City ended in the ranks of the poor and swelled the slum populations of the Tenderloin, San Juan Hill or Harlem. To many northern Negroes, who had never known or had since forgotten the restrictive conditions in the South, the life of the typical migrant seemed no great improvement on his former condition.

The average Negro migrant to New York City obviously found life harsh and difficult. For those who came, however, conditions in the North did offer a measure of self-respect and the possibility for future advancement that was generally denied the Negro in the South. "To many of them oppressed within the limitations set up by the South," wrote Ray Stannard Baker, "it is indeed the promised land."[116]

Alienation: New York and the Negro

"And the Nation echoed . . . : Be content
to be servants, and nothing more; what
need of higher culture for half-men."
—W. E. B. DuBois, 1903

"This is a mass in the midst of . . .
an alien and hostile people."
—*Harper's Weekly*, 1900

I

For the Negroes of New York City the years after 1900 marked not
only a new century but a breaking point in a way of life. As the
Negro population of New York and other northern cities increased,
so did racial antagonism, violence and patterns of social and residential segregation. "One of the striking developments of very recent
years," one white northerner noted in 1906, "is the recrudescence
of . . . prejudice against people of African descent. . . ."[1]

At no period in the history of New York City were Negroes
accepted as full American citizens. Restrictions on Negro voting,
equal access to public facilities and education were maintained even
after emancipation was proclaimed in the early nineteenth century.
Jim Crow street stages, with "For Colored People Only" signs hung
over their sides, ran along Manhattan streets until the eve of the Civil
War. Colored people sat in special Negro pews (whites called them
"Nigger Pews") or in the balconies of white churches: "Negroes were
not permitted to sit in any public assembly, court or church, except in
the particular quarter set apart for them, [and] generally in the most
remote and worst situation." In 1837, *The Colored American* denounced the "Negro Pew" as a technique which whites used to
degrade Negroes.[2] The only minority group to suffer franchise re-

strictions in the state was the Negro. Negroes were forced to meet property qualifications for voting after these had been abolished for all other New Yorkers in 1821, and they were further subject to longer residential requirements for voting than whites.[3] Although racial prejudice was never absent from city life, it was not always uniformly intense. The attitudes of New Yorkers toward Negroes— sometimes eased, at other times hardened—wavered with national trends of racial adjustment.

In the late nineteenth century, and especially in the 1870's and 1880's, most northern communities made significant progress in attacking *institutionalized* racial prejudice. Laws were passed in most state legislatures, including New York's, which attempted to guarantee equal rights for Negroes. The motivating force for this liberal attitude toward the Negro was undoubtedly a spirit for racial reform which came in the aftermath of the Civil War and Reconstruction. Serious restrictions on Negro rights that had existed in some form since colonial times were done away with. In New York State, Negroes were given the right to vote without impediment by the Civil Rights Act of 1873, and this was followed by two other civil rights acts before the end of the century. New legislation permitted Negroes to travel on transportation facilities, attend theaters, eat at restaurants, and be buried in all cemeteries which served the public. Acts which had previously outlawed intermarriage were repealed, and insurance companies were specifically prohibited from charging Negroes rates higher than those paid by white clients.[4] The first Negro to serve as a juryman in Manhattan did so in the 1880's.[5] In 1884, the last three Negro public schools in the city were made ward schools, thus ending the tradition of separate education which had existed in New York City since the eighteenth century. In 1895 the first permanent appointment of a Negro teacher to a predominantly white public school was made. Susan Elizabeth Frazier, a graduate of Hunter College, won an extended legal battle with the school board. After Miss Frazier's breakthrough other Negroes received similar appointments. Statewide, the *coup de grâce* to separate Negro education came through a general education act passed in 1900.[6]

Negro and white people in New York were aware of the change in racial status typified by these acts. Cases of discrimination in public places continued to occur,[7] but it was generally recognized that significant progress was made in the area of race relations subject to law since the end of the Civil War. Jacob A. Riis commented on the "wavering color line" in New York City in 1890,[8] and Samuel R. Scottron later wrote of the "decline of color prejudice" in these years.[9] When southern Negro politicians passed through New York City in the 1880's they lived in the most exclusive hotels. P. B. S. Pinchback regularly stayed at the Hoffman House, John Mercer Langston at the Fifth Avenue Hotel, John R. Lynch at the Metropolitan Hotel.[10] The Negro *New York Freeman,* in an 1887 editorial, said that "Now in many of the best restaurants, hotels and churches decent colored people receive courteous treatment."[11] "Respectable colored men have little trouble in finding accommodations in the very best hotels," a Negro New Yorker indicated in the 1880's.[12] It was the easing of racial tensions in the North in these years that rekindled the traditional drive of the Negro middle class for total acceptance as Americans, not Negroes, within our society: "From the earliest times the attitude of the free negroes has been opposed to any organization or the segregation of the negroes as such," W. E. B. DuBois wrote in 1901. "Men like Fortune, McCune Smith, and Redmond [*sic*] insisted that they were American citizens, not negroes. . . ."[13]

II

In spite of the attack on institutionalized discrimination, however, there was very little (if any) change in the stereotyped conception of the Negro that most white Americans held. With rare exception, even in the North during the late nineteenth century, there was general agreement on what contemporaries called the "peculiar genius" of the Negro people.[14] The stereotyped image of the "sensuous," "lazy," "good-natured," "childlike," "faithful" Negro was presented by defenders as well as critics of the race—both Negro and white. The literature of the time abounds with relevant examples of this image. A New York rabbi, for example, in a sermon at Temple Emanu-El in 1906, attacked the vicious racism embodied in the Reverend Thomas Dixon, Jr.'s, novel, *The Clansman.* (Dixon's trilogy on race relations, of which *The Clansman* was a part, was the basis for the successful movie *The Birth of a Nation,* a film which Negroes have protested against for five decades.)[15] The rabbi defended "the faithful, loyal Negro—his humor, his pathos, his geniality, his shrewdness, his love of his master . . . his sympathy and charity, his even childlike patriotism, and love of freedom."[16] An Episcopal clergyman advocated the extension of church services to Negroes in the city in 1884: "The negro is exacting," he said, "therefore, let the Church . . . arouse him. If he is emotional, let the Church meet these emotions with a lively service, and thus subdue them. The negro is imitative," he concluded.[17] Train and hire Negro workers and they will always be loyal and never strike, a southern Negro educator told a group of northern businessmen in 1902: "Look at the great strikes you are having, and every time you have to make concessions," he said. "But if you educate this million and a half colored boys and girls and make skilled laborers of them they will take the place of these strikers."[18] "The negroes are . . . good-natured and happy under all circumstances," concluded a late-nineteenth-century writer.[19]

Negroes of prominence of New York City were often considered dark counterparts of white leaders. The Negro abolitionist Samuel Ringgold Ward was popularly known as a "Black Daniel Webster" prior to the Civil War.[20] After the war, a well-known Negro singer was called "Black Patti," and another "Colored Jenny Lind."[21] Three local colored politicians were respectively: "Black Depew," "Colored Croker," Negro "Mark Hanna."[22]

Popular images of the Negro were portrayed to New Yorkers in the numerous vaudeville and minstrel shows which regularly appeared in the city. New York City was the theater capital of America at the turn of the century and Negro vaudeville reached the height of its popularity then.[23] Many of the performances, including the Creole shows which specialized in presenting scantily clad and beautiful Negro women, were hits.[24] The hackneyed themes running almost without exception through all these plays were, in exaggerated form, a reflection of the generally accepted attitudes of white America toward Negro life. For the most part, they presented a comic and derisive caricature of an entire people: "The 'darky' to the white man is grotesquely amusing," Mary White Ovington wrote.[25]

The Negro of these plays was a ludicrous figure of a man—he was "darky," he was "coon." Williams and Walker, for example, were billed as the "Two Real Coons."[26] Such plays as the *Gentlemen Coons' Parade* (Chorus: "You'll find no common second-class nigs/ In the gentlemen coons' parade"), *The Coon at the Door, The Coon Musketeers, Dat Famous Chicken Debate* ("Resolved, That Stealing Chickens Ain't No Crime"), *Dat Watermillyon, The Coonville 'Ristocrat Club, The Coon and the Chink, Jes' Like White Folks, The*

Irishman and the Coon, The Policy Players, The Sons of Ham, In Bandanna Land, In Dahomey, In Abyssinia and dozens of others were performed on the stage in New York City and cities throughout the country.[27] Songs such as "All Coons Look Alike to Me," "Coon, Coon, Coon," "I Wish My Color Would Fade," had "wide currency" in New York City in the 1890's. "It was no longer the 'darkey melody' [that was popular in the 1890's] but the 'coon song.'" New York historian Henry Collins Brown noted. These songs presented a "ribald school of 'babies,' 'honies,' mercenary wenches . . . and sundry 'no account niggers.'"[28] Characters like "Useless Peabody," "George Washington Jones," "Moses Abraham Highbrow," "John Jacob Astor House" (crushed silk hat, big bow tie, long white gloves, worn-out shoes), were always about to steal a chicken or a watermelon, or pretending to be something they were not. "Sam Lightfoot," the waiter in *Badly Sold,* changed his attitudes to suit the customer, or lied to get a bigger tip.[29] "Careless Cupid" applied for a job in a bakery and listed the following qualifications to his prospective employer: "I kin eat an' I kin sleep, and de res' ob de time jes' lay round. Say, boss, whar's yo lounge? I's gettin' tired standin' yere. . . . I'm a straight out nigger, I am, yessir."[30] Sam Caesar, Pompey Ducklegs, Julius Crow, Doolittle Black, were waiters, porters, servants, butlers, confidence men, who shuffled along in baggy pants, liberally used ungrammatical language, loved whiskey, shot dice, seemed eternally shiftless or carefree. The covers of *Denison's Black-Face Series* showed a broadly smiling, white-toothed Negro woman whose hair was always tied with white bows and curlers, or a white-haired old Negro man strumming on a banjo. James Weldon Johnson, who was personally involved in the production of some of these shows in New York City, summed up the themes that ran throughout them: "The Negro songs then the rage were known as 'coon songs,'" he wrote, "and were concerned with jamborees of various sorts and the play of razors, with the gastronomical delights of chicken, pork chops and watermelon, and with the experiences of red-hot 'mammas' and their never too faithful 'papas.' These songs were for the most part crude, raucous, bawdy, often obscene."[31]

Many Negroes seriously objected to these ludicrous characterizations of Negro life. "It is humiliating to be regarded as a curiosity," wrote one man in 1895. *The New York Age* angrily denounced "plays which burlesque the character of a people and tend to degrade them in the estimation of their fellow citizens." It proposed that they "be prohibited."[32] Negro performers attempted to gain recognition for themselves as true artists, not hacks, but they were unable to convince theater managers that anything but the standard fare was profitable: "Every show had to be studied carefully for anything that might offend white prejudices. . . ."[33] In speaking of his friend Bert Williams, the most famous Negro comic of the early twentieth century (whites called him "the darky comedian"), James Weldon Johnson later wrote that he expressed "only certain conceptions about Negro life that his audience was willing to accept and ready to enjoy."[34] "My job," said Bert Williams simply, "is to make them laugh."[35]

> Why should the world be otherwise,
> In counting all our tears and sighs?
> Nay, let them only see us, while
> We wear the mask.[36]

What was most striking about the Negro stereotype was the way it portrayed a people in an image so totally the reverse of what Americans considered worthy of emulation and recognition. The major and traditional American values were all absent from the Negro stereotype. The Negro was conceived of as lazy in an ambitious culture; improvident and sensuous in a moralistic society; happy in a sober world; poor in a nation that offered riches to all who cared to take them; childlike in a country of men. He seemed more fit to be a servant, a "half man," than anything else: "And the Nation echoed . . . : Be content to be servants, and nothing more; what need of higher culture for half-men."[37] "Let the Negro learn," said a *New York Times* editorial in 1900, "to clean stables, care for horses, feed and harness and drive them, run lawn mowers, make and keep gardens, and also keep engagements. . . ."[38] Negroes hoped for full acceptance in a culture which mocked their aspirations.[39]

III

With the increased migration of Negroes from the South, the brighter side of race relations in the city—the softening of institutionalized prejudices—came to an end. Among white people, Kelly Miller remarked in 1906, there was a "prevailing dread of an overwhelming influx from the South."[40] Even during the late nineteenth century

Negroes argued that most white northerners knew little, and cared even less, about Negro life: "The Northern white man knows practically nothing of the Negro; he is looked upon more as a problem than as a factor in the general weal, with the same desires, passions, hopes, ambitions as other human creatures," a journalist concluded.[41] "Do we ever think of how such people live?" a reviewer of Dunbar's *The Sport of the Gods* wrote. "It is a . . . whole stratum of society of which all of us are densely ignorant and of whose very existence most of us are wholly unaware."[42] As the population increased, however, the city became more aware of its Negro residents, and responded by reversing the trend in formal race relations that had typified the 1870's and 1880's. The early twentieth century in New York City and in the North generally was a period of intensified racial alienation.

Racial antagonism was rekindled in a variety of ways. White churches, for example, which had formerly allowed small numbers of Negroes to participate in regular services, now attempted to ease their Negro members out: "In each of these churches when the number of Negro communicants was small the colored brother was accorded a hearty welcome, but as the Negro population steadily increased . . . from the white members would be heard generous suggestions that the Negro members get a place of worship of their own."[43] An Episcopal church in the area of San Juan Hill resolved its problem by holding separate services for Negroes.[44] Once the Negro population of Harlem expanded, the pastor of one white church told Negro members they were "Not Welcome," and then gave them an ultimatum to join one of the Negro institutions moving into the neighborhood: "When there were few black and colored communicants in the Harlem district the white . . . churches received them," a Negro New Yorker observed in 1913. "Of late years conditions have greatly changed. . . ."[45] "Trinity Vestry, in New York City, is making arrangements to provide a separate place of worship for the colored members," the NAACP journal *Crisis* recorded in 1914. "At present all worship at the same place."[46]

The separation that was evident in the churches was true of many other areas of racial contact in the city. When the "Colored Men's YMCA" was opened on West Fifty-third Street, it was taken for granted that Negroes would use these facilities exclusively rather than those Y's which catered to white people.[47] White fraternal organizations brought suit against Negro societies which used the same names.[48] The New York State Boxing Commission outlawed bouts between Negro and white fighters, and American society longed for a "White Hope" to defeat Negro heavyweight champion Jack Johnson.[49] There were innumerable legal suits brought by Negroes against white hotels, restaurants and theaters for refusing them service in the early twentieth century: "Northern Negroes believe this discrimination in public places against the black man [is] increasing in New York," Mary White Ovington noted.[50] Union restrictions and racial barriers in industry were so widespread that Negroes were largely excluded from "employment along lines other than those of beggarly paid menials."[51] As a result of these exclusions, the urban Negro continually represented a large group of unemployed workers readily available for strikebreaking: "In this matter of excluding colored men from unions, skilled mechanics must remember that they run the risk of building up in the United States a great body of justly indignant and always available STRIKE BREAKERS," a white journalist wrote in 1910. In 1895, 1904, 1907, 1910, 1911, 1912, 1916 and 1920 Negro strikebreakers were used to help break strikes of New York City longshoremen, laborers, street cleaners, baggage handlers, hod carriers, waiters, and garment workers.[52] There was even an unsuccessful attempt in 1910 to re-establish the state law barring intermarriage. The proposed "Act to Amend the Domestic Relations Law, in Relation to Miscegenation," proposed to void all marriages *"contracted between a person of white or Caucasian race and a person of the negro or black race."*[53] Negroes organized to oppose these new "Black Codes."[54] Assemblymen were urged to defeat the miscegenation bill. It was, a Negro New Yorker thought, but one part of a general "sentiment . . . that would 'Jim Crow' us at every turn, and that sentiment is growing in this State."[55] Negro Harlem was created in these years. It was a world within a world that reflected the subtle and radical changes then taking place in many areas of life in major cities of the North.

Was there any solution to the problems created by the migration and the intensified racial hatreds? With almost no exception the only opinion that was publicly stated was that it was necessary to convince Negroes their proper place was in the South. Booker T. Washington made a tour of the tenement districts of New York City in 1904. One journalist said that his trip would be of great value because Washington could then return south and describe the poverty he saw. He would tell the "country negroes [to remain] on the farms in the South rather than [come] to an overcrowded city" where they certainly would die.[56] "Northern men visiting southern colored industrial schools advise[d] the pupils to remain where they [were]," a white reformer noted in 1910.[57]

IV

The migration of southern Negroes also created antagonisms which were intraracial in nature. Negroes who had lived in the city for generations, especially those who gloried in the easing of racial tensions during the late nineteenth century, blamed the southern migrant for reversing this trend. Similar antagonisms were evident among most immigrant groups—Jews, Italians, Greeks, and others— when earlier generations seemed overwhelmed by the problems of later arrivals from their countries. Negroes of "the old Knickerbocker stamp," "the old time aristocracy bearing Knickerbocker names" ("the best people," "aristocratic dark race circles"), some of whom were members of the Negro Society of the Sons of New York, railed against the lower-class southern Negro with the virulence of good white racists: "The taint of slavery was far removed from these people," Mary White Ovington remarked, and they "looked with scorn upon arrivals from the South."[58] "These people are thoroughly embarrassed by the raucousness, vulgarity, and violence with which they find themselves surrounded," a Negro clergyman concluded. "They do everything possible to disassociate themselves from it." Middle-class Negroes in Chicago, Philadelphia and Boston reacted in a similar manner.[59]

To many New York Negroes the migrants were "riff-raff," "illiterate," "thoughtless," "lazy," "overdemonstrative," "boastful," "uncouth," "undesirable," "common." It was the southerner, they said, who created the "epidemic of negrophobia," the recent "spread of race antipathy in the North."[60] They listened too readily to "Tramp Preachers," and were too dirty—they were "the low element to our race . . . the class who own a lot of dirty rags and dogs and crowds of children," a correspondent of Booker T. Washington said.[61] The "Old Settlers" struck out against "the lower masses of their people" with an automatic, instinctive drive for "self-defense and self-preservation," DuBois wrote.[62] "We have too much unwarranted criticism to fight to be handicapped in this way," a Negro New Yorker complained in 1905.[63]

> God knows
> We have our troubles, too—
> One trouble is you:
> you talk too loud,
> look too black,
> don't get anywhere,
> and sometimes it seems
> you don't even care.[64]

The only solution that these people had to offer was basically the one that white New Yorkers proposed—keep the migrants in the South. In the 1880's, prior to any significant migration, *The New York Age* encouraged Negroes to flee the social and economic proscriptions of the South: "Why should they not seek in other sections to better their social, material and civil condition," it said. When migrants came in larger numbers, however, the *Age* changed its tune: "It will well repay them to consider whether it will not be better to bear some of the ills they now do, than fly to others they know not of." "We believe the South is the best place for the great masses of the Afro-American people."[65] This same theme was emphasized and re-emphasized in a whole spate of articles, editorials and speeches printed in Negro journals in the years preceding the First World War. The interracial Committee for the Industrial Improvement of the Condition of the Negro in New York, established in 1906, sent circular letters to southern newspapers, churches and schools discouraging any thoughts of migration to New York City.[66] Kelly Miller and Booker T. Washington wrote numerous articles on "The Farm" as the "Negro's Best Chance," and on the evils and destructiveness of life in northern cities. Only "country life" and "working on the soil" would "uplift" the Negro, it was argued. "There should be organized . . . a bureau of information which should furnish the masses of the race . . . accurate knowledge of the evil of indiscriminate influx to the North," Miller thought.[67] But "even while they exclaimed," Paul Laurence Dunbar said, "they knew there was no way, and that the stream of young negro life would continue to flow up from the South. . . ." ("I was born and raised in the country/But Mamma I'm stayin' in town.")[68]

V

This negative view of the migration expressed by Negroes and whites was felt most intensely in the working-class districts of the city into which migrants moved. Interracial conflicts became so common at the turn of the century, it will be remembered, that San Juan Hill was named as a parody on them. Small but regular clashes ordinarily involving Negroes and the Irish were recorded in the New York press then. The antagonism between these two peoples was undoubtedly one of the harshest intergroup hatreds in American history. The deep strain of nativism that traditionally runs through American Negro thought was especially evident during this period of overwhelming foreign immigration. The Negro, born in the United States, commonly expressed his antagonism for foreigners in general and for the Irish immigrant in particular: "It is to be regretted," the Negro journalist John E. Bruce said, "that in this land of Bibles where the outcasts—the scum of European society—can come and enjoy the fullest social and political privileges, the Native Born American with woolly hair and dark complexion is made the Victim . . . of Social Ostracism." Such statements as "These low-foreheaded, beetle-browed fellows . . . driven from Europe"; "tens of thousands of aliens are being landed on these shores and freely given the employment which is denied Negro citizens"; "his brogue was so heavy it sounded like he had marbles in his mouth"; "the time is upon us when some restriction will have to be placed upon the volume and character of European immigration," were written by Negroes. A Negro journal spoke of "the open dislike of the Irish and colored people. . . ." One man put it tersely. Whatever the Negro is, he said, "he is no hyphenate."[69]

The Irish immigrant, in turn, was given full leeway by American society to look with disdain upon the Negro. A European traveler to the city in the 1860's maintained that Irish immigrants considered Negroes "a soulless race." "I am satisfied that some of these people would shoot a black man . . . as they would a hog," he concluded. "Pat O'Flannagan does not have the least thing in the world against Jim from Dixie," a Negro educator remarked in 1909, "but it didn't take Pat long after passing the Statue of Liberty to learn that it is popular to give Jim a whack." "It is quite remarkable how easily

. . . foreigners catch on to the notion . . . to treat Afro-Americans disdainfully and contemptuously," *The New York Age* noted.[70]

Throughout the nineteenth century this mutual antipathy erupted into violence many times. Since the Draft Riots of 1863, however, there were no major clashes between Negroes and Irish in New York City. Now, with increased racial tensions pervading the city, especially in the neighborhoods where the two groups had closest contact, there was a revival of bitterness. The Tenderloin was a common battleground.

A major race riot occurred in New York City in 1900. It was the first serious outbreak of racial violence since the Draft Riots. The riot of 1900 was a symbol of the entire new trend of increasing racial alienation and violence taking place throughout the city. The generally apathetic response of the white community to the demands Negroes made after the riot for justice was a reflection of the growing lack of concern of white New Yorkers for the increasingly serious impediments to Negro equality.

VI

In August 1900 New York City was in the midst of a heat wave. The weather bureau recorded stifling temperatures throughout the month: "The warmest August since the Local Bureau kept track of it." At noon on August 12, the temperature reached 91 degrees. New Yorkers spilled out of their tenements seeking relief. Stoops in the Tenderloin were crowded throughout the night. Local saloons were packed to capacity.[71]

Arthur J. Harris left his house at 241 West Forty-first Street on the evening of August 12 to buy some cigars and pass some time at McBride's Saloon. Harris, twenty-two, was typical of many young Negroes who came to New York City at that time. Born in Richmond, Virginia, of an unstable family (his mother lived in Washington, D.C., in 1900, his father in Cranford, New Jersey), he had left home at fourteen and lived in Washington for seven years. In 1899 he came north to visit his father and find work. The Washington police never had any trouble with him, his record showed "No Prior Convictions." When asked about his previous education, he responded "Yes"; he could read and write.[72] He called himself a Protestant.[73]

In Jersey City in 1899, he had picked up money working at odd jobs—as a cook, baker, carpenter and poolroom attendant—and lived with 20-year-old May Enoch, who had left the husband she had married at sixteen. Harris and "his woman," or, as he often referred to her, "my wife," came to Forty-first Street at the beginning of August 1900, rented a room at Annie Johnson's, and said they were looking for work. At 2 A.M. on August 13, May came down to McBride's: "I says to Harris, 'Kid come on up home.' "[74] While she waited for him at the corner of Forty-first Street and Eighth Avenue, Robert J. Thorpe, a plain-clothes policeman, approached her and charged her with "soliciting." To Harris he looked like a white man who was mishandling his woman: "The policeman grabbed my girl. I didn't know who he was and thought he was a citizen like myself," he maintained later at his trial. Harris was clubbed in a struggle with the policeman. He said the policeman pummeled him with his club and shouted, "Get up you black son-of-a-bitch." "I thought the man was trying to kill me, and I believed that he would kill me if I didn't protect myself." Harris pulled out a knife and "cut him twice." May ran home where she was later picked up and arrested; Harris took a train to his mother's home in Washington; Thorpe died in Roosevelt Hospital the next day.[75]

Little more was needed to set off the racial tensions that now lay so near the surface of everyday life in the Tenderloin. A Negro, a recent southern migrant, had killed a "cop"—the son-in-law to be of the acting captain of the local police station. Rumors of violence spread throughout the Negro sections. One woman went to the police and begged for protection: "the tenants of her house were terror-stricken," she said. "They had been warned of an attack in the late night."[76] "Feelings against the Negroes in the neighborhood of Thorpe's late home had been at white heat for a couple of days," it was reported. Large crowds, including sixty members of the Thirty-seventh Street station house, gathered at the home of the Thorpe family to pay their respects.[77]

The immediate cause for the outbreak was a fight between a Negro, Spencer Walters, and a white man, Thomas J. Healy. The Police Board, in its official findings on the riot, claimed that Walters attempted to shoot Healy on the night of August 15. The fight took place near Thorpe's home the evening before the burial. Negroes said that Walters had been set upon by some hysterical people who just visited the Thorpe family.[78] It makes little difference who was right. If it was not this, there would have been some other excuse for violence.

The entire neighborhood went wild with rage. Walters was immediately attacked by a mob. He "was a wreck when placed under arrest." "If there had been a carefully arranged plot and this had been the agreed signal, the outbreak could not have been more spontaneous," a journalist reported. "Men and women poured by the hundreds from the neighboring tenements. Negroes were set upon wherever they could be found and brutally beaten."[79] The word spread that a "nigger chase" was on.[80] Up and down the streets, through hotels and saloons, in cellars and streetcars, Negroes were attacked and beaten. White street gangs mobbed the electric cars on Eighth Avenue ("Nigger, nigger never die, black face and shiny eye"), pulled Negroes off at random and beat them: "Every car passing up or down Eighth Avenue . . . was stopped by the crowd and every negro on board dragged out. . . . The police made little or no attempt to arrest any of [the] assailants," *The New York Times* noted. One man brought a clothesline, tied it to a lamppost, and looked for someone to lynch.[81]

A group of Negro waiters at a midtown hotel remained there all night rather than tempt the mob. Stephen Small and Adolphus Cooks were beaten by the police and decided to hide in a cellar all night. Zeb Robinson, a Negro barber, was attacked on the streets and taken to Bellevue in a disheveled state. Charles Mitchell became hysterical after repeated "blows on the head."[82] A friend of James Weldon Johnson never fully recovered from the beating he received with a lead pipe.[83] Affidavits were later collected from eighty Negroes— waiters, porters, elevator operators, chimney sweeps, laborers, longshoremen—attesting to police and mob brutality. Although there are no reliable estimates of the number of persons injured in the riot, any Negro who happened to be on the streets of the Tenderloin that night was attacked and beaten. That serious injury was done to many is attested in the individual complaints collected in *Story of the Riot* (1900). Others never bothered to protest.

Acting Captain Cooney of the Twentieth Precinct called out the reserves to quell the trouble. However, the predominantly Irish police force hardly acted as detached enforcers of the law. Some did protect Negroes, but most, at the height of the frenzy, encouraged the rioters:

"It was said freely by witnesses of the disorderly scenes of Wednesday night that the police had done as much as anybody to encourage and promote the abuse of inoffensive negroes," a reporter indicated. Policemen often led mobs that attacked Negroes. Some dragged Negroes off streetcars and beat them. Others looked the other way rather than witness trouble. A white woman, Mrs. Davenport, sheltered a few Negroes in her home on the night of August 15. When she refused to turn them over to the police, they replied: "What kind of woman are you to be harboring niggers?" It seemed their ambition to "club the life out of a nigger," a witness said.[84]

William J. Elliott, a Negro waiter, was arrested for carrying a revolver. Reporters saw him entering the Thirty-seventh Street station house uninjured. When he left the next morning he was beaten and bloody. Elliott told the Police Commissioners that as he passed through the muster room the lights were turned out and he was kicked, punched and clubbed into insensibility.[85] As he could not identify any specific assailant, however, the Commissioners found this evidence "contradictory," and ruled that "no conviction of a violation of the Rules of the Department could be sustained [on it]."[86]

At about 2 A.M. on August 16 a providential summer thunderstorm drenched the city. It ended the initial violence. Emergency staffs on all-night duty at Roosevelt, Bellevue and New York hospitals handled the many cases of battered heads. The local police courts were jammed to capacity—with Negroes. One of the magistrates criticized the police and asked to see "some of the white persons who participated in this riot." By 1:30 A.M. his request was fulfilled. A teenager, Frank Minogue, was brought in and charged with trying to trip a policeman who was dispersing a crowd of rioters.

VII

Although the riot had ended, the neighborhood remained tense. Negroes began to arm. Revolvers and other weapons were easily purchased at local pawnshops and hardware stores. In a survey made of the Tenderloin, just one day after the riot, it was found that 145 revolvers and a substantial amount of ammunition had been sold— "all had gone to negroes."[87] Lloyd Williams, a Negro bartender, was seen leaving one store with an arsenal of weapons. When asked what he was going to do with them, he replied: "I understand they're knocking down negroes 'round here. The first man tries it on me gets

this. . . ." Other Negroes warned that no white men were going to
bother them. As policemen patrolled the Negro blocks they were
showered with bricks, bottles and garbage from rooftops and tenement windows. They fired back with revolvers. It seems miraculous
that no one was killed then.

Orders went out to keep the Negroes off the streets. Paul Laurence
Dunbar went into the Tenderloin, visited Negro homes and attempted
to restore peace. Innumerable arrests were made, practically all of
Negroes, on the charge of carrying concealed weapons. For more
than a month after the riot there were almost daily clashes between
individual Negroes and whites. At least two people were killed in
these fights. Slowly, the Tenderloin returned to its normal state of
semipeace.

VIII

The whites were shocked.[88] Editorials appeared throughout the press
criticizing the police for their brutality and the vicious for their violence. The tone of the responses, however, lacked sympathy for the
injured Negroes. The riot was made a political issue as the Republican press and the Good Government Society attacked Tammany Hall.
The *New York Daily Tribune* printed a cartoon of a massive Tammany tiger in police uniform swinging a club. Huddled on the floor in
the background was a bloody Negro. The caption read: "He's On the
Police Force Now." The "Respectable Citizenry" attacked the "white
trash" and advised Negroes to vote Republican.[89]

Negro leaders demanded punishment of the guilty and compensa-
tion for the injured. The Reverend Dr. W. H. Brooks of St. Mark's
Methodist Episcopal Church led the protest. Brooks, born on a
Maryland plantation, had been at St. Mark's since 1897—well
equipped with a voice that could drown out the clatter of elevated
trains that ran near his church.[90] One of the most important leaders
of the city's Negro community, he later became a founder of the
NAACP and the National Urban League. From his pulpit, and from
the pulpits of all the Negro churches in the city, the mobs and police
were vilified. An honest public investigation was demanded,[91] and
prominent members of the Negro community—lawyers, clergymen,
politicians, businessmen—were urged to use their influence to seek
justice.[92] An *ad hoc* defense committee, the Citizens' Protective
League, was organized at a meeting in St. Mark's on September 3. Two

lawyers, Frank Moss and Israel Ludlow, were hired. Moss vowed never to let the riot "fade into forgetfulness." Suits were filed for damages against the city in the names of persons injured by the police.[93] At a mass meeting at Carnegie Hall to raise money and gain public support, some speakers urged caution and peaceful agitation. D. Macon Webster, a Negro lawyer, wanted justice done for the "humblest citizen." "One might think we [were] all aliens" from the manner in which we were treated, he concluded.[94] Others, more belligerent, urged Negroes to arm and defend their homes.[95] All agreed that right must be done.

The protests were militant and idealistic, the results cold and bleak. There was no mass response to the appeal for public support: "I heard many native Americans . . . say after the riot," a contemporary noted in *Harper's Weekly,* "that they would have been glad if many of the negroes had been killed." "This is a mass in the midst of what is . . . an alien and hostile people," another believed.[96] The August Grand Jury refused to indict a single policeman, alleging that accusations were brought against groups rather than individuals. When cases were presented against individual policemen, they too were dismissed.[97] The Police Board set up a committee of investigation, which refused Moss and Ludlow permission to cross-examine witnesses, and concluded in its report that "there is nothing in the evidence taken by your committee which will justify preferment of charges against any officer. . . ."[98] The *Tribune* quipped: "The Police Board wants it understood that the riot inquiry is to be full and impartial, only no evidence against the police will be admitted."[99] Arthur J. Harris was arrested in Washington for killing policeman Thorpe, tried in New York, found guilty of murder in the second degree, and "sentenced to the State Prison at Sing Sing at hard labor for the term of his natural life."[100] The Reverend Dr. Brooks created "The Arthur J. Harris Liberation Fund" and continued to fight for his release, but Harris died in prison on December 20, 1908.[101] The Citizens' Protective League simply ceased to exist. It accomplished nothing. The little power it could wield ran into an almost solid wall of indifference and opposition. "It is like sheep proclaiming the law of righteousness to a congregation of wolves," Kelly Miller commented on another occasion. "A complaint is effective only in so far as there is power to enforce it."[102]

And the Police Department, in its *Annual Report,* provided its own conclusion to the sad affair: "In the month of August the west side of the city was threatened with a race war between the white and colored citizens. . . . Prompt and vigorous action on the part of the Police . . . kept the situation under control, and . . . quiet was restored in districts . . . which were affected."[103]

Was the riot and the reaction to it a sign of intensified racial alienation in New York City, as some people claimed? No, said a columnist for *The New York Times* in an emphatic rejoinder. There is no "settled race hatred . . . in New York. There are no signs that the citizen of African descent is distrusted or disliked. . . . His crude melodies and childlike antics are more than tolerated in the music halls of the best class."[104]

CHAPTER 4

Urban Progressives: Negro and White

"To my amazement I learned that
there was a Negro problem in my
city. I had never honestly thought
of it before."
—Mary White Ovington, 1900

"We seem to be doing things in the
same old unprogressive ways as when
society was less complex. . . ."
—Frances A. Kellor, 1907

I

The emergence of racial violence and antagonism and the increasing number of complex social problems created by the urbanization of the Negro produced a need for racial reform in the North in the early twentieth century. The movement for social and economic reform in northern cities, a vital part of the national Progressive movement, showed deep concern for the welfare of the Negro people.[1] The years preceding World War I found a revitalization of interest in Negro life among urban reformers in every major northern city to which migrants came in large numbers. When "Race was against the colored man," a Negro New Yorker recalled, "the reformers turned out. . . ." These Progressives were, in the words of a Negro businessman, the "doers," not the "talkers," of American society.[2]

The white people involved in this movement were primarily social workers and urban reformers who attempted to improve living conditions in the industrial and tenement house areas of northern cities. Those who established settlement houses for immigrants in the 1890's also founded similar institutions for Negroes. In the first decade of the twentieth century, Progressives organized the Frederick Douglass Center in Chicago, the Robert Gould Shaw House in

Boston, the Eighth Ward Settlement in Philadelphia, the Stillman House and two Lincoln Settlements in New York City. Frances Bartholomew, Carl Kelsey and R. R. Wright, Jr., in Philadelphia; Isabel Eaton, who had worked with DuBois on his study of Philadelphia Negroes, in Boston; Celia Parker Woolley, Sophonisba Breckinridge, Mary E. McDowell and Louise DeKoven Bowen in Chicago; Mary White Ovington, Elizabeth Walton, Victoria Earle Matthews and William Lewis Bulkley in New York City were all actively engaged in social work among Negroes.[3] Perceptive studies of Negro society were undertaken as well in these years, in the first major scholarly effort to analyze America's racial problems since the abolitionist era. In typical Progressive fashion, volumes of facts and statistics were gathered to learn how best to improve living conditions. "We must not forget," W. E. B. DuBois wrote in 1903, "that most Americans answer all queries regarding the Negro *a priori,* and that the least . . . human courtesy we can do is to listen to evidence."[4] Between 1899 and 1915 a number of books on race problems appeared, among them DuBois' *Philadelphia Negro* (1899), Ray Stannard Baker's *Following the Color Line* (1908), R. R. Wright, Jr.'s, *The Negro in Pennsylvania* (1908), Mary White Ovington's *Half A Man: The Status of the Negro in New York* (1911), George Edmund Haynes' *The Negro at Work in New York City* (1912), Louise DeKoven Bowen's *The Colored People of Chicago* (1913), Frank U. Quillin's *The Color Line in Ohio* (1913), John Daniel's *In Freedom's Birthplace: A History of the Boston Negro* (1914), William A. Crossland's *Industrial Conditions Among Negroes in St. Louis* (1914), and Frances Blascoer's *Colored School Children of New York* (1915). Numerous articles on Negro life were printed in contemporary periodicals early in the century. In 1909–1911 the first national Negro defense and improvement agencies were founded—the NAACP and the National League on Urban Conditions Among Negroes—both in New York City.

II

Concern for the welfare of Negroes among white people in New York City had traditionally been associated with religious groups, and most particularly with the Society of Friends. Quakers, leading abolitionists in New York City, played an important role in founding free schools for Negro children. After the Civil War, the only white organization that continued its works among the city's Negroes was the New York Colored Mission, founded by the Quakers. A few Negro churches in these years gave some assistance "to needy persons who find themselves in the great city without a home for a few days," but this effort was not highly organized.[5]

The "Friends' Mission," as some contemporaries called it (more vituperative observers christened it "Nigger School"),[6] offered missionary work and "Christian Fellowship"[7] to Negroes, distributing religious tracts, temperance literature and Bibles by the thousands to the city's Negro population.[8] Before its incorporation in 1871, the society was called the "African Sabbath School Association," and its first home was over a stable. When incorporated, it conceived of its task basically as a religious one: "To conduct in the City of New York a Sabbath School for Religious Instruction," and hold "Social, Religious Meetings."[9] Whatever practical assistance the organization would give Negroes was considered secondary to its religious obligation. The City Mission and Tract Society contributed enough money to the Colored Mission to permit it to purchase a building of its own in the Tenderloin, its motto: "Inasmuch as ye have done it unto one of the least of these my brethren, ye have done it unto me."[10]

But, as the Negro population of Manhattan increased, slightly in the 1870's and 1880's, more rapidly in the 1890's, the Colored Mission was slowly transformed into a social service agency. It conducted an employment bureau, provided temporary housing and inexpensive meals for migrants (a "Sunday bowl of soup and slice of bread"), opened a small "infant school" which cared for and fed Negro children for five cents a day, and bought glasses for Negroes who wanted to learn how to read (most wished to read the Bible). Destitution was so widespread in the depression winter of 1893–1894 that the Colored Mission distributed tons of coal and barrels of food to Negro families—flour, corn meal, oatmeal, hominy, rice, bread, beans, pork, milk. "The records of those months are so sad that one shrinks from recurring to them," the society's missionary recorded in his journal. "No fire, no food, dispossession impending, illness, death . . . confronted us. [People] were found actually dying of want."[11] Between the Civil War and the 1890's, with this one modest exception, no organizations in New York City were concerned with the welfare of Negroes. By 1915 there were more than a dozen.

III

Increasing interest in Negro life developed in the 1890's and first decade of the twentieth century among white and Negro reformers. The movement was widespread and involved people who disagreed with one another on the over-all methods of improving the status of the Negro in American society. Some were avid supporters of the gradualism of Booker T. Washington, others more militant followers of W. E. B. DuBois. Mary White Ovington, for example, considered herself "an ardent disciple of the DuBois School."[12] Whatever theoretic differences existed among them, they held basic agreement on the need for immediate practical reforms to improve the generally harsh lives of Negroes in the city. Urban reformers' primary concern was to find jobs and decent homes for Negro migrants, to open playgrounds for Negro children, to break the color barrier in businesses and unions, to improve health, educational and sanitary conditions in the Tenderloin, San Juan Hill and Harlem, and to protect Negro domestics from the exploitations of city employment bureaus.

The first organization this spirit of "social justice" produced, founded in 1897, was the White Rose Industrial Association; the "White Rose Working Girls' Home," as the sign which hung over its door read. A Negro, Mrs. Victoria Earle Matthews, the youngest daughter of a Georgia slave,[18] organized the society. Born in slavery herself just one month after the Civil War began, she came to New York City with her mother and family in the 1870's. She was young enough to attend the Negro public schools; after graduation she became a writer, and her stories and articles were published in white and Negro journals. She thought of herself as an emancipated woman, founded a Negro protest and women's rights society in the city (the "Women's Loyal Union of New York and Brooklyn"), supported Ida B. Wells' antilynching crusade, and delivered lectures on "The Awakening of the Afro-American Woman." When she learned of the "unscrupulous employment agents who deceived the unsuspecting girls desiring to come North," "those unprincipled men who haunted the wharves," she decided to "check the evil."[14]

Mrs. Matthews' association provided lodgings and meals for women until they could find work. The society kept agents at piers— "meeting the boats" it was called—in Norfolk as well as New York

City to answer questions, escort women to their places of employment or, instead, to the White Rose Home: "Our principal object is to protect our girls, to direct and help them amid the dangers of our great city." The White Rose Home became a settlement house as well as a temporary lodging place for migrants. The classes presented there in domestic training and "race history," the library of books on Negro life, and the facilities for recreation admitted the public as well as residents of the home. Paul Laurence Dunbar and Booker T. Washington gave lectures at the settlement. The White Rose Home continued its work among Negroes even after Mrs. Matthews' death in 1907, and finally moved to larger quarters in Harlem in 1918.[15]

The fear of exploitation of Negro women by "intelligence agents" that motivated Victoria Earle Matthews also led to the founding of an organization which attempted to do on a national scale what the White Rose Home did for Negro migrants who came to New York City. The initiator of this movement, a white reformer, Frances A. Kellor, wrote a perceptive series of articles on criminality among Negroes, one of the earliest sociological analyses of racial problems in the city.[16] She also spent a good part of her early crusading career attacking the corruptions of private employment bureaus. In 1903, the Woman's Municipal League of New York hired Miss Kellor to collect as much data on employment agencies as a thorough investigation could produce.[17] She gathered information from 732 private employment bureaus, published her findings in 1904 in an important book of the Progressive era, *Out of Work: A Study of Employment Agencies,* and bombarded municipal officials with the information she uncovered. Her criticisms and prodding led to the creation of the Office of Commissioner of Licenses in New York City, and helped establish the first state-controlled employment bureau in New York in 1911.[18]

Frances A. Kellor and other municipal reformers interested in job placement believed that many employment agents were dishonest and treated their clients in a shoddy manner, and, even worse, that many agencies served as subtle guises to draw women into the arms of "the alluring procuresses of the city."[19] Some Negro women found their jobs as maids and cooks to be in what Miss Kellor called "sporting houses." "They are often threatened until they accept positions in questionable places and are frequently sent out without knowing the character of their destination," she wrote in *Out of Work.*[20] In

Chicago also, Louise DeKoven Bowen discovered that "most of the maids employed in houses of prostitution were colored girls. . . ."[21] The recruitment of women for "immoral purposes" by "intelligence agents" was the first point the New York City Commissioner of Licenses listed in a memorandum which explained why the office had been created.[22] "The southern states, especially Virginia and Georgia, are honey-combed with the slick agents of these employment bureaus," Miss Kellor said in 1905. ". . . Good wages, easy work . . . and good times, are promised. . . . To them, going to Philadelphia or to New York seems like going to Heaven, where the streets will be paved with gold, all will be music and flowers!"[23]

The disparity between image and reality led Miss Kellor to establish a society for the protection of Negro women—the National League for the Protection of Colored Women. The League had offices in New York City and Philadelphia and agents in many southern port cities. It distributed literature to southern Negro pastors and schools urging them to "educate the women on these conditions."[24] Like the White Rose Home, and sometimes in conjunction with it, the League stationed workers at the major depots within the city and offered general fellowship and advice to country strangers who came to town for the first time: "It is the aim of the League to furnish helpful information to colored girls who are intending to come North, to protect them during the journey . . . and to find work or friends or homes for them [when they arrive]."[25] The National League for the Protection of Colored Women continued this work until 1911, when it became one of three Negro reform agencies to consolidate into the National League on Urban Conditions Among Negroes.

IV

Reformers Victoria Earle Matthews and Frances A. Kellor had concentrated on a single aspect of the problem—the exploitation of Negro domestic workers. Mary White Ovington became the first prominent New Yorker to devote herself to the improvement of all aspects of Negro life in New York City, and eventually in the entire nation.

Miss Ovington, like many other urban reformers of her generation, grew up in comfort and gentility. She was the daughter of a well-to-do New York merchant. Her home in an exclusive section of Brooklyn lay not far from the working-class districts, but it was as separate from them in spirit as two distinct worlds could be: "In my youth," she recalled in an autobiographical sketch, "no place was more remote than the section of the city in which persons of different caste lived."[26]

With the typical education of a young woman of refinement, Miss Ovington had studied as a child exclusively in private schools, and then went to Radcliffe. Her family expected her to take her proper place in society—"what we called 'going into society,'" she remarked. But the quiet, secure and stable world into which Miss Ovington was born seemed too remote in the America of the 1880's and 1890's. Massive industrialization and urbanization created major social dislocations on a scale unequaled in the previous history of the nation. It created urban slums, and the immigrants who lived in them often experienced poverty, distress, illness and a sense of hopelessness difficult for the socially conscious to overlook: "I found out about conditions in my own city of which I was utterly ignorant."[27]

Miss Ovington's reaction to these new conditions, similar to the responses of other Progressives, was positive and optimistic. Involvement in a movement for social reform also gave added meaning and fulfillment to her own life. There was, she recalled, a "fervor for settlement work in the nineties, for learning working-class conditions by living among the workers and sharing to some small extent in their lives. . . . The desire for such knowledge was in the air—*hope was in the air*." In 1896, with the financial assistance of civic leader Frederick B. Pratt, Miss Ovington opened a settlement house "among white working-class people" in Greenpoint, Brooklyn. Her five-room home grew into a forty-room settlement in the seven years she remained there. "That I should later work for the Negro never entered my mind," she wrote.[28]

Her first awareness of the seriousness of urban problems among Negroes came at a lecture given by Booker T. Washington. The "Social Reform Club," of which she was a member (she was also a member of the Socialist Party), invited Washington to speak before it: "To my amazement I learned that there was a Negro problem in my city. I had honestly never thought of it before." At that time she decided to find out more about these conditions and, from 1904 till her death in 1951, devoted her life to improving them.[29]

Although Washington's descriptions may have appeared new and shocking to her as an adult, Mary White Ovington had heard similar stories as a child. The Ovington family was one of those ubiquitous New England families that controlled much of New York commerce, and much of the mercantile operations of all the seaboard cities, for a good part of the nineteenth century. William Lloyd Garrison had been a friend of her grandmother's and Miss Ovington, born in 1865, grew up when memories of the "Great Rebellion" were very much alive. She listened attentively to her grandmother's tales of abolitionism, the Underground Railroad, anti-abolitionist rioting in Boston, and the preaching of Garrison's close friend and follower, the Reverend Dr. Samuel J. May. She was taught to despise Daniel Webster and Henry Clay for compromising on the slavery issue. When Frederick Douglass came to speak at Plymouth Congregational Church, Miss Ovington went to see one of her idols. "I was," she wrote, "a sympathetic listener." Garrison "was my childhood's greatest hero."[30]

Mary White Ovington's parents were abolitionists too. Her father told her he severed connections with Plymouth Congregational Church because Henry Ward Beecher supported a missionary association which dealt with a slaveholder. He joined a Unitarian congregation, and his daughter continued in this religion, led by an abolitionist "of the strictest brand." Her brother later became a lifetime member of the NAACP. "Ours was an abolition family."

The Ovington family, like many other supporters of abolitionism, lost contact with Negro life after the Civil War. Slavery had been the great evil, they thought, and it was now destroyed. The Thirteenth, Fourteenth and Fifteenth Amendments were passed and Negroes were *legally* made equal American citizens. It seemed to them that nothing was left to be done: "Slavery was ended," she said. "That was the great point."

Booker T. Washington reawakened Miss Ovington's interest in the Negro people. She decided to open a settlement house for Negroes in New York City and asked Mary Kingsbury Simkovitch of Greenwich House for advice. They both decided the first step was to gather as much specific information as possible on Negro urban problems. Miss Ovington was appointed Fellow of Greenwich House in 1904 and began the studies which led to the publication of *Half A Man* seven years later.[31]

One of the enduring problems of the twentieth-century city has been its inability to supply decent and inexpensive living accommodations to Negroes: "The need for model tenements for colored people is perhaps the greatest of all . . . our's city's population," a group of tenement house reformers indicated in the early twentieth century. Miss Ovington, impressed with the desire of urban Negroes for "wholesome homes," decided to do something about it. She sought to contact Henry Phipps, steel magnate and philanthropist, who previously constructed model tenements for immigrants in New York. The City and Suburban Homes Company, incorporated in 1896, managed the houses built by Phipps and other patrician reformers—Alfred T. White, the Phelps Stokes family, and others—and they accepted a modest profit of five per cent on their investments.[32] It seemed an artful combination of philanthropy and sound business. Miss Ovington and Phipps had a mutual friend, John E. Milholland,[33] whom she went to see. Milholland was another early supporter of the civil rights cause and a good friend of W. E. B. DuBois. In 1904 he founded the Constitution League in New York City, and the League tried to breathe some life into the dormant post-Civil War constitutional amendments.[34] Milholland, convinced of the need for the project, in turn persuaded Phipps to construct a model tenement for the Negroes of San Juan Hill. When the new Phipps Houses were completed on West Sixty-third Street in 1907 they seemed an incongruity in the neighborhood. These fireproof, steam-heated, roof-gardened, six-story houses stood out against the older rundown tenements on the West Side. (The Phipps apartment houses have somehow survived a half-century of urban renewal and may be seen today.) Miss Ovington also hoped that Phipps would support a settlement house for Negroes in the building, and decided to live there herself: "I hoped by quietly renting on my own account, to persuade him to add social work," she wrote to a Negro friend.[35]

Mary White Ovington moved into the model tenement, the only white person in the entire house, in January 1908. There she gathered information for her book, became a close friend of the Reverend Dr. George H. Sims of Union Baptist Church on the block, attended his services occasionally, and read *Peter Rabbit* and other stories to the Negro youngsters who knocked at her door. (She later published stories for Negro children.) Miss Ovington lived on West Sixty-third Street for eight months, but failed to get the philanthropist to support a Negro settlement house.

In September 1908, after having attended meetings of the Negro

Niagara Movement, she read an article in *The Independent* which diverted her attention to national civil rights problems, and redirected the course of her life. William English Walling's since-famous article, "The Race War in the North," attacked the growing racial antipathy and apathy evident in the North and called for a revival of "the spirit of the abolitionists. . . ."[36] Miss Ovington responded to this appeal and called a small meeting of her friends to discuss what could be done to counteract this burgeoning racism. A National Negro Conference met in 1909 at the Henry Street Settlement and the National Negro Committee was established at this gathering. The NAACP had been born. Mary White Ovington spent the rest of her career within this organization.[37]

Although her main energies were channeled into the NAACP—she was called "Mother of the New Emancipation"—she remained active in social work among the city's Negroes. She was an executive of the Committee for Improving the Industrial Condition of the Negro in New York City, chairman of its "Neighborhood Work" subcommittee, president and main fund-raiser of the Lincoln Settlement, which she helped found for Negroes in Brooklyn, and organizer of the West End Workers' Association, active among the Negroes on San Juan Hill.[38] Her Negro secretary from 1905 to 1951 remembers Miss Ovington as a person totally dedicated to the struggle for Negro rights and honestly devoid of any racial prejudice.[39] Negro poet and novelist Claude McKay, in florid tones, wrote that "her personality radiated a quiet silver shaft of white charm which is lovely when it's real."[40] "No white woman's life in America has been colored more by the clash of color and race," concluded a Negro newspaper in an editorial.[41] "That the sincerity of my friendship has never been doubted has been my greatest joy," Miss Ovington said on her resignation as Chairman of the Board of Directors of the NAACP.[42]

V

The reforming zeal evident in Mary White Ovington reached a high point with the founding of the Committee for Improving the Industrial Condition of the Negro in New York (CIICN) in 1906. The primary motivation for the creation of the CIICN was the desire to broaden employment opportunities for the city's Negroes. Its members, supporters, directors and subcommittee chairmen were the most important municipal reformers in New York in the Progressive era, many later active in founding the NAACP. Interracial in structure, the CIICN included social workers, philanthropists, educators, clergymen, writers, publishers, physicians, supporters of Hampton and Tuskegee and businessmen.[43] The founder of the CIICN was a Negro principal in the New York City school system, Dr. William Lewis Bulkley. Bulkley decided to organize the Committee, he said in 1906, after seeing Negro students leaving his schools "to open doors, run bells or hustle hash" for the rest of their lives. "On every hand avenues of employment are shut tight, discouragement begins and [Negro children] leave school to work at any menial employment that offers itself," Bulkley observed. "The constant cry of the negro," another man wrote, "is for 'a white man's chance.' "[44]

Bulkley was the leading Negro educator in New York City in the early twentieth century, a bright, idealistic and ambitious man who rose from the slavery in which he was born in 1861 to earn a doctorate in ancient languages and literature from Syracuse University. As a boy he attended the local log cabin school in Greenville, South Carolina, and finally was graduated from Claflin University, in his home state, in 1882. Bulkley came north to Wesleyan University in Connecticut and continued his studies in France and Germany. In 1893, after completing his master's degree, he earned the Ph.D. at Syracuse.[45]

For a time, Bulkley taught as professor of Latin and Greek at Claflin, but as a student, he worked as janitor, steward, cook and salesman. To save the little money he earned this way he scrimped wherever he could. His meals often consisted of oatmeal and water, he washed and darned his own clothing, and pressed socks and handkerchiefs between the pages of books or under the mattresses on which he slept. William Lewis Bulkley, in the language of his day, achieved "Success Under Difficulties." The "Slave Boy Now a Professor" was "A Noble Example of the Triumph of Perseverance."[46]

Bulkley thought of himself as a southerner driven from his home by racism: "There is not one of us who would not gladly go back home if we did not know that every right dear to any full man has been ruthlessly torn from our grasp," he said in 1909. He longed to share the "soul-refreshings that only a [southern] Negro revival can give."[47] Bulkley came to New York City in the 1890's and was appointed seventh grade teacher in a lower Manhattan public school. In 1899 he became principal of P.S. 80 on West Forty-first Street in the Tenderloin.[48] This school, in the heart of the Negro district, had formerly been an all-Negro institution which was made a ward school in the integration of 1884. In 1909, despite protest meetings and petitions from the teachers of P.S. 125, Bulkley became the first Negro principal of a predominantly white school in city history.[49]

William Lewis Bulkley insisted that Negroes be given full equality in American society—constitutional, political, social, economic—immediately. He supported the demands made by W. E. B. DuBois along these lines, and became a founder of the NAACP. During his summer vacations he was a temporary expatriate who lived in Switzerland and France with his wife and children. His family sometimes remained in Europe when he returned to resume his duties in the fall. On retiring from the New York City school system in 1924 he left the country and established a private school in France. He died in Paris in 1933.[50] That a supporter of DuBois should found an organization to foster practical, industrial employment for the Negroes in the city seemed the height of inconsistency to Booker T. Washington's supporters. "You will see that this opponent of industrial education is not practicing what he preaches," one of them wrote. "This is inconsistency with a vengeance." Washington even had agents attend meetings of the CIICN to check the activities of "Bulkley and his crowd. . . ." "It is hard to carry out plans if our friends are in the minority," Washington observed.[51] White social workers, like Mary White Ovington, Jane Addams and Julia Richman, on the other hand, thought highly of Bulkley's work.[52]

A pragmatist, Bulkley met conditions in the city as he saw them and tried to improve them immediately as best he could. He "set out to make his school a social center," a contemporary journal commented. Soon after becoming principal of P.S. 80, for example, he opened a kindergarten to relieve the working mothers of the neighborhood. He delivered special lectures to parents and students five times a semester on proper nutrition and sanitation, health and other social problems. He visited homes, addressed church groups, attended parents' meetings, wanted "to awaken [Negroes] to a larger self respect and aspiration for better living."[53] In 1903 he started an evening school in the building which specialized in industrial and commercial training. Some of the most diligent students in the school were elderly Negro men and women, some in their seventies and eighties, who had no opportunity for education as youngsters but now wanted to learn to read and write.[54] Bulkley invited friends and associates to visit the school.[55] Members of the Board of Education, on one inspection tour, described it as "the most successful evening school that ever was established in New York. . . ."[56]

The idea of a permanent industrial organization to assist Negroes in New York City apparently originated with William H. Baldwin: President of the Long Island Railroad, philanthropist, and one of Booker T. Washington's key financial supporters. Bulkley, however, initiated the movement which led to the creation of the CIICN.

Bulkley had agitated since 1902 for an organization to do on a broad scale what he attempted to do as an individual at his school: "With an Afro-American population in New York increasing yearly at a very great, I had almost said alarming rate," he maintained in one speech, "it behooves every thoughtful man and woman in this city to stop long enough to think what it may mean to us and to them."[57] Early in 1906 he began a series of local meetings to discuss the subject. He, Mary White Ovington and others lectured these gatherings on the harsh facts of Negro urban life. Finally, in May 1906, at a meeting of some sixty Negro and white New Yorkers, Bulkley's hope became reality. The CIICN was founded and issued a public statement on its goals. "Here at home," the report maintained, "conditions are piling up which must be met at once." The Committee would endeavor to provide equal "economic opportunities" for all citizens: "A square deal in the matter of getting a livelihood is held to be fundamental."[58] William Jay Schieffelin, philanthropist, urban reformer, heir to the Jay family abolitionist tradition, and president of the Board of Trustees of Hampton's Armstrong Association, was appointed chairman. Schieffelin immediately began to contact friends to mobilize support for the new organization. With "seventy thousand Negroes in New York," he wrote in a letter, "we ought to feel a responsibility concerning them."[59]

The CIICN was divided into subcommittees, each headed by an eminent specialist in a particular area of service—"Employment," "Neighborhood Work," "Craftsmen," "Publication," "Trade Schools," "Social Centers," "Legal Affairs," "Public Meetings." They canvassed Negro streets in the city to gather information on social problems which seemed most pressing. Regular public meetings in Negro churches stimulated interest in the Committee's work and provided a sounding board for local discontent. An employment bureau located and helped create jobs for Negroes. The names of skilled Negro workers were collected and these craftsmen were organized into small trade units for dressmakers, printers, mechanics, waiters, carpenters and the like. The policies of racial restriction normally adhered to by unions cracked a bit when, under prodding from the CIICN, the Grand United Brotherhood of Carpenters and Joiners of America issued a charter to a Negro local in the city. Plumbers, construction workers, painters, bricklayers, masons, decorators, found jobs. Subway companies were asked to hire Negro motormen. The subcommittee on Trade Schools, headed by a New York City school superintendent, collected a thousand names on a petition for new night schools in the Negro districts. Two more evening schools primarily for Negroes began in these years. The City and Suburban Homes Company was encouraged to build additional model tenements for Negroes.[60]

The CIICN also co-operated with the other Negro reform agencies in the city. In 1908, for example, it began to send people to the docks to assist Frances A. Kellor's organization. When the Committee on Urban Conditions Among Negroes was established in New York in 1910, the CIICN sent spokesmen to the new organization to map out lines of co-operation with it. The problems which emerged from Negro migration grew more complex each year. In response to the obvious waste of a number of separate bodies' defining their spheres as particular aspects of what was really one broad and interrelated problem, a general agreement for consolidation in 1911 merged the CIICN, the National League for the Protection of Colored Women, and the Committee on Urban Conditions Among Negroes. A new and stronger society, which is still operating today, resulted—the National League on Urban Conditions Among Negroes (National Urban League). William Lewis Bulkley was its first vice-chairman. He probably originated in one of his speeches the phrase "Not Alms, But Opportunity," which became the organization's motto. "We do not ask for charity," he said in 1909, "all we ask is opportunity. We do not beg for alms; we beg only for a chance."[61]

The founding of the two most prominent national Negro organizations, the NAACP and the National Urban League, was a culmination and fulfillment of individual local reform efforts begun in the North in the first decade of the twentieth century. The serious revitalization of concern with racial problems this demonstrated was evident in New

York City in a variety of other ways as well. Each year brought to spontaneous life some new Negro welfare institution. Two settlement houses, one a branch of the Henry Street Settlement, were founded for Negroes in 1904 and 1907. In 1911 they consolidated into one large unit, the Lincoln Settlement House. Lillian D. Wald sent Negro nurses into the Tenderloin, San Juan Hill, and Harlem to help these communities with their medical problems; they still offer free nursing service today. A Negro Music School Settlement, numerous free nurseries, kindergartens, homes for delinquent girls and two new Negro Y's began. Housing bureaus attempted to clean up the streets of Negro slums and locate clean, respectable and inexpensive homes for Negro families. New York City's Board of Health conducted special evening classes for colored people in tuberculosis prevention.[62] Some migrants, fresh from the country, received rudimentary lessons in the use of modern sanitary and plumbing devices.[63] A Negro Fresh Air Committee was established in 1905; playgrounds and summer camps for Negro children were opened.

When the new century began the prevailing attitude toward the Negro in New York City had been one of hostility and increasing alienation. And as far as the majority of the population was concerned, there was no change in this dominant reaction of the city to the Negro people. The racial antagonism of the majority made necessary the creation of segregated communities like Harlem. But a sense of renewed promise and hopefulness among Negroes was born of the important reform movements that coped with the problems of rapid Negro urbanization. In 1900 Booker T. Washington and W. E. B. DuBois would have agreed that American reform seemed to overlook the Negro. Ten years later, both recognized a new "awakening" of interest in Negro life.[64] Some may question the degree of commitment and success this basically middle-class reform movement reflected. It obviously could not end the deep strains of racism that pervaded American culture, and it remained a minority movement. Yet these urban reformers were the first major group of Americans to manifest a serious concern with racial inequities since the abolitionist era. To some Negroes they were "a veritable god-send to the colored people."[65]

PART TWO

The Making of a Ghetto

CHAPTER 5

A Genteel Community: Harlem, 1890

"A great city is developing north
of Central Park."
—*Harlem Local Reporter*, 1889

"It is evident to the most superficial
observer that the centre of fashion,
wealth, culture, and intelligence,
must, in the near future, be found in
the ancient and honorable village of
Harlem. . . ."
—*The Harlem Monthly Magazine*, 1893

I

In the last three decades of the nineteenth century Harlem was a community of great expectations. During the previous quarter century it had been an isolated, poor, rural village. After the 1870's, however, it was transformed into an upper- and upper-middle-class residential suburb—Manhattan's first suburb.

Prosperity had come to Harlem before.[1] Throughout the colonial period its lands brought wealth to farmers. The estates of some of America's most illustrious colonial families were located there—Delanceys, Beekmans, Bleeckers, Rikers, Coldens, Hamiltons and others.[2] The stamp of respectability and distinction colored Harlem's name and later settlers recalled its past glories proudly: "Who among [you] then," a lecturer on the history of the community said in 1882, "with Harlem's . . . history before you, and the goodly prospects in store, are not proud of being called Harlemites. . . . The spirit which animated their [the founders'] breasts," he concluded romantically, "is rooted in the soft rich soil of Harlem. . . ."[3]

For some two hundred years the village of New Harlaem remained remarkably stable. Most of its small population, following the general ethnic patterns of New York City's population (as it would continue

71

to do in the future), descended from Dutch, French and English pioneers. The surnames of Harlem's residents in the late eighteenth century recall those of the seventeenth century.[4] Generations quietly passed into generations: ". . . Old Resolved Waldron built himself a house . . . where his children were born and where he finally died. His son inherited the home . . . reared his family under its roof, and was likewise buried from it. This homestead has been in the possession of the lineal descendants of Mr. Waldron ever since," a journalist recorded in 1883.[5]

There was no need for town government in a community of this size and social structure. Committees and magistrates appointed at town meetings settled matters of public concern. So it had been in 1667, so in 1774 and again in 1820. The commission appointed to lay out the streets of New York City in 1811 did not think Harlem would be "covered with houses for centuries to come."[6] In the 1820's the ninety-one families of the "delightful village" of Harlem had one church, one school, one library.[7]

And this tradition was not completely extinct in the late nineteenth century. Harlem always remained a strange combination of the old and new. A fifth-generation descendant of a man who came to Harlem in 1667 continued proudly to live on part of the family estate at the turn of the century.[8] At least four other heirs to seventeenth-century land titles lived in Harlem in 1882: Bensons, Montagnes, Hoppers, Raubs.[9] The Watt Mansion, originally built by John Delancey in the eighteenth century, was standing to meet the twentieth.[10] Hamilton Grange, completed in 1803–1804, may still be seen today, and the Hamilton Estate owned Harlem land in the 1890's. (In 1904, a hundred years after Hamilton's death, the community publicly honored his memory.)[11] Scattered throughout the area were other formerly stately colonial homes, two erected prior to 1670,[12] others "yet in good repair."[13] A boy fishing in Harlem Creek could still find a button from the uniform of a soldier of the American Revolution.[14] In 1910, the Collegiate Reformed Church, founded in 1660, celebrated its 250th anniversary, a solid reminder to newcomers of Harlem's distinguished past.[15]

II

To most residents of Harlem in the 1840's and 1850's, however, these were skeleton remains of a never-known age. Harlem's decline began when its lands, worn out after centuries of use, lost their former productivity. Hamilton's widow, for example, had abandoned the Grange because the farm was "yielding trifling returns."[16] Others, rather than eke out a grudging existence in an America of great opportunity, simply deserted the seemingly worthless property and went elsewhere. Formerly great estates were sold at public auction.[17] The city acquired much property and resold it.[18] In 1838 the New York City Board of Aldermen described Harlem as a "third or fourth-rate country village."[19]

Into this decaying community came groups of people to whom the once productive soil seemed less forbidding. Those in search of cheap property bought land there and built one- and two-story frame houses. Others, including many newly arrived and destitute Irish immigrants—some of whom remained in Harlem to see the twentieth century—squatted on the forsaken land or lived in mud flats at the river's edge. They created Harlem's shantytowns and lived in two-room cottages pieced together with any material that could be found: bits of wood, twigs, barrel staves, old pipes, tin cans hammered flat.[20] In the backwash of a growing metropolis, Harlem's squatters made money by raising animals and vegetables for local markets. Geese, cows, horses and "genus goat of the Harlem species" roamed over the area. There were so many hogs in one section of One Hundred and Twenty-fifth and One Hundred and Twenty-sixth Streets that it came to be known as Pig's Alley.[21] Parts of Harlem Plains[22] were marshes, which reeked so badly that they could "knock the breath out of a mule!"[23] Harlem at midcentury was largely "a village of shanties and huts with here and there a farm house. . . ."[24] And so it remained until the pressure of urban population growth and the subsequent need for living space restored value to Harlem lands.

With the exception of the marshes, Harlem's topography maintained much of its earlier beauty. Relatively untouched for centuries, it had the physical possibilities of becoming the country retreat of a burgeoning metropolis: "Everything that is lovely and much that is grand are assembled in a moderate space. Hill and dale, stream and wood, rock and meadow . . . river views . . . of surpassing magnificence," a historian noted in the 1890's. "The walks through the woodland shade . . . are always charming. . . . The clear brooks, the yellow leaves of autumn, the birds . . . lead one to forget the city and all its toils. . . . "[25]

Of a Sunday, from the 1860's on, the residents of Harlem shanties would find "downtowners" wandering about on country jaunts. They could walk to Harlem Lane (St. Nicholas Avenue) and watch men of the "exclusive class," "the horse-racing fraternity," "swells"—Commodore Vanderbilt was probably the most prominent—working out their "fast trotters": "Any fine afternoon you could see the wealthy horse-fanciers driving their . . . sulkies through Central Park on their way to 'the road' as they called Harlem Lane."[26] After a day in the country these "fashionable people" might stop at Toppy McGuire's Clubhouse or sip wine at the intriguing Brossi's Tunnel, bored out of rock at One Hundred and Twenty-second Street. "Harlem had become the rural retreat of the aristocratic New Yorker," an old Manhattanite recalled, and its "chief charm [was] its well-bred seclusion. . . ."[27]

In the late nineteenth century, this remoteness from city life served as the one great barrier to Harlem's development as a residential community. Harlem was approximately eight miles from City Hall and, under no great urgency to be otherwise, its transportation facilities remained rudimentary. The New York and Harlem Railroad ran trains from lower Manhattan to Harlem after 1837.[28] Horsecars started opposite City Hall and stopped at Forty-second Street. At this junction the horses were replaced by a locomotive and the train went directly to One Hundred and Twenty-ninth Street. The entire trip, scheduled to take forty minutes,[29] often took much longer. Young boys ran alongside the tracks and jeered:

> The Harlem Road is a smashing line,
> It starts at four and stops at nine,
> And if you want to go to town,
> The quickest way is to foot it down.[30]

There were other means of transportation to the city. Stage lines on the east and west sides operated after the 1830's as well ("Murphy's Economical Accommodation Line" was one), but they were even less reliable than the Harlem Railroad. Under ideal conditions they took an hour and forty minutes to the city but in the winter often bogged down in the snow.[31] After 1856 the picturesque steamboats of Sylvan Line, remembered with great fondness by Harlem's older residents, made the trip to Manhattan in thirty minutes, but closed during the winter months as ice clogged the East River.[32] Such a transportation system obviously did little to encourage settlement in Harlem.

III

The phenomenal growth of Harlem in the late nineteenth century
was a by-product of the general development of New York City.
From the 1870's on, the foundations of the modern metropolis were
laid. This urban revolution was characterized by improvements in
methods of sanitation, water supply, transportation, communication,
lighting and building.[33] As the city expanded, so did its population.
In 1880, for the first time in its history, and in the history of any
American city, the population of Manhattan alone passed the one
million mark (1,164,673),[34] and "New Immigrants" had just begun
to arrive. This increase in population coincided with an expansion of
commercial and industrial activity and both made serious inundations
on living quarters in formerly staid residential sections. The only way
for the island city to grow was northward. Many older residents and
older immigrants, attempting to avoid the bustle of the new metropolis and escape contact with its newest settlers, looked to Harlem as
the community of the future: "In our family, we were always careful
to explain that we lived in Harlem, not in New York City," a man
whose family moved uptown in these years recalled. "It was our way
of avoiding contact with such uncouth citizens as might be found
downtown. . . ."[35] The neighborhood would become "the choicest
residential section of the city," predicted another resident. "Upper
Seventh Avenue in Harlem has become one of the finest streets in
New York. . . . Rows of trees and pretty gardens . . . lend to it a
semi-suburban aspect."[36]

Harlem expanded gradually in the 1860's and was annexed to New
York City in 1873.[37] The city filled some 1,350 acres of marshland
in 1870, sold them to the public, and constructed houses over them.
A few city fathers in the heyday of the Tweed Ring appropriated
promising lands for themselves and built fashionable homes there.[38]
The turning point in Harlem's history came in 1878–1881. During
these years three lines of the elevated railroad came as far north as
One Hundred and Twenty-ninth Street and, by 1886, the elevated line
came even further north.[39] Rows of brownstones and exclusive
apartment houses appeared overnight: "Business grows, blocks and
flats go up with apparently so little effort, that the average Harlemite
is in a continuous swim of development and prosperity," the local
newspaper commented in 1890.[40] Practically all the houses that
stand in Harlem today were built in a long spurt of energy that lasted

from the 1870's through the first decade of the twentieth century. Electric lights were first installed in 1887 and the telephone followed the next year.[41] Shanties, doomed by "the wilderness of brownstone, brick and mortar . . . ,"[42] took with them Harlem's celebrated goat, the subject of much newspaper lampooning. An irate "Harlem Goat" begged the *New York Herald* to leave it in peace: "I feel as if my browsing days in Harlem are over, and I can hardly find a . . . blade of fresh grass. . . ."[43] "No more goats in Harlem/There's prosperity in Harlem," sang the Harlem Board of Commerce at a neighborhood fete. "When Harlem was a Prairie," echoed the motto of the Harlem Old-Timers Association.[44] An Irish resident of the community since the 1840's saw a "one horse town . . . turned into a teeming metropolis. . . ."[45]

Speculators made fortunes buying Harlem land, holding it for a short while, and reselling at great profit. Builders purchased land, constructed houses and sold them as soon as they were completed. They used the profits for reinvestment. Oscar Hammerstein I, Henry Morgenthau, and August Belmont were among them. "Hammerstein bought and sold properties in that area with great speed and generally at a profit," his biographer wrote.[46] Edward H. W. Just, another speculator, born in Eisleben, Germany, in the 1830's, came to New York City as a young man when the ready-made clothing industry was becoming a major source of city wealth. He became a successful shirt manufacturer and invested heavily in Harlem property. When he died in 1893 he left an estate worth more than $2,000,000.[47] One plot of land purchased in 1852 for $3,000 was worth $200,000 in 1890.[48] "When I see the prices that real estate is now bringing in Harlem," one old-timer bemoaned in 1889, "it makes me feel that I was a fool for not making . . . investments years ago when property was so cheap. Twenty years [ago] the meadow lands of Harlem were not considered worth paying taxes for. . . ."[49]

IV

If this man thought himself a fool, those who previously abandoned or sold their Harlem property felt cheated: "The country town grew, until this . . . almost valueless land has become worth millions." Descendants of Harlem settlers, some tracing their rights to the earliest seventeenth-century grants, now attempted to reclaim what they maintained was still their property. The first man to do so, Alfred E.

Tilton, gathered his old land titles and brought suit against the city in the 1870's, but he died in 1876 before any settlement was made. His idea, however, was exploited for more than a generation as the heirs of other settlers organized and tried to do in grand style what Tilton attempted to do as an individual. The movement to reclaim Harlem lands had all the overtones of a great land grab: "the Great Harlem Land Claim," newspapers called it.[50]

In 1883, the Harlem Commons Syndicate was organized and incorporated. Descendants of earlier residents, sought throughout the country, were made shareholders, for a price, in the great scheme. General John C. Frémont, a Harlem heir himself, became president of the corporation. Schuyler Colfax, former Vice-President of the United States, was a claimant. Every available scrap of information—genealogical data, wills, letters—was gathered to prove that descendants still held valid rights in the old commons land and in the recently filled marshes. The Syndicate pressured for congressional intervention and brought suit against New York City, but all efforts proved unsuccessful. The corporation finally collapsed in 1895.

The fortune-hunting temptation outlived the Harlem Commons Syndicate in the Harlem Associated Heirs Title Company, founded immediately after the demise of the Syndicate, in another group active at the turn of the century and still another as late as 1932.[51] Each, of course, sold shares to Harlem heirs. Genealogical information collected by researchers went for a price—$10 to $15. Stock was sold to some 1,400 persons. Two claimants of a family sued each other over contested rights to property neither legally owned. Provisions in old leases and sales were carefully checked for possible discrepancies, and many were supposedly uncovered. Books were written to show these claims valid and one man even tried to demonstrate by scripture that the cause was a righteous one: that "divine direction constituted the sole motive for the recovery of . . . Harlem rights and properties. . . ." Terrestrial forces, however, proved obdurate in their refusal to share Harlem's new-found prosperity, and these efforts were as unsuccessful (for all save the promoters, perhaps) as those of the Harlem Commons Syndicate.[52]

V

People generally took it for granted that Harlem would develop into an exclusive, stable, upper- and upper-middle-class community: "a neighborhood very genteel." The newly built elevator apartment houses, many equipped with servants' quarters, rented for prices that could be paid only by the wealthy. The most magnificent was a group of spacious, luxurious brownstones built on One Hundred and Thirty-eighth and One Hundred and Thirty-ninth Streets in 1891. Stanford White, the well-known architect so closely associated with the architectural history of the city (he designed Madison Square Garden, Washington Arch, Grand Central Station), had been commissioned to build one hundred and six distinguished homes, each with ten to sixteen rooms and flower-bedecked driveways. They were advertised to be as "distinctive as a suburban colony but with all the advantages of city life": "These driveways are ornamented at their intersections by circular beds of flowers, making a decorative feature even of their utility. Great care is taken of the property to preserve its exclusive appearance, and a general air of being well-looked-after pervades the surroundings." Houses set back twelve feet from the street added privacy and rear entrances "permitted the business of housekeeping to be kept out of sight." In a society whose working-class families paid an average of $10–18 a month rent, the rents for these homes *started* at just under $80, and ranged between $900 and $1700 a year.[53]

Another group of twenty-eight three-story exclusive homes, Astor Row, constructed in the 1890's on West One Hundred and Thirtieth Street, provided large porches and shade trees. They were known "as one of the most attractive and exclusive home centres" in Harlem, and "presented a picture of domestic tranquility and comfort which few other . . . blocks in the city possess," a *New York Times* reporter noted. In spite of high rentals Astor Row had a long waiting list of prospective tenants.[54]

Prosperity and optimism seemed the order of the day. One merchant built a large department store on One Hundred and Twenty-fifth Street in 1890 and had such confidence in Harlem's future that he offered to pay half the rent for five years of any businessman who followed him.[55] Local citizens could attend the Harlem Opera House, built by Oscar Hammerstein I in 1889, or go to one of Harlem's many theaters.[56] In 1900 they might dine at the luxurious German Pabst Harlem: "Where Gentlemen and Ladies can enjoy good music and a perfect cuisine amid surroundings which have been rendered as attractive to the eye and senses [as] good taste, combined with expenditure, could make them."[57]

The people attracted to this "residential heaven" were obviously older and wealthier New Yorkers—"people of taste and wealth."[58] Few neighborhoods in the entire city at the turn of the century had so disproportionate a number of native Americans or immigrants from Great Britain, Ireland and Germany, including German Jews, living in it. In 1902, of the 103,570 families in the Twelfth Ward, only 10,786 could be classified as "New Immigrants."[59] Many late-nineteenth-century Harlemites were born in downtown Manhattan or immigrated to America in the years 1830–1850, and subsequently moved to the community after 1870.[60] One man came to visit a friend in Harlem in 1889 and was surprised "to see so many downtowners who have come here to live. It looks as if everybody will be rushing up here from downtown before long," he said.[61] A future director of the Harlem Board of Commerce moved to the neighborhood in the 1880's and was surprised to meet so many Greenwich Village friends there.[62] The homes of municipal and federal judges, mayors, local politicos (including Tammany boss Richard Croker), prominent businessmen and state politicians (Chauncey M. Depew, for example), were scattered throughout Harlem.[63] Their children attended Grammar School 68, "referred to as the 'Silk Stocking School' of the City" because its "pupils were practically all from American families, and . . . more or less prosperous people."[64] Their daughters could go to "Mme. De Valencia's Protestant French and English Institute for Young Ladies," one of the many private schools for the wealthy that flourished in the nineteenth-century city.[65] A young Jewish boy moved to Harlem from the Lower East Side in the first decade of the twentieth century and recalled seeing rich German Jews, "Uptown Jews," strutting down Seventh Avenue in top hats, black coats and canes.[66]

Among the institutions developed to service Harlem's newest residents was Calvary Methodist Episcopal Church, organized in 1883 with forty members, but ten years later the congregation worshiped in a magnificent Gothic structure. Its membership had increased to over a thousand and two missions were in the process of being established.[67] Nor was this a unique story. New churches proliferated in Harlem in these years. Between 1870 and 1894, for example, six

Presbyterian churches were founded there.[68] Harlem had a First German Baptist Church, a Temple Israel of Harlem, and a St. Charles Borromeo Roman Catholic Church, to mention just a few.[69] There were German *Turnvereins,* cafés and choirs, German-Jewish fraternal societies, a Harlem Catholic Club, the elite Harlem Club (initiation fee $100), a Harlem Yacht Club, a Harlem Literary Society, active local Democratic and Republican clubs, a branch of the YMCA, a Harlem Philharmonic Orchestra, and even Harlem orders of the Daughters of the Revolution and Loyal Women of American Liberty: created "to defend our free institutions."[70] The Twelfth Ward Savings Bank, founded in 1889, moved to larger quarters three times by 1896.[71] Harlem supported a monthly literary magazine, a weekly magazine of Harlem doings, and bi-weekly newspaper.[72] It was a vital, ever-growing, genteel community of great promise whose future seemed boundless.[73]

To the generation that remembered only this Harlem, those who had never known the Harlem of squatters, shanties and mud flats (and would little understand the causes for its future changes), its memory remained warm and bright. It was a neighborhood "old-timers have cherished," a resident wrote years later. Few could disagree with the editor of *The Harlem Monthly Magazine* who saw Harlem developing as a "district . . . distinctly devoted to the mansions of the wealthy, the homes of the well-to-do, and the places of business of the tradespeople who minister their wants. . . ."[74] "We have no adequate idea of . . . the greatness that lies in store for Harlem," another thought in 1890.[75]

The Other Harlem: Roots of Instability

"Foreigners are crowding up the whole
length of the island."
—*The Harlem Local Reporter,* 1893

"The existing speculation in flats and
tenements surpasses . . . anything of the
kind which has previously taken place
in the real estate history of the city."
—*Real Estate Record and Builders' Guide,* 1904

I

Within the general prosperity and optimism characteristic of the Harlem community in 1890 a few sources of possible instability could be noted. Much of the neighborhood was rebuilt in the 1870's and 1880's but some sections along the waterfront and others inaccessible to transportation remained undeveloped. One Hundred and Thirty-eighth to One Hundred and Forty-eighth Streets west of Eighth Avenue was unfilled marshland, known locally as "Canary Island." A gang of youths who lived nearby called themselves the "Canary Island Gang," and guarded their territory like an armed brigade when Negroes began moving into the Canary Island neighborhood in the early twentieth century. "The Irish boys on Eighth Avenue wouldn't let the other races come on Eighth Avenue at all," an early Negro resident recalled. "Up here . . . we had the Canary Island gang. . . ."[1]

Other low and marshy sections of what were then the fringes of the community served as garbage dumps, one on West One Hundred and Forty-first Street between Fifth and Lenox Avenues and another at West One Hundred and Twenty-ninth Street. In the early 1890's it was generally believed that apartment houses would be constructed on these grounds in the near future, and that the garbage piled ten to twelve feet high would act as filler and save future work.[2] Residents

81

of the neighborhood complained to municipal officials about these health hazards, spawning grounds for all kinds of disease. One prominent local businessman admonished the city fathers for failing to clean up the dumps: "You must remember, gentlemen," he protested, "that Harlem is no longer a country village."[3] "Fill in the Flats," a local newspaper said in an editorial.[4]

When the flats were filled in the late 1890's, they helped initiate another wave of land and property speculation in Harlem. In the aftermath of the collapse of this second speculative mania, during the first decade of the twentieth century, Negroes moved to Harlem in considerable numbers.

II

Near the less attractive areas of Harlem, on the periphery of the middle-class community, lived people by-passed by Harlem's late-nineteenth-century affluence. Italian immigrants crowded in "common tenements"[5] from One Hundred and Tenth to One Hundred and Twenty-fifth Streets, east of Third Avenue to the river. This section, the future bailiwick of La Guardia and Marcantonio, was "as thoroughly Italian as Rome, Naples, Palermo or Messina," a journalist noted. In the 1890's the poverty of "Harlem's Little Italy" seemed a glaring incongruity in a neighborhood known as the home of "the great middle-class population, the very cream of our citizenship."[6] Italians were the first New Immigrant group to come to Harlem and a source of embarrassment and displeasure to the richer people who lived nearby. The smells that emanated from their "vile tenements," one critic said in 1894, "annoyed their brownstone neighbors."[7]

The "Italian Colony" appeared like a "Foreign Village" to one man. Inquisitive Harlemites would stroll across town on religious holidays and feast days to gaze at the strange doings. They could see a marionette show or men grinding their street organs: the "boxes full of music that come around on four wheels everyday."[8] Pushcart peddlers hawking their wares upset the quiet demeanor of the neighborhood and a campaign was waged by local businessmen and street cleaners to keep them off the streets. In 1891 the city opened an area along the East River for use as a produce market: "Adieu! Peddlers Forever!"[9] The poorest of the poor groveled for leftover food in garbage dumps and trash cans: "Here can be found the refuse of Italy making a poor living on the refuse from Harlem ashbarrels," a caustic reporter commented.[10]

Those who lived through the transition of Harlem to a Negro ghetto tended to forget that substantial numbers of Negroes were also scattered throughout the neighborhood in the late nineteenth century. It seemed to many that Negroes came to Harlem suddenly in the twentieth century; older white residents never really understood the nature of the change that reshaped their entire community.[11] In reality, the Negro sections of Harlem predated those of its late-nineteenth-century residents. The first Negroes to live and work in Harlem were slaves and references to them are found in seventeenth-century documents. The original wagon road constructed between New Amsterdam and Harlem was built by the "Dutch West India Company's Negroes."[12] Slaves worked on farms and estates in Harlem in the seventeenth and eighteenth centuries and colonial Harlem even had its own "Negro Burying Ground." One local farmer bequeathed his slaves to his children in 1752.[13] The New York Census of 1790 listed 115 slaves for the "Harlem Division," just under one-third of its total population.[14]

With freedom Negroes continued to live in the general area. A white Methodist church in Harlem had some Negro communicants in 1832,[15] and Negro squatters and farmers settled in the community at the time Irish immigrants came in the 1840's and 1850's.[16] Harlem African Methodist Episcopal Zion Church ("Little Zion") was constructed as a mission to Harlem's Negroes by the downtown "Mother Zion" Church. In 1843 its sixty-six members worshiped in a small brick building on East One Hundred and Seventeenth Street. "Little Zion," a center of Negro life in Harlem throughout the nineteenth century, became an independent church in the twentieth.[17] There was a branch of Bethel African Methodist Episcopal Zion Church in Harlem in the 1840's,[18] and a Negro public school there in the 1850's.[19] Draft Rioters tramped through Harlem in 1863 destroying Negro cottages in their rage: "Many of them went through 125th Street carrying clubs toward the east side where they burned almost an entire block at 130th Street and the Harlem River," a white resident remembered.[20]

Harlem's small Negro community gradually increased in size in the late nineteenth century as colored servants worked in homes of the wealthy who moved into the neighborhood. One family paid for the passage of a Negro woman from Virginia in 1875 ("a genuine Virginia darkey," they recalled),[21] and later brought her daughter to Harlem also. Occasional advertisements for jobs by Negroes appeared in local periodicals: "Colored woman wants family washing."[22] William H. Butler, a Negro musician, offered lessons to the public.[23] A Harlem tenement house, "Hooker's Building," which had once been occupied by Irish refugees of the Famine, "fell an easy prey to the negro" in the 1890's, a white Harlemite recalled.[24] Salem Church, a mission of St. Mark's Methodist Episcopal Church, was founded in a Harlem store at the turn of the century.[25] Other Methodist and Baptist storefront missions "up in Harlem [were] doing much-needed work for colored servants" in 1900, the *New York Sun* observed.[26]

In fact, a substantial Negro population lived in Harlem at the turn of the twentieth century. Though much smaller but more disparate than the Negro sections in the Tenderloin and San Juan Hill, it included occasional Negro blocks distributed throughout Harlem: "they are found clear across the city from river to river," a Columbia University student wrote in 1898.[27]

In the 1880's and 1890's Negroes lived on East One Hundred and Twenty-second, One Hundred and Twenty-fourth and One Hundred and Twenty-sixth Streets, and on West One Hundred and Twenty-fourth, One Hundred and Twenty-fifth, One Hundred and Twenty-sixth and One Hundred and Thirty-fourth Streets.[28] There were two Negro apartment houses, the Garrison and the Sumner, of One Hundred and Twenty-fifth Street and Broadway in 1890.[29] West One Hundred and Forty-sixth Street had "a large colony of the poorest colored people" in the 1890's, and was popularly known by the choice epithet "Nigger Row."[30] The "Negro tenements" on West One Hundred and Thirtieth Street were called Harlem's "Darktown."[31] Colored Knights of Pythias had a lodge in Harlem, Negro churches used the Harlem and East Rivers for baptisms, public outings were held in Sulzer's Harlem Park.[32] In 1891 a Negro political organization conducted public meetings in a Harlem assembly hall.[33] "Colored Tenants Preferred," "The Neatest Apartments in Harlem," "Desirable Properties for Colored People," and similar signs appeared on tenements in Harlem in the 1890's.[34] In 1902 the New York City Tenement House Commission made a block-by-block survey of Manhattan's population. Its records present an exact description of the *distribution* of Harlem's Negro population at the turn of the century.

DISTRIBUTION OF NEGRO FAMILIES IN THE TWELFTH WARD, 1902[35]

Families	Streets	Avenues
50	88th and 89th	2nd and 3rd
24	94th and 95th	2nd and 3rd
77	96th and 97th	2nd and 3rd
50	97th and 98th	Lexington and 4th
72	97th and 98th	3rd and Lexington
19	97th and 98th	2nd and 3rd
40	99th and 100th	3rd and Lexington
15	99th and 100th	2nd and 3rd
11	102nd and 103rd	2nd and 3rd
29	103rd and 104th	2nd and 3rd
17	114th and 115th	Madison and 5th
11	121st and 122nd	1st and 2nd
46	122nd and 123rd	1st and 2nd
13	123rd and 124th	7th and 8th
16	123rd and 124th	Pleasant and 1st
51	124th and 125th	7th and 8th
56	124th and 125th	Pleasant and 1st
16	125th and 126th	Amsterdam and Broadway
28	125th and 126th	Columbus and Amsterdam
27	125th and 126th	8th and Columbus
16	126th and 127th	Columbus and Amsterdam
46	126th and 127th	2nd and 3rd
14	127th and 128th	2nd and 3rd
12	130th and 131st	Broadway and West to River
39	133rd and 134th	Lenox and 7th
30	133rd and 134th	5th and Lenox
74	134th and 135th	Lenox and 7th
101	134th and 135th	5th and Lenox
48	135th and 136th	5th and Lenox
56	146th and 147th	7th and 8th
23	147th and 148th	8th and Bradhurst

III

The Negro and Italian sections of Harlem seemed, when thought of at all, curiosities, sources of minor annoyance or objects of charity to the typical Harlemite of the 1880's and 1890's. Women's clubs and religious organizations offered varieties of assistance to the poor of these neighborhoods. A young Negro educator from the South, known even then as a level-headed fellow, visited the Lenox Avenue Unitarian Church in 1893. He gave a lecture and appealed to Harlem's "substantial citizenry" to raise money for his small school in Alabama, and undoubtedly left the community with a sizable contribution.[36] He was Booker T. Washington.

The Republican Ladies Auxiliary of Harlem gave lessons in American democracy and voting to residents of the "Italian Quarter." (It was reported they taught immigrants to make the "X" next to the Republican column.)[37] In the Depression of 1893, the Harlem Relief Society, composed of volunteer workers from the local branch of the Charity Organization Society, was founded. The Society distributed food, clothing and fuel to the poor in the winter of 1893. (Winters in the city were always harshest for the poverty-stricken who lived in cold-water flats.)[38] In response to widespread economic distress churches in the neighborhood took up collections for the needy.[39] A Society for Befriending the Poor Catholic Children of Harlem was organized.[40] Tammany politicians opened "People's Restaurants" to offer decent five-cent meals to the hungry.[41] (Make the "X" next to the Democratic column.) With the growth of the Negro population of Harlem, the Relief Society boosted its work among colored people and eventually hired a Negro nurse and social worker to visit their homes. "No white person can quite understand the underlying thoughts and actions of this race," the Society said in explaining its reasons for hiring a Negro assistant. "Our work among Negroes increases year by year."[42]

The concern of Harlemites for the lower classes, Negro or white, was not always charitable. Newspapers mocked what they considered the peculiar social and religious lives of Negroes and Italians. *The Harlem Local Reporter,* typical of its age, made light of the "colored pussons" who attended the wedding of a Negro janitor, spoofed the Negro "ristocrats" who danced the Cake Walk (a cake or pie was given to the winning couple).[43] Harlemites who laughed at *A Trip to Coontown* and *In Old Kentucky* made them highly successful vaudeville shows.[44] Italian immigrants seemed to some knife-wielding members of the Mafia. Articles described "Harlem's Bowery Sights."[45] No one suspected that these minority groups and others who settled in Harlem in the early twentieth century would eventually become a serious threat to the stability of the community.

IV

Harlem life altered radically in the first decade of the twentieth century. The construction of new subway routes into the neighborhood in the late 1890's set off a second wave of speculation in Harlem land and property. Speculators who intended to make astronomic profits when the subway was completed bought the marshes, garbage dumps and lots left unimproved or undeveloped in the 1870's and 1880's. Between 1898 and 1904, the year that the Lenox Avenue line opened at One Hundred and Forty-fifth Street, "practically all the vacant land in Harlem" was "built over," the *Real Estate Record and Builders' Guide* noted in 1904. "The growth of . . . Harlem . . . has been truly astonishing during the last half dozen years."[46]

The real estate boom created a wave of new building activity in Harlem dominated primarily by speculators, although some individuals made long-term investments. It was taken as business gospel that investments would be doubled and trebled after the completion of the "tunnel road." "Even a 5-story single flat in Harlem would net . . . at the end of . . . three to five years . . . at the utmost . . . a very handsome unearned increment," a realtor concluded. "It would be impossible to err."[47] Another supposed expert in urban real estate maintained that no "other class of public improvements had such a great, immediate and permanent effect upon land values as rapid transit lines. . . ."[48]

Speculation in Manhattan land along the routes of new transportation facilities originally occurred when charters were granted to horse-car companies in the early nineteenth century.[49] Trafficking in city lots throughout urban America proved often more lucrative than speculation on the western frontier. At the turn of the century the "grey wolves" who dominated so many other urban commercial and industrial enterprises in the Gilded Age controlled New York City's building industry: "expert professional operators [who raised] amounts of money varying between a few thousand and many million dollars. They . . . eagerly scan . . . New York real estate values, and . . . make a rush for any section in which they see possibilities of profit."[50] The Equitable and Metropolitan Life insurance companies invested heavily in Harlem land. "The existing speculation in flats and tenements," an observer wrote at the turn of the century, "surpasses . . . anything of the kind which has previously taken place in the real estate history of the city."[51]

This real estate fever "seized upon [the Jewish] Ghettos of Greater New York" too. Offices were set up in people's homes, investments were discussed in Lower East Side restaurants, as workers with modest savings conceived themselves as budding realtors. Abraham Cahan, the well-known Jewish newspaper editor and novelist, graphically described the "boom atmosphere" which even pervaded the immigrant ghettos of the city: "Small tradesmen of the slums, and even working-men, were investing their savings in houses and lots. Jewish carpenters, house-painters, bricklayers, or instalment peddlers became builders of tenements or frame dwellings, real-estate speculators. Deals were being closed and poor men were making thousands of dollars in less time than it took to drink a glass of tea or the plate of sorrel soup over which the transaction took place. Women, too, were ardently dabbling in real estate. . . ."[52]

In the section of Harlem north of Central Park to One Hundred and Twenty-fifth Street, and west of Lexington Avenue to Seventh Avenue, new tenements and apartment houses went up in the late 1890's. These properties seemed to offer "good profit on investments," as East European Jews spilled out of the Lower East Side in search of better homes[53]—part of the migration to lower Harlem and other boroughs that reflected their economic mobility. The disintegration of the Jewish sections on the Lower East Side that began in the first decade of the twentieth century continued for thirty years. As Russian and Polish Jews replaced German Jews in the garment industry in these years, they now began to encroach on the residential center of "Uptown Jewry." To live in lower Harlem became a symbol of good times to many East European Jews. Some families who moved into the neighborhood, one contemporary recorded, "speak apologetically and at times are actually embarrassed when their former residence in the lower parts of the city is mentioned." The newspapers called this section of Harlem "Little Russia."[54]

The University Settlement, founded on the Lower East Side, followed its people to Harlem. An "Experimental School in Harlem" established in 1902[55] became the "Harlem Guild of the University Settlement" in 1903.[56] Maurice H. Harris, a social worker, started another settlement on East One Hundred and Fifth Street in 1906. "It is from the inspiration . . . I obtained from your Settlement that I have been enabled to start a humble venture of my own," he wrote his mentor Lillian D. Wald.[57] Jewish synagogues bought property in the neighborhood: "Calvary Presbyterian Church is now one of the prettiest little Jewish synagogues in . . . New York."[58] A variety of social institutions arose: the Harlem Home of the Daughters of Israel, Harlem Hebrew School, Harlem Hebrew Educational Institute, Harlem Hebrew Retail Grocers' Association, and so on. Local libraries began to acquire books of Jewish history and Yiddish literature for their newest readers.[59]

Older residents objected to the "migration of the better class of East Side Jews into the district north and east of the Park, then the new quarter of the most prosperous Russian Jews,"[60] in terms similar to those previously reserved for Italian immigrants and Negroes. "Foreigners are crowding up the whole length of the island," the *Harlem Local Reporter* said in an editorial.[61] Elmer Rice and his family, like many of their Harlem neighbors, moved away from One Hundred and Sixth Street in 1903 because the "neighborhood had been growing less 'refined'. . . ."[62] The sometimes bitter response of German Harlemites to the settlement of East European Jews in their community was symbolized by a to-let sign which hung on one building: *Keine Juden, und keine Hunde.* [No Jews, No Dogs.][63]

V

More luxurious apartment houses were built around 1900 in West Harlem, along Seventh and Lenox Avenues in the One Hundred and Thirties and One Hundred and Forties, the first section of the neighborhood to become Negro Harlem. Contemporaries called these blocks "the best of Harlem." This section of the community suffered most from inaccessibility in the 1880's and 1890's,[64] and hardly an edition of the local newspaper in the 1890's failed to demand improved transportation facilities there. To contemporaries this "old, old story of rapid transit" would make Harlem "even more popular than it is as a place of residence. . . ."[65]

Speculation in these properties was probably more widespread and involved larger expenditures than realty manipulations in other sections of Harlem or the city. Two brothers, John D. and Thomas F. Crimmins, for example, bought the entire blocks of One Hundred and Forty-fourth and One Hundred and Forty-fifth Streets between Lenox and Seventh Avenues in 1895, thinking the "Lenox Avenue electric car" would "greatly enhance the value of the property."[66] In keeping with the traditions of the neighborhood and the type of homes constructed in the 1880's, it was believed richer people who wanted "high-class flats," "costly dwellings," and who earned enough to afford them, would come to West Harlem. Many of the newly constructed buildings were equipped with elevators, maid's rooms and butler's pantries.[67] In 1899 William Waldorf Astor erected an apartment house on Seventh Avenue at a cost of $500,000.[68] Sunday real estate sections of New York City newspapers at the turn of the century bristled with full-page advertisements and pictures of the elegant homes in West Harlem.[69] The revived building activity of these years created the physical foundations for what became the most luxurious Negro ghetto in the world.

Speculation in West Harlem property led to phenomenal increases in the price of land and the cost of houses there—increases inflated out of all proportion to their real value. John M. Royall, Negro realtor, recalled that "from 1902 to 1905 real estate speculative fever seized all New York City. The great subway proposition . . . permeated the air. Real estate operators and speculators [imagined] becoming millionaires, and bought freely in the West Harlem district in and about the proposed subway stations. Men bought property on thirty and sixty day contracts, and sold their contracts . . . and made substantial profits. I have known buyers to pay $38,000 and $75,000 for tenements which showed a gross income of only $2600 and $5000 a year. On they went buying, buying. . . ." Houses continually changed hands. Each time a house was sold, Royall said, it brought a higher price. In the urge to get rich quick on Harlem property, few persons realized how artificial market values had become.[70]

The inevitable bust came in 1904–1905. Speculators sadly realized afterward that too many houses were constructed at one time. West Harlem was glutted with apartments and "excessive building . . . led to many vacancies."[71] No one knew exactly how long it would take to construct the subway and many houses built four and five years in advance of its completion remained partly unoccupied. The first of them to be inhabited by Negroes, for example, was never rented previously.[72] Rents were too high for the general population ($35–$45 per month) and precluded any great rush to West Harlem even after the subway was completed.[73] There was a widespread "overestimation of . . . rental value," a contemporary remarked. When the market broke, landlords competed with each other for tenants by reducing rents, or offering a few months' rent-free occupancy to them. Local realtors unsuccessfully attempted to eliminate these cutthroat practices.[74]

By 1905 financial institutions no longer made loans to Harlem speculators and building-loan companies, and many foreclosed on their original mortgages. The inflated prices asked for land and property in West Harlem "solemnly settled beneath a sea of depreciated values."[75] In the aftermath of the speculative collapse, and as a consequence of the initiative of Negro realtors, large numbers of colored people began to settle in West Harlem.

CHAPTER 7

Race Enterprise:
The Afro-American Realty
Company

"The books of the Afro-American Realty Company
are now open for stock subscription. Today is
the time to buy, if you want to be numbered
among those of the race who are doing something
toward trying to solve the so-called 'Race
Problem.' "
—The Afro-American Realty Company, *Prospectus,* 1904

"In numerous conversations with you both, I have
urged that the very least the Company could do,
since it has ceased to do business, is to make . . .
an Explicit statement giving the reasons which
led to . . . failure. . . ."
—Emmett J. Scott to Philip A. Payton, Jr., and Fred R. Moore, 1908

I

The individuals and companies caught in Harlem's rapidly deflated
real estate market were threatened with ruin. Rather than face "financial destruction" some landlords and corporations opened their
houses to Negroes and collected the traditionally high rents that colored people paid.[1] Others used the threat of renting to Negroes to
frighten neighbors into buying their property at higher than market
prices. Shrewder operators (contemporaries called them "clever buyers" and "white blackmailers," present-day realtors refer to them as
"blockbusters") hoped to take advantage of the unusual situation by
"placing colored people in property so that they might buy other
parcels adjoining or in the same block [reduced in price by] fear on
the part of whites to one-half of the values then obtaining," John M.
Royall noted. By using these techniques "a great number" of property
owners were able "to dispose of their property or . . . get a . . .

more lucrative return from rents paid by colored tenants," he concluded.[2]

The existence of a loosely rooted Negro population ready to settle in Harlem was primarily the result of ever-increasing Negro migration to the city. Further, the destruction of many all-Negro blocks in the Tenderloin when Pennsylvania Station was built in the first decade of the twentieth century, part of a more general commercial expansion in midtown Manhattan, dislocated the Negro population. Negro businessmen who owned property in the Tenderloin made substantial fortunes by selling and moving uptown. Negro tenants, offered decent living accommodations for the first time in the city's history, "flocked to Harlem and filled houses as fast as they were opened to them."[3]

This situation offered unusual money-making opportunities to a Negro realtor, Philip A. Payton, Jr. Payton was keenly aware of the housing needs of New York City's growing Negro population. His plan seemed foolproof, and guaranteed to satisfy Harlem's white landlords, the Negro people and himself. Payton offered to lease Harlem apartment houses from white owners and assure them a regular annual income. He, in turn, would rent these homes to Negroes and make a profit by charging rents ten per cent above the then deflated market price.[4] Many Negroes were willing to scrimp to live in beautiful apartments in an exclusive section of the city and Payton's initial operations were highly successful. His name became a respected one in Negro New York.

II

Phil Payton, as his friends called him, was born and brought up in Westfield, Massachusetts. His father, a southerner by birth, was an educated man—a graduate of Wayland Seminary in the District of Columbia. The elder Payton came north in 1872 and earned his living as a merchant and barber. His barber shop was a gathering place for the small Negro community in Westfield. In 1873, he married a Baltimore girl, and Phil was born three years later.[5]

The younger Payton's career started in similar fashion. He went south for his education and was graduated from Livingston College in Salisbury, North Carolina, in 1898. When he married and came to seek his fortune in New York in 1899 he worked at odd jobs to support himself. At first he was a handyman at six dollars a week, then a barber (a trade he learned in his father's shop), and finally a janitor in a real estate office. Payton became intrigued with the real estate business in the boom atmosphere that pervaded the housing market at the turn of the century, and also picked up a touch of the speculator's urge himself.[6] In 1900 the twenty-four-year-old Philip A. Payton, Jr., decided to go into business for himself: "Management of Colored Tenements A Specialty."[7]

At first the nascent entrepreneur was far from successful. In fact, he did so little business initially that he could not pay rent on his office and was evicted from his apartment. Payton's first break came as a result of a dispute between two landlords. In an interview in 1912 he described the incident: "I was a real estate agent, making a specialty of the management of colored tenement property for nearly a year before I actually succeeded in getting a colored tenement to manage," he said. "My first opportunity came as a result of a dispute between two landlords in West 134th Street. To 'get even' one of them turned his house over to me to fill with colored tenants. I was successful in renting and managing this house, and after a time I was able to induce other landlords to . . . give me their houses to manage."[8] Within a short time Payton began to advertise his services in white real estate journals:

Colored Tenements Wanted[9]

Colored man makes a specialty of managing colored tenements; references; bond. Philip A. Payton, Jr., agent and broker, 67 West 134th.

By 1904 the young man who four years earlier could not afford a decent meal[10] became the most prominent Negro realtor in New York City.

Payton was a light-skinned man of medium height and build. He wore pince-nez glasses and could easily have passed for a young teacher or clergyman, but his physical appearance belied his personality.[11] Friends knew him as an ambitious and impetuous man, the archetype of a hard-driving salesman. When it was rumored that he was going to visit Liberia, for example, one of them wrote: "You had better cause the Liberians to be notified of his approach that they might get out their padlocks, and nail down everything that's lying around loose."[12]

Payton's business success brought him public recognition. By the first decade of the twentieth century he was an intimate of Negro politician and Internal Revenue Collector Charles W. Anderson, and a friend of Fred R. Moore, editor of *The New York Age*[13] and general manager of the National Negro Business League. He was on the closest terms with practically every other member of the small Negro business and professional community in the city. Payton corresponded with Booker T. Washington and Washington's secretary, Emmett J. Scott. He was president of a short-lived local Negro defense society organized to protest police brutality in 1905, and a respected member of Washington's National Negro Business League.[14] Payton certainly conceived himself as a leader of the race and his public and private statements tended to foster this impression. When Emmett J. Scott learned that white landlords in Harlem were organizing to prevent the settlement of Negroes there, Payton told him not to worry: *"The fight that I am making,"* he replied, *"has got to be made sooner or later and I see no better time than now."*[15] Four of the apartment houses he rented to Negroes in 1906 were called "The Washington," "The Langston," "The Douglass," "The Dunbar."[16] When asked about his role in securing homes for Negroes in Harlem, Payton emphasized his personal importance: "By opening for colored tenants first a house on one block and then a house in another I have finally succeeded in securing . . . over two hundred and fifty first-class flats and private dwellings," he said in 1912.[17] The letters "P A P," in red and black, appeared on all the houses Payton controlled. Philip A. Payton, Jr., has been called the "Father of Colored Harlem."[18]

There is no serious question of Payton's personal honesty, although he was later sued for fraud by some stockholders in the Negro real estate company he founded—the Afro-American Realty Company. He was, however, a young man who clearly saw the possibilities of exploiting Harlem's depressed real estate market for his own as well as for the race's interest. He seemed to have complete confidence in his own business judgments. He got rich almost overnight, and made deals involving large sums of money before he had much practical business experience. Sometimes his activities as a businessman were less than exemplary. He could, for example, forget to file his corporate financial statements at the proper time, as he did in 1910, and thereby make himself liable to penalties of $1,000 to $10,000. His friend, Collector of Internal Revenue Charles W. Anderson, got him out of this jam by extending the filing date: "Payton went away without arranging for any report of his corporations, as required by the corporation tax law," Anderson wrote. "Learning of this, I availed myself of the authority conferred on collectors in the law to extend the time . . . thirty days."[19]

Nor could Payton hold on to money once he made it. One of his properties, at One Hundred and Thirty-second Street and Lenox Avenue, was hopefully to become the site of the "Payton Building." He confessed to a friend that he sold the land for $10,000 in cash instead, and quickly spent it all: ". . . It is all gone," he lamented, "and now I need some more." Alluding to a commonly held stereotype that Negroes spent money freely, he concluded sadly, "I am colored, too."[20]

III

Payton's activities in Harlem real estate reached a high point in 1904 with his founding of the Afro-American Realty Company. The company had its genesis in a partnership of ten Negroes organized by Payton. This partnership specialized in acquiring five-year leases on Harlem property owned by whites and subsequently renting them to Negroes. In 1904, Payton conceived of reorganizing this small concern into a regular real estate corporation, capable of buying and constructing homes as well as leasing them. The company, incorporated on June 15, 1904, was permitted to "buy, sell, rent, lease, and sub-lease, all kinds of buildings, houses . . . lots, and other . . . real estate in the City of New York. . . ." It was capitalized at $500,000 and authorized to issue 50,000 shares at $10 each. Ten of the eleven original members of the all-Negro Board of Directors subscribed to 500 shares each. The company began with an estimated capital of $100,000.[21]

Some of the important backers of the Afro-American Realty Company were Negroes who succeeded in what the Negro press called "Race Enterprise." Wealth in the Negro community came principally from businesses which provided services to Negroes, or larger extensions of such businesses. Real estate men, undertakers, lawyers, barbers, hair stylists—small entrepreneurs of all kinds—were the leading figures in the Negro business world. They supported the new corporation.

James C. Thomas, first president of the company, was probably

Payton's key backer initially. (Payton, the real power of the corporation, held the offices of vice-president and general manager.) Thomas was born in Harrisburg, Texas, on Christmas Day in the year of Emancipation, 1863. As a young man he worked as a cabin boy on steamers that plied their way between Galveston and ports of the northeast. In 1881, at the age of eighteen, he came to New York City and never left.[22] He worked as a steward in some of Manhattan's private clubs; like many other Negro businessmen of his generation he found it necessary to accept service positions in the early years of his career. (Payton, a college graduate, was a porter and barber; the Reverend Dr. Adam Clayton Powell, Sr., was employed as a waiter in Atlantic City even after his ordination;[23] a Negro public school teacher earned her education by working as a janitress;[24] Negro educator William Lewis Bulkley was a cook, janitor and waiter.)[25] While working as steward Thomas attended a local embalming school and was graduated as registered undertaker.

After a short-lived partnership with another Negro undertaker in the 1890's, Thomas opened his own business in the Tenderloin. A good funeral was all that many Negroes could look forward to—death was often the high point of life—and Thomas, tall and distinguished-looking in his Vandyke beard, was known as the man to do a proper job. His business was so successful that he purchased two buildings on Seventh Avenue at the turn of the century. Thomas' luck was with him in the selection of these houses—they were near the site of the future Pennsylvania Station. He later sold them for $103,000 and, shortly afterward, moved his establishment to Harlem. By 1907 he was known as "the richest man of African descent in New York. . . ."[26]

James E. Garner and Wilford H. Smith also served as officers in the Realty Company. Garner, corporation secretary and treasurer, had been born a slave in Charles County, Maryland. He grew up in the District of Columbia and worked as a porter in a drugstore and as a waiter when he came to New York City. In 1880 he established a small janitorial service in the Tenderloin. By the turn of the century, Garner's Manhattan House Cleaning and Renovating Bureau regularly employed thirty to thirty-five workers. When the National Negro Business League was founded in 1900, he was appointed treasurer of its New York branch.[27] Smith, another southern migrant, was the corporation's lawyer, a close friend of Booker T. Washington, and one of the most esteemed Negro lawyers in Manhattan in the early twentieth century. Initially, Smith, Garner, Thomas and Payton held all the offices in the Afro-American Realty Company. In the next few years other well-known Negroes became directors and investors: Emmett J. Scott, the Reverend Dr. W. H. Brooks, Fred R. Moore and Charles W. Anderson.[28]

IV

The Afro-American Realty Company was founded with high hopes of success—hopes which proved unfounded. At first, the corporation seemed to have sound financial backing and the support of eminent members of the Negro community. "The personnel of the Board of Directors of the company is bound to commend it to the respect, trust and confidence of even the most skeptical of our race," its prospectus stated. "Most of them are men who have made a success in their individual lines and are well-known in New York City for their ability, worth and integrity."[29] Early company transactions were profitable and tended to verify Payton's optimistic judgments. In 1904, for instance, the Afro-American Realty Company sold three of its newly acquired houses on West One Hundred and Thirty-fifth Street to a white real estate concern, the Hudson Realty Company. Hudson Realty proceeded to evict its Negro tenants in order to replace them with whites. Payton, in turn, "blocked the game" by buying two other houses on the same street and evicting the white tenants in them. Within a short time, he was able to repurchase the original three (at 40, 42 and 44 West One Hundred and Thirty-fifth Street), "filling the houses with Afro-Americans." These first highly publicized transactions boosted the reputation of the Realty Company. They "gave great publicity to the existence of the Afro-American Realty Company," *The New York Age* concluded in 1905.[30]

Payton did not let the company rest on its laurels. To attract financial support from the Negro working class he advertised regularly in the Negro press and promised the average investor much more than he was able to fulfill later. (The prospectus offered profits of seven to ten per cent, the weekly advertisements omitted the seven.)[31] Investment would not only yield "Tempting Profit," Negroes were told, but it was also their obligation to support an enterprise which would help end "relentless race prejudice": "To-day is the time to buy, if you want to be numbered among those of the race who are doing something toward trying to solve the so-called 'Race Problem,' " it was argued. The anticipated success of the company would become a symbol of Negro business acumen and would end racial segregation in urban housing: "A respecting, law-abiding Negro will find conditions can be so changed that he will be able to rent, wherever his means will permit him to live," the *Prospectus* maintained. Race prejudice would be turned into "dollars and cents" for *Negroes,* not whites.[32] Although public reports showed stocks being sold rapidly, privately the company found it necessary to hire a salesman to drum up business at a commission of 20 per cent. And stocks were sold, usually to individuals who could afford only a few shares at a time.[33]

The Realty Company promised the world and delivered little. It had hopefully been incorporated for fifty years, but folded after four. During its short and hectic existence it was wracked with internal dissension. In four years there were three major reorganizations of its Board of Directors and officers. James C. Thomas and James E. Garner severed connections with the company in its first year. Wilford H. Smith was later influential in bringing suit against Payton for fraud. The final reorganization, in 1906, left Payton as president and general manager. It was formal recognition of the power he had wielded since the founding of the corporation.

V

In September 1905 Fred R. Moore, then secretary and treasurer of the corporation, wrote that the "Realty Company is coming on slowly. . . . If a conservative policy is followed profits can be made. . . ."[34] Payton played for bigger stakes. As general manager, he finally leased or purchased on loans and mortgages, at high interest rates, some twenty-five houses, the majority in Harlem.[35] The paper value of this property was estimated at $1.1 million and its annual rental income at $114,500.[36] Some members of the company objected to Payton's management, but they apparently had little say in the day-to-day operations of the corporation. The "directors," Wilford H. Smith wrote in 1906, "exercise no control. I think the near future will reveal all that I do not care to say."[37] Booker T. Washington, on close terms with all the officers of the Afro-American Realty Company, received regular reports of its progress. He was also a sounding board for the internal opposition to Payton's control. In May 1906, for example, Smith informed him he was severing connections with the corporation. "I still believe that if the Company is properly handled, it will pay each investor well," he wrote, "but I do not believe it will ever be handled in the interest of the stockholders as long as the present manager is in control."[38]

The dissension came into the open in October 1906 when forty-three dissatisfied stockholders, represented by Smith, sued Payton and the Realty Company for having issued a "fraudulent prospectus"; one which "intended to mislead and deceive, and to cheat and defraud the general public, and especially the colored people. . . ." The specific charge leveled at Payton was that he held absolute control of the company and was therefore personally liable for any misrepresentation. All the initial statements of the corporation's financial stability and the amount of property it owned were highly exaggerated, the accusation ran. Charles J. Crowder, the stockholder in whose name the suit was filed, charged that $100,000 in stock "had not in fact been honestly subscribed for," but issued to Payton and his associates on "fictitious values"; that the contracts for the ten apartment houses the Realty Company claimed to control on five-year leases contained sixty- and ninety-day cancellation clauses, and that "nearly all of them had been cancelled" when the prospectus was issued; and, finally, that most of the houses the company claimed to own were, in reality, mortgaged nearly to their "full value." Crowder and another litigant, Frank S. Armand, each held one hundred shares of the corporation's stock. Practically all the others involved in the suit owned one to ten shares.[39]

A touch of the ludicrous ran through the case. Payton, arrested in January 1907, immediately won release in the custody of one of his lawyers. The order of arrest was itself declared illegal and vacated when the judge ruled the suit a civil not a criminal action.[40] The lawyer for the plaintiff, Wilford H. Smith, had been the corporation's lawyer at the time of the writing of the supposedly fraudulent prospectus. During the trial, Payton's attorney introduced a manuscript copy of the original prospectus containing penciled corrections and revisions by Smith himself. The specific charge of fraud against Payton was dismissed on the grounds that he was only one of the officers in the corporation. The Realty Company itself, however, was found

guilty of misrepresentation and Crowder and other stockholders recovered their initial investments plus damages and legal costs. Justice
Victor J. Dowling cited the company for claiming it owned property
without restriction, when all its houses were heavily mortgaged.[41]

VI

The Afro-American Realty Company, with Payton as president, continued to do business through 1907 and the early part of 1908. After
some prodding from stockholders, and in an attempt to restore confidence in the company's name, the first (and last) dividend was
declared in June 1907.[42] Further attempts to stimulate interest in the
company after the bad press it received from Crowder's suit—letters
sent to officers and stockholders asking them to encourage friends to
invest, a stockholders' meeting in Mercy Baptist Church at which
participants were "requested to bring any friends whom you think
will be interested in subscribing to our Capital Stock"[43]—were unsuccessful. Before the end of the year the Afro-American Realty
Company floundered and, by 1908, it ceased to do business.

The corporation had been confronted with the first organized effort
of white property owners in Harlem to prevent the sale of houses or
the rental of apartments to Negroes, but this movement itself did not
do any serious damage to the company. Payton himself scoffed at its
importance. "I have taken no steps," he told his friend Emmett Scott,
"without serious talks with some of the *large Real Estate interests in
our City.*" Any fear on this account, he concluded, "is ground-
less. . . ."[44] Payton's connections must have been solid for, once
the company was in financial trouble and no longer met its mortgage
payments, some of the receivers gave it leeway. They initially permitted the Realty Company to collect rents and apply this money to
its indebtedness: "the receiverships are friendly," Fred Moore wrote
in the winter of 1907.[45] The suit against Payton, however, was certainly harmful for the company's reputation. He and his friends said
that *all* the troubles of the company were caused not by any opposition to his business methods but by personal enmity. "The purpose of
the action seems only to be to harass and discredit me," Payton
claimed. "The past grand masters of the United Orders of Envy and
Jealousy are arraying themselves against Mr. Payton," one of his
friends wrote.[46] When Payton was asked about the higher rents he
charged Negroes, he justified them on the grounds that he was forced

to borrow money at higher interest rates and had to pay more for his options than white realtors did.[47]

In spite of charges and countercharges the major burden for the failure of the Afro-American Realty Company was Phil Payton's speculations. He had continued to buy property at a rapid pace even after Crowder's suit, and refused to listen to those who counseled a more moderate policy of acquisition. Rather than encourage interest in the corporation, this tended to further alienate other stockholders: "No matter how friendly we may feel for Mr. Payton there seems to be an opposition in the Company against him as its head that prevents it from making any progress," Fred Moore told Emmett Scott in 1907.[48] Payton's management and continued purchases finally led to an overextension of the company's holdings. The success of the Afro-American Realty Company, as with all Race Enterprise, was inextricably tied to the earning capacity of the city's Negro community. This predominantly lower-class group was always hardest hit by economic recessions. The recession of 1907–1908 coincided with Payton's speculations and left the company with many new tenements, but few tenants. "The cause of . . . the trouble," Fred Moore explained privately, "was due to taking on some property which remained unoccupied for months, and the money received from the property which was occupied had to go toward keeping up the unoccupied property. . . ."[49] The Realty Company could not generate enough income to meet its mortgage and interest payments in 1907. It needed the comparatively small sums of $10,000 to $20,000 to keep solvent, but simply could not raise the money. In November 1907 Moore wrote: "The Realty Co. is [in] a bad way, am trying to help straighten it out by persuading Payton to resign."[50]

By the end of 1907 it was evident to the officers, only Moore and Payton then, that the corporation was on the verge of collapse. Payton tried desperately to keep the company from going under. Since he could no longer borrow any money on his name ("He has tried all the white folks who have money without result"),[51] he wrote Booker T. Washington for a letter of introduction to Andrew Carnegie. "The Doctor," as Washington was known to intimates, refused to intercede in what was a business not a philanthropic matter.[52] Payton went to see Carnegie anyway and Oswald Garrison Villard as well, but he won no support from either of them. Their response might have been different, Moore told him, if the Realty Company charged Negroes modest rents: "If, as I told him, we could show that we were housing these people at a nominal rent, and the rents were very much lower than those charged by the white people, then perhaps they might look into it."[53]

In a final gesture to keep the corporation in business Booker T. Washington himself was asked to underwrite the company's notes due on January 1, 1908. "I have promised to advise all parties as soon as I hear from you," Moore told him. Washington rejected this proposal and the last thread of hope was cut.[54] By 1908 the Afro-American Realty Company collapsed, and all its properties were lost.[55]

The underlying causes for the failure of the company were never made public—they have remained hidden in private correspondence for more than half a century. Emmett J. Scott, who fully supported Payton throughout "his hour of trial," and who lost $500 in the corporation's demise, addressed an angry letter to the officers. He criticized them for permitting the company to fail without "a single word" of explanation to the stockholders. "In numerous conversations with you both," he told Payton and Moore, "I have urged that the very least the Company could do, since it has ceased to do business, is to make a statement, to be signed by you both . . . an Explicit statement giving the reasons which led to the failure of the Company. As honorable men I do not see how the Company could do less than this."[56]

Payton was out of town when Scott's letter arrived in July 1908. Moore promised to issue such a statement "if I have to do it myself. . . ."[57] By October, Moore was still promising to do so "at the very first opportunity."[58] No public statement was ever issued.

Payton was "down but not out."[59] He continued to operate in Harlem real estate as a private businessman and seems to have been successful in later ventures. His public reputation remained untainted, for all except those who lost their investments in the Realty Company. In one Negro encyclopedia he is remembered as "without a doubt the greatest Negro real estate dealer that ever lived."[60]

The Afro-American Realty Company played a significant part in opening homes for Negroes in Harlem. Philip A. Payton, Jr., owned and managed apartment houses and brownstones in sections never previously rented to Negro tenants. His holdings were scattered throughout Harlem from One Hundred and Nineteenth to One Hundred and Forty-seventh Streets. When the company folded, white realtors and mortgagors took over its property but the Negro tenants remained. The new owners continued to advertise the Negro company's former houses in the colored press.[61] The speculations of Philip A. Payton, Jr., led to the downfall of the Afro-American Realty Company, but they also helped lay the foundations of the largest Negro ghetto in the world.

CHAPTER 8

A Neighborhood Transformed

"The agents promise their tenants
that these houses will be rented
only to WHITE people."
—Harlem realtors, 1910

"The colored [people] are in Harlem
to stay, and they are coming each year by the thousands."
—John M. Royall, Negro realtor, 1914

I

The pressing need and desire for accommodations to house an expanding Negro population made the founding of the Afro-American Realty Company possible. This need continued to exist with greater intensity after the company's demise, and Negroes found other means to buy or rent homes in Harlem. The "border line" which separated whites and Negroes "rapidly receded" each year, and by 1914 some 50,000 Negroes lived in the neighborhood.[1]

But not all property owners were ready to open their houses to colored people. It seemed unbelievable to some that theirs, one of the most exclusive sections in the entire city, should become the center of New York's most depressed and traditionally worst-housed people. Some owners banded together in associations to repulse what they referred to as the Negro "invasion" or the Negro "influx." The language used to describe the movement of Negroes into Harlem—the words "invasion," "captured," "black hordes," "invaders," "enemy," for example, appear repeatedly in denunciations of Negroes—was the language of war.[2]

In the 1880's and 1890's Harlemites annually celebrated the historic Revolutionary Battle of Harlem Heights. These patriotic fetes were symbols of community pride and pamphlets were widely distributed informing the neighborhood of the dignitaries participating in them.[3] In the early twentieth century, however, Harlem's residents gathered not to preserve the memory of a Revolutionary conflict, but to fight their own battle—to keep their neighborhood white.

Most of the formal opposition to Negro settlement in Harlem centered in local associations of landlords. Some were committees representing individual blocks, others were community-wide in structure. Property owners on West One Hundred and Fortieth, One Hundred and Thirty-seventh, One Hundred and Thirty-sixth, One Hundred and Thirty-fifth, One Hundred and Thirty-first, One Hundred and Thirtieth, One Hundred and Twenty-ninth Streets, and so on, in descending order as the Negro community spread southward, and along the avenues, signed restrictive agreements. Each swore not to rent his apartments to Negroes for ten or fifteen years—till when, it was thought, "this situation . . . referred to . . . will have run its course": "The premises, land, and buildings of which we . . . are the owners . . . shall not be used as a . . . Negro tenement, leased to colored . . . tenants, sold to colored . . . tenants . . . or all [other] persons of African descent," one agreement reads. "Each of the parties," another maintains, "does hereby covenant and agree [not] to . . . hereafter . . . cause to be suffered, either directly or indirectly, the said premises to be used or occupied in whole or in part by any negro, quadroon, or octoroon of either sex whatsoever. . . ." Some covenants even put a limitation on the number of Negro janitors, bellboys, laundresses and servants to be employed in a home. Following a pseudo-legal procedure which was supposed to make these agreements binding, each signer paid all the others a fee of one dollar. The finished products were notarized and filed at the County Clerk's Office in the New York City Hall of Records where they may be read today.[4] The streets covered by such restrictive codes were known in the Negro community as "Covenant Blocks," and Negroes took pride in being the first colored landlords or tenants to live in them: "to knock [the covenants] into a cocked hat," one said. "Although organizations to prevent the settling of colored citizens in certain . . . sections of Harlem mushroom overnight," the *Age* quipped, "the colored invasion goes merrily along."[5]

Other community groups led by white realtors, businessmen, journalists, clergymen, members of the Board of Commerce and local citizens tried to hold back the Negro's "steady effort to invade Harlem." One realty company dealing in upper-Manhattan property was called the Anglo-Saxon Realty Corporation. Such organizations as the West Side Improvement Corporation, the West Harlem Property Owners' Association, the Save-Harlem Committee, the Committee of Thirty and the Harlem Property Owners' Improvement Corporation were formed. Each planned to arouse the interest of all white Harlemites in what they called "the greatest problem that Harlem has had to face."[6]

The Harlem Property Owners' Improvement Corporation (HPOIC), active from 1910 to 1915, was the most forceful of these organizations. "We are approaching a crisis," its founder, John G. Taylor, said in 1913. "It is the question of whether the white man will rule Harlem or the negro." Taylor hoped to organize the entire white community "to fight the common enemy." "We believe," he wrote on another occasion, "that real friends of the negroes will eventually convince them that they should buy large tracts of unimproved land near the city and there build up colonies of their own." "Drive them out," Taylor shouted in an angry tirade at another time, "and send them to the slums where they belong. . . ."[7]

The HPOIC found active support in the local press. *"When will the people of Harlem wake up to the fact that they must organize and maintain a powerful anti-invasion movement if they want to check the progress of the black hordes that are gradually eating through the very heart of Harlem?"* the *Harlem Home News* said in an editorial in 1911. "They must wake up and get busy before it is too late. . . . Are we to give Harlem over to the negroes altogether?"[8] Stories about Negroes in the *Home News* were generally accompanied by such abusive epithets as "coon," "darkey," "nigger," "black plague," "black hordes." Its journalists quoted Negroes in exaggerated dialect.[9] Meetings of property owners were held, some in white churches, and programs introduced which proposed evicting all Negroes in Harlem and outlawing future sale and rental of property to colored people. At one session, Taylor suggested that whites who lived on streets bordering Negro blocks build twenty-four-foot fences to separate themselves from Negro neighbors.[10] Advertisements for white tenants were printed in dailies with city-wide distribution, and *Harlem Magazine,* organ of the white Harlem Board of Commerce, publicized the activities of the HPOIC. It pleaded with whites to join the anti-Negro crusade: "Will You Help Yourself?"; "Help Protect Your Property"; "Will you do a little to save yourself?"; "Do you wish the influences which have tended to depreciate your realty values to be removed?" To participate in the restrictive movement, it maintained, would "be the most vital and useful thing that you have ever done."[11]

Negro realtors were contacted and told not to try to find houses on certain streets: "We herewith resolve that every colored real estate broker be notified as to the following: That the owners of this section have unanimously agreed not to rent their houses for colored tenancy. . . ."[12] Like an enemy negotiating a line of truce, whites called a meeting of Negro real estate men to attempt to draw a voluntary boundary line that would permanently separate the white and Negro communities—a "dead line," it was called.[13] Four members of Harlem's Church of the Puritans attended meetings of the New York Presbytery to protest the proposed movement of the Negro St. James Presbyterian Church into the neighborhood.[14] Others called on city fathers to try to prevent the licensing of a Negro-owned movie house on Lenox Avenue.[15] The Lafayette Theatre, on Seventh Avenue, permitted Negroes to sit only in its balcony.[16] People who signed restrictive covenants and subsequently broke them were brought to court.[17]

These movements permitted whites the opportunity to vent their anxieties and the chimerical hope that restrictive agreements "safe-guarded the neighborhood . . . for all time," but they did not end Negro settlement in Harlem. All the organizations failed. That it was necessary to found so many in a relatively short period of time was a reflection of the general failure of each. Private housing covenants had not, during the life of the HPOIC, been ruled constitutional (from 1917 to 1948 the United States Supreme Court barred segregation by public ordinance but not separation in private agreements). Although at least two people were sued in New York City for violating their original commitments, local courts never convicted them. Negro realtors, like John M. Royall, ridiculed the proposal for a voluntary line of segregation as an agreement to "capitalize on prejudice," and "a joke."[18] In spite of protests of Harlemites—"can *nothing* be done to put a restriction on the invasion of the Negro into Harlem?"—St. James was permitted to move into the area and even granted a large loan from the Presbytery to build a new church.[19] Its success forced it to move to larger quarters twice in the next decade. In 1913 the Lafayette Theatre was sold to promoters who realized it was foolish to run a segregated theater in "what is destined to become a colored neighborhood." The new owners encouraged Negro patronage—"Our Doors Are Open To All"—and even contributed regularly to Negro charities. The large basement of the building in which the theater was housed, Lafayette Hall, was later leased as a temporary armory to Harlem's Negro National Guard unit. For a short time the entire building, including the theater, was controlled by a group of Negro businessmen. In the twenties, the Lafayette was advertised as the "Most Widely Known Negro Theatre in America"; "America's Leading Colored Theatre."[20]

The basic cause of the collapse of all organized efforts to exclude Negroes from Harlem was the inability of any group to gain total and unified support of all white property owners in the neighborhood. Without such support it was impossible to organize a successful neighborhood-wide restrictive movement. Landlords forming associations by blocks had a difficult time keeping people on individual streets united. There also continued to be speculators, Negro and white, who, as in 1904 and 1905, sought to exploit the situation for their own profit. They bought tenements and opened them to Negroes to try to force neighbors to repurchase them at higher prices.[21] Nor was it possible, and this is the major point, to create a well-organized and well-financed movement of Negro restriction (the HPOIC plan called for the contribution of one-half of one per cent of the assessed valuation of all property to a community fund)[22] in the disrupted and emotional atmosphere that pervaded Harlem in the first two decades of the twentieth century. The very setting in which whites were confronted with Negro neighbors for the first time led to less than level-headed reasoning. The first impulse of many "in a rather panicky state of mind"[23] was to sell at whatever price their property would bring and move elsewhere. Realtors called this "panic selling" and, in spite of efforts to prevent it, it continued.[24] Between 1907 and 1914, two-thirds of the houses in or near the Negro section were sold—practically all at substantial losses to the original owners. Since the already weak real estate market was flooded with property in a short time, and only a relatively few Negroes were wealthy enough to buy—"there was no market for real estate among the newcomers"— prices continued to depreciate rapidly: "realty values have tumbled by leaps and bounds." "The coming of Negroes to this locality without any financial backing brought about a decided change, as the colored people . . . were unable to adhere to the standard formerly observed by the whites," a Harlem banker wrote. "Hence there was a deterioration in values. . . ."[25] In the 1870's and 1880's fortunes were made in soaring Harlem land prices; by 1917 white realtors tried to encourage interest in the neighborhood by advertising how cheap property had become: "Changes in the character of Harlem population," a member of the Harlem Board of Commerce wrote, have led "to remarkable bargains, both for rental and purchase. . . . Such properties in good condition can now be purchased at less than the assessed value of the land alone."[26] In the 1920's, as will be shown, this situation changed radically.

The minority of Harlem landlords who adhered to their original restrictive covenants suffered serious economic consequences. Many were unable to find white people willing to rent their apartments. To encourage white tenants already in them to remain, some were forced to reduce rents drastically: "The introduction of negro tenants . . . has caused . . . many white tenants to move and [has] required a substantial reduction of rents to those who remained," a group of Harlem landlords complained.[27] Those who had mortgage payments to meet were threatened with foreclosure by banks and other lending institutions, and many found it "impossible . . . to hold out."[28] The opponents of Negro settlement faced the dilemma of maintaining a "White Only" policy and probably losing everything, or renting to Negroes at higher prices and surviving. Most chose what seemed to them the lesser of two evils. The following "Notice," one of many, appeared on a Harlem tenement in 1916:[29]

NOTICE

We have endeavored for some time to
avoid turning over this house to
colored tenants, but as a result of . . .
rapid changes in conditions . . . this
issue has been forced upon us.

II

The creation of Negro Harlem was only one example of the general development of large, segregated Negro communities within many American cities in the years *preceding* and following World War I. Harlem was New York's equivalent of the urban ghettos of the nation. "The Negroes are being relegated to the land of Goshen in all our great cities," Kelly Miller commented.[30] "Niggertowns," "Buzzard's Alleys," "Nigger Rows," "Black Bottoms," "Smoketowns," "Bronzevilles," and "Chinch Rows" developed elsewhere, North and South, by 1913—and they would continue to emerge in the future. The District of Columbia was noted for its supposedly decadent Negro alleys: "Tin Can Alley," "Coon Alley," "Hog Alley," "Moonshine Alley," and "Goat Alley." (Life in "Goat Alley," was the subject of a play by that name in the 1920's.) "So closely have the terms Alleys and Negroes been associated," a historian of Washington's Negro section wrote, "that in the minds of the older citizens they are inseparable." "There is growing up in the cities of America a distinct Negro world," George Edmund Haynes said in 1913. These were neighborhoods "isolated from many of the impulses of the common life and little understood by the white world," he concluded.[31]

Among these urban ghettos Harlem was unique. Initially, its name was a symbol of elegance and distinction, not derogation; its streets and avenues were broad, well-paved, clean and tree-lined, not narrow and dirty; its homes were spacious, replete with the best modern facilities, "finished in high-style."[32] Harlem was originally not a slum, but an ideal place in which to live. For the first and generally last time in the history of New York City, Negroes were able to live in decent homes in a respectable neighborhood, "the best houses that they have ever had to live in": "It is no longer necessary for our people to live in small, dingy, stuffy tenements," *The New York Age* said in an editorial in 1906.[33] Harlem was "a community in which Negroes as a whole are . . . better housed than in any other part of the country," an Urban League report concluded in 1914.[34] "Those of the race who desire to live in grand style, with elevator, telephone and hall boy service, can now realize their cherished ambition."[35]

It was expensive to live in "grand style." The rents paid by Harlem's Negroes were higher than those charged in any other Negro section of New York City and they continued to rise rapidly after World War I. In 1914 the average Negro family paid $23.45 per month for apartments in Harlem, and rents in the most elegant houses were much higher.[36] As Negroes moved into the neighborhood they complained of being overcharged by landlords and, as a rule, most were paying higher rents than their incomes would warrant.[37] Although the cost of living was certainly high by the standards of a low-income group, few of Harlem's rentals, *prior to World*

War I, were extortionate. Houses were originally constructed for the well-to-do, "the class above the ordinary." "Harlem tenements," one Negro wrote, "were built for persons of larger incomes than Negroes receive."[38] Since the beginning of the century, however, rents steadily declined, and they were usually lowered even further immediately before Negroes occupied a house. When homes were opened to Negroes it was the general practice to increase rents, but rarely prior to the First World War did prices return to their original levels.[39]

Those Negroes who could afford to pay high rents began moving into the neighborhood at the turn of the century. William H. Smith, caterer, businessman and member of Negro Manhattan's social set, bought a home on West One Hundred and Thirty-fourth Street in the 1890's. Another Negro merchant owned property on the same block at the turn of the century[40] and one wealthy Negro clergyman lived in Harlem in 1895—attended by white servants and chauffeured about in an expensive carriage.[41] As the housing market deteriorated in the early twentieth century other private homes were made available to "respectable colored people." By 1910 many of the city's most prominent Negroes lived in Harlem—the Reverend Dr. Adam Clayton Powell, Sr., Bert Williams, James C. Thomas, Charles W. Anderson and others. Madame C. J. Walker built her mansion on West One Hundred and Thirty-sixth Street in 1913.[42] A student of the Negro Tenderloin found every colored pastor of the churches he visited "living in Harlem" in 1912.[43] The less respectable middle class—gamblers, prostitutes and the like—could also afford high rents. One house was occupied by individuals who represented such an inordinate variety of occupations that Negroes called it "Noah's Ark."[44]

As Harlem became a Negro section its "modern houses" and "better homes" attracted many people from the older Negro sections of Manhattan. Negro women in the Tenderloin hoped "to marry and go get a home in Harlem."[45] Negro businessmen, finding customers moving uptown, sold their property and moved northward. "The massing of the large Negro population in the Harlem district," a journalist observed in 1910, "has been the making of many successful Negro . . . businessmen."[46] San Juan Hill (usually called Columbus Hill after the First World War) "was fast pouring its people into Harlem [as the] exodus from the downtown districts continues with great activity."[47] By 1920, the former Negro sections of Manhattan were terribly rundown backwash communities inhabited by Negroes who, as a rule, desired to live in Harlem but could not afford to pay the high rents charged there. A survey of Columbus Hill in the early 1920's classified 63 per cent of its houses as "absolutely undesirable," and 21 per cent as "passable." "Tenements show thirty to forty years of hard wear," T. J. Woofter recorded in *Negro Problems in Cities*. "Paving is noisy granite block, sidewalks are broken, and fire escapes are hung with bright garments. . . . On the avenue . . . are filthy stores, poolrooms filled with boys and men from morning to late night, with drunks and frowsy street-women. Families are shiftless. . . ." The older model tenements built early in the century were surrounded by houses noted for their congestion, filth and vice. "In regard to the Tuskegee," the City and Suburban Homes Company noted, "the caretaker reports that she cannot interest respectable colored persons in even looking at the vacancies. This has become a very bad street frequented by a most undesirable class of people and our tenants fear for their safety in going through it." One Negro woman, ashamed that she was left behind in a downtown tenement, proudly told an investigator: "I'd like to show you Harlem."[48]

III

After the collapse of the Afro-American Realty Company, Negro churches played a more important role in the development of Harlem than all other institutions in the Negro community. The primary reason for this was that the church had traditionally been the most stable and wealthy Negro institution. As the Negro population expanded rapidly in the early twentieth century the influence and wealth of the church increased phenomenally. Membership in older churches doubled and trebled, and they continually moved to larger quarters; little missions which began in storefronts or in private homes became independent and built or bought stately structures in which to worship; new churches were founded. Mercy Street Baptist Church, for example, was organized in Harlem by seven Negroes at the turn of the century. At first the small congregation met in a house owned by the Baptist City Mission. By July 1907 the congregation, supported by eight hundred communicants, moved to a new building. Population pressure made these facilities inadequate—"Standing room is always at a premium"—and the congregation, under its new name,

Metropolitan Baptist, negotiated the sale of a white Presbyterian church in 1918. Harlem Presbyterian had been "one of the finest church buildings in Harlem." Metropolitan Baptist has remained there ever since.[49]

Salem Memorial Mission, founded in a small room in Harlem in 1902 by the Reverend F. A. Cullen, foster father of the gifted poet Countée Cullen, had a similar history. The first service was attended by three women and the Reverend Mr. Cullen received nineteen cents for his efforts. Ten years later Salem Memorial Methodist Episcopal Church moved into quarters vacated by a white congregation and, in 1923, it moved again. Its final home, the former Calvary Methodist Episcopal Church, was a plush structure, the old meeting place of "one of the most prosperous congregations of the denomination in Manhattan." "The white people have moved away to such an extent," the minister of Calvary Church explained shortly before its sale, "that it is difficult now to continue the most limited church activities or finances. . . ."[50]

Similar changes occurred throughout Harlem in the early twentieth century. Exclusive white denominations left the neighborhood and sold their property to Negro Baptists, Methodists and others. "Little Zion," the uptown branch of "Mother Zion," remained in a small wooden building on Harlem's east side for three-quarters of a century before it constructed a new church on the west side in 1911. "Not in seventy years has there been so much real enthusiasm in the Harlem A.M.E. Zion Church," one member commented.[51] Ministers in all the churches preached in quarters inadequate to seat those who wished to attend, and some were forced to hold five or six services each Sunday.[52] New Negro Moravian, Seventh Day Adventist, Roman Catholic and evangelical churches were established in Harlem prior to and after the First World War. Before all the downtown congregations moved to Harlem they too opened branch Sunday schools and Bible classes in public halls and theaters. Mass services were sometimes held in "gospel tents," "mammoth tents," pitched on Harlem's empty lots, as clergymen sought to "Harvest the Souls" of the ungodly.[53]

Pastors of Negro churches, as they had done in the nineteenth century, planned to follow their congregations to the new Negro neighborhood. The Reverend Dr. Adam Clayton Powell, Sr., repeatedly preached his sermon "A Model Church," encouraging his congregation to move Abyssinian Baptist to Harlem and to purchase property there while prices were low. "It was apparent as early as 1911," he later wrote, "that Harlem would be the final destination of the Abyssinian Church."[54] "On to Harlem"[55] movements began in downtown churches and, prior to 1914, three of the oldest and most distinguished Negro churches, Bethel African Methodist Episcopal, African Methodist Episcopal Zion ("Mother Zion") and St. Philip's Protestant Episcopal Church moved into the section. By the early 1920's practically every established Negro church in Manhattan was located in Harlem, and most occupied exceptionally beautiful buildings.

But the Negro churches did more than simply follow their members to Harlem. Many were able to realize large profits by selling property in the midtown area at high prices and moving uptown where land and property had depreciated in value before World War I. The more important and wealthy congregations not only built new churches in Harlem, but invested heavily in local real estate. Negro churches became the largest Negro property owners in Harlem. St. Mark's Methodist Episcopal, Abyssinian Baptist, and "Mother Zion" owned houses in Harlem prior to 1915. After the war, they and other Negro churches continued to invest heavily in land and homes. Some of the houses purchased by churches were on blocks covered by restrictive covenants, but nothing could be done to prevent such transactions. By becoming landholders, Negro churches helped transform Harlem to a Negro section.

The Negro church most actively engaged in buying Harlem real estate was St. Philip's Protestant Episcopal Church. Throughout the nineteenth century St. Philip's was reputed to be the most exclusive Negro church in New York City. Its members were considered "the better element of colored people," and its services were dignified and refined. This reputation as a fashionable institution made membership in St. Philip's a sign of social recognition and many of the more prominent Negroes of the city were its communicants. It was the only Negro church in Manhattan with a "Pew System" in the nineteenth century—by which members outbid each other for choice seats in the chapel.[56] St. Philip's was also recognized as the "wealthiest Negro church in the country," and this reputation has continued to the present.[57]

The growth of St. Philip's was similar to that of many other important Negro churches. Founded by a small group of Negroes in the Five Points districts in 1809, it held its first formal services in 1819 in a wooden building, 60 feet by 50 feet, on what is now Centre Street. In 1856 St. Philip's moved to a former Methodist church on Mulberry Street and, in 1889, following the Negro population to the Tenderloin, it came to West Twenty-fifth Street. St. Philip's remained in the Tenderloin until 1910, when it moved to a newly constructed church in Harlem.[58]

Because of the opposition of Harlem property owners, the first transactions in the developing Negro section were made in subterfuge. The Reverend Dr. Hutchens C. Bishop, pastor of the church, came to New York City from Charleston, South Carolina, in 1886. He was a tall, thin and almost bald man who easily passed for white. From 1906 through 1910 the Reverend Dr. Bishop bought houses and land in Harlem in his name, including a site for a new church. Some white landlords were happy to sell him their houses and told him they would never sell to Negroes. In 1910 the pastor turned all the property he bought over to the church and prepared to move his congregation to Harlem.[59]

Aside from the church building which St. Philip's owned on West Twenty-fifth Street, it also acquired a number of lots on West Thirtieth Street in the 1830's. This property, originally donated to the church as a cemetery, was valued at the time of acquisition at $9,000. As real estate prices rose in mid-Manhattan the value of St. Philip's holdings skyrocketed. In 1909 the church sold its building on West Twenty-fifth Street for $140,000; the cemetery land was put on the market two years later and brought in $450,000.[60]

When the church site in the Tenderloin was sold in 1909, the Reverend Dr. Bishop attempted to purchase a white Protestant Episcopal church in Harlem. He offered the Church of the Redeemer $50,000 for its property on West One Hundred and Thirty-sixth Street. The neighborhood around the church was obviously changing, its members were moving away, and it would have been to the church's advantage to sell then at a reasonable price: ". . . the coming of so many negroes to the locality had made the property undesirable," its pastor said, "most of the members of the congregation having moved away."[61] West One Hundred and Thirty-sixth Street was a Covenant Block, however, and many of the vestrymen of the white church felt morally bound (if that is the proper term) to their original agreement. They rejected the offer and St. Philip's built its new church a few blocks away. (In 1913 the Church of the Redeemer put its property on the market for sale. For one year the vestrymen unsuccessfully tried to find a white buyer. In 1914, adhering to the letter not the spirit of the Covenant, the Church of the Redeemer was sold to a white woman who immediately resold it to the African Methodist Episcopal Zion ["Mother Zion"] Church for $22,000.[62] Within ten years "Mother Zion" outgrew the premises.)

The new St. Philip's, designed by Negro architects, as Madame Walker's mansion had been, was completed in Harlem in 1911. The church was always moderately wealthy, but it never before controlled the vast sums accumulated through the sale of its property in the Tenderloin. Taking advantage of the depressed condition of the real estate market, the decision was made to invest the church's capital in Harlem apartment houses. In 1911 St. Philip's bought a row of ten new apartment houses on West One Hundred and Thirty-fifth Street between Seventh and Lenox Avenues for $640,000—the largest single real estate transaction, involving Negroes, in the city's history at that time. Before the sale, signs which hung in renting offices of the white realtors who managed these buildings read:

> The agents promise their tenants that
> these houses will be rented only to
> WHITE people.

Shortly after the transfer of this property to St. Philip's and after its remaining white tenants were evicted, a new sign was displayed, telling prospective Negro tenants to contact colored real estate agents:

For Rent, Apply to Nail and Parker[63]

IV

John E. Nail and Henry C. Parker handled the transactions which led to the sale of St. Philip's downtown property and the purchase of its One Hundred and Thirty-fifth Street holdings. They continued to act as agents for the church after 1911 when St. Philip's invested more heavily in Harlem real estate. Jack Nail, as he was known to his friends, was a member of the church and undoubtedly played a vital role in advising the Reverend Dr. Bishop on possibilities of making money in Harlem property. The firm of Nail and Parker, through these and other major transactions (for example, they acted as agents for the downtown YMCA when that body decided to move to Harlem, and later handled the transfer of the Stanford White houses), became the most important Negro real estate company in Harlem. Nail, president of the corporation, was an active participant in community affairs. He was first president of Harlem's Negro Board of Trade, vice-president of the exclusive and predominantly white Republican Business Men's Club of New York City, a member of the Mayor's Housing Committee and the first Negro elected to the Real Estate Board of New York. When President Hoover created a national commission to investigate American urban housing, Nail was brought in as consultant. Throughout his life he raised money for the New York Urban League and was elected one of its officers. John E. Nail was one of the most respected businessmen in New York City.[64]

Nail was the son of a well-known Negro saloon owner. The elder Nail, John B., migrated to the city from Baltimore in 1863, and began his career as an attendant in white gambling houses. Apparently more successful than most patrons, he saved enough money to open a café in the Tenderloin in the 1880's—a gathering place for theatrical people.[65] John B. Nail was another Negro businessman who made substantial profits from selling his downtown property and moving to Harlem in the early twentieth century: "Mr. Nail had been in business for about thirty years when he found that his community was on its way to Harlem and better housing," a student recorded. "Noting this trend—especially from his dwindling income—he sold his business and the building it occupied." He used the money to buy five newly built apartment houses.[66]

Henry C. Parker was a North Carolinian by birth and, like many other southern migrants, returned to Rocky Mount each year to visit his family and friends. The younger Nail and Parker learned about the real estate business as salesmen for Philip A. Payton, Jr. When, in December 1907, it was obvious the Afro-American Realty Company would fold, John E. Nail and Henry C. Parker established their own real estate corporation. Their business was highly successful (until the Great Depression) and they have sometimes been called the "Little Fathers" of Negro Harlem.[67]

The success that Nail and Parker achieved was typical of many other Negro realtors. As each year passed it became more evident that Harlem was to become a Negro section permanently: "The colored [people] are in Harlem to stay, and they are coming each

year by the thousands." White landlords and corporations hired
Negro managers to deal with their new Negro tenants. By 1914, 37
per cent of the Negro tenements in Harlem were managed by "colored agents," although less than five per cent of these houses were
owned by Negro landlords. In 1920 there were twenty-one Negro real
estate firms with offices in Harlem, specializing in uptown property,
and real estate dealers composed the largest single Negro professional
group at the time of the 1930 census.[68]

Compared with holdings of white landlords, insurance companies
and business firms, Negro ownership of Harlem property was, and
always remained, limited. After 1914, however, when houses were
made available to Negroes in larger numbers, a significant increase in
the amount of Negro capital invested in the area took place. Negro
businessmen from the South and other sections of the country,
smelling success and opportunity in Harlem, sent agents there. Local
realtors, like the dogged Philip A. Payton, Jr., closed deals involving
more than a million dollars. A month before his death, in August
1917, Payton and his associates, many of them Negro businessmen
from the South, bought six elevator apartment houses, "the last word
in high-class apartment house construction," and immediately opened
them to Negroes:

The World's Finest Housing Proposition
Catering Exclusively to
Refined Colored Tenants

Each house bore the name of a distinguished Negro, and at the center
of every hall was a picture of the dignitary: Toussaint, Wheatley,
Attucks, Dunbar, Washington, Douglass.[69] Watt Terry, a successful
Negro businessman from Brockton, Massachusetts ("Watt Terry of
Brockton and New York"), came to New York City and founded
another Negro realty corporation in Harlem—the Terry Holding
Company. Terry, a Virginian who came north in 1901, was reputed
to be one of the wealthiest Negroes in America—if not *the* wealthiest.
In story-book fashion his original "capital stock" of fifteen cents, as
he once described it, was somehow transformed into a sizable fortune
through speculation in Massachusetts land. He came to New York
City in 1917 and made it his permanent residence. In the 1920's
Terry built a real estate empire in Harlem.[70] Wealthy Negroes from
Georgia, Florida, Pennsylvania, and the District of Columbia followed his path. The Sarco Realty Corporation, controlled by a man

who originally owned a house-cleaning business, bought the stately Smithsonian Apartment House, constructed in 1899. In 1919 the Equitable Life Assurance Society, after restricting ownership to whites for two decades, put the lovely brownstones designed by Stanford White on the market. The Negro press was plastered with advertisements for their sale; within eight months practically all were sold to well-to-do Negroes. They were called "the finest group of Negro residences in the country." Since then, within the Negro community, the Stanford White houses have been known as "Striver's Row." Buildings of the old Astor Estate, second in reputation and quality only to "Striver's Row," were also sold to Negroes in the early twenties.[71]

Practically every major Negro institution moved from its downtown quarters to Harlem by the early 1920's: the United Order of True Reformers; Odd Fellows, Masons, Elks, Pythians and other fraternal orders; the Music School Settlement; the Coachmen's Union League; the African Society of Mutual Relief; *The New York Age*; West Fifty-third Street YMCA and YWCA; almost all the Negro social service agencies, including local offices of the Urban League and NAACP; the AME Home and Foreign Missionary Society; all the major churches.[72] The virtual monopoly *The New York Age* had for generations as the city's only leading Negro journal was broken, and two other weeklies were established: the *New York News* and the *Amsterdam News* ("boasting local sheets," the *Age* called them). The *Age* continued to be a staid newspaper in the tradition of nineteenth-century journalism, although it too began to change in the 1920's. Its competitors were tabloids whose blaring and sensational headlines appealed to mass audiences and mirrored the highly successful white dailies. P.S. 89, on Lenox Avenue, three-quarters Negro by 1915, opened a night school, reading room and a community center for Negro youth. Within a short time it became one of the most run-down public schools in the city. P.S. 68, the former "Silk Stocking" school, was now noted for its regular skirmishes between white and Negro pupils. The *Harlem Home News* moved to the Bronx in 1913. A historic landmark of an earlier Harlem, Watt Mansion, was first transformed into a cafeteria, "the Lybia," and finally torn down. The famous Pabst Restaurant became a Kress five-and-ten-cent store in 1920, and Horton's Ice Cream Parlor, a well-known meeting place owned by the "Grand Old Man" of white

Harlem, was transformed into a shoestore. The most famous institution of white Harlem, Collegiate Reformed Church (Second Dutch Reformed Church), held out against the inevitable longer than most—in 1930, however, it became the Negro Ephesus Seventh Day Adventist Church, and has remained that to the present.[73]

Those who remembered the expectations of previous generations—Germans, German-Jews, Irish, and others—sadly moved away. "Harlem has been devastated as a result of the steady influx of Negroes," an old resident bemoaned in 1913. "The best of Harlem was gone," another thought in the same year, and it "will be all colored in ten years." In 1922, *The New York Times* reported that "very few of the old families remain which made . . . Harlem . . . a delightful . . . residential locality a quarter of a century ago. . . ." Harlem's Old-Timers changed their tune. When they met in their midtown clubhouse they no longer sang of Harlem's prosperity, but of how "everything has changed except our friendship."[74]

Merchants left behind as their former clientele departed attempted to adjust to new conditions, although a few refused to accept the change. H. C. F. Koch, for example, owned one of the largest department stores in Harlem. Koch moved into the German section of the community and opened a business on One Hundred and Twenty-fifth Street in 1890. When Negroes came to Harlem, Koch and his children ignored their trade or treated them discourteously: "The Koch family paid scant attention to colored . . . customers," a Negro wrote. Rather than continue business in a Negro section the family sold the store in 1930.[75]

Most businessmen remained. L. M. Blumstein, a German-Jew, opened his store in Harlem in 1896. Blumstein was as much opposed to Negro settlement as Koch, and refused to hire Negroes for other than menial positions until 1930. In that year he employed Negro elevator operators but still refused to hire Negro salesmen, clerks and cashiers. Negroes forced him to change his mind through the pressure of a successful boycott during the Great Depression. Blumstein remained in the neighborhood and the department store founded in 1896 remains one of Harlem's most successful businesses.[76]

As merchants saw it, the problem was to change the neighborhood's image to attract new industry. The Harlem Board of Commerce conducted an "elaborate campaign to advertise Harlem . . . telling of the advantage of Harlem from a business standpoint. . . ."

The community advertised as a place of exclusive residence in the 1880's and 1890's was now claimed to be the perfect area in which to locate factories. Land was cheap, it was argued in 1917, transportation good, and the neighborhood overflowing with unskilled, low-income families willing to accept any kind of employment. The heterogeneity of Harlem's population was then seen as one of the community's principal assets: "Only 17 per cent of its people are native white of native parents," a survey of the Harlem Board of Commerce concluded in 1917. "Racial colonization shows distinctly." "Let us consider Harlem as it is to-day," Charles H. Fuller of the Board of Commerce noted. "The zenith of its prosperity and utility as a residential section has . . . passed. . . . The hope of the future lies in the development of its manufacturing." Carnivals, pageants, fairs and parades were held regularly to stimulate public interest in Harlem's business opportunities. The community which formerly denounced street-hawkers and peddlers seemed to have gone into business for itself.[77]

The larger the Negro population became, the more often businessmen spoke of their community as "Greater Harlem"—an undefined term which apparently included surrounding white areas. In the 1920's, when Americans came to know Harlem as the "Negro Capital of the World," *Harlem Magazine* argued the impression was "erroneous." Negroes occupied only "a small fraction of *Greater Harlem*," it maintained. By 1932 the Harlem Board of Commerce gave up its mirage. It changed its name, and the name of its journal. "While the decision of the Board to adopt a new name . . . is certain to cause deep regret," the final issue of *Harlem Magazine* editorialized, "it must be apparent to all . . . that such a step was inevitable. [Harlem has] a new and entirely different meaning to the present generation." "How our old Dutch burghers would writhe," an old resident commented, "if they could be reincarnated for just long enough to grasp the modern idea of what once was their cherished "Nieuw Haarlem!"[78]

In 1914 Negroes lived in some 1,100 different houses within a twenty-three-block area of Harlem. After a house-to-house survey in that year, the Urban League estimated Harlem's population at 49,555—the entire Negro population of Manhattan in 1910 was 60,534. *Prior to World War I*, the neighborhood was already the "largest colony of colored people, in similar limits, in the world"—

and it continued to expand. By 1920 the section of Harlem bordered approximately by One Hundred and Thirtieth Street on the south, One Hundred and Forty-fifth Street on the north and west of Fifth to Eighth Avenue was predominatly Negro—and inhabited by some 73,000 people. Two-thirds of Manhattan's Negro population lived there in 1920. "If my race can make Harlem," one man said, "good lord, what can't it do?" Harlem had become "the Mecca of the colored people of New York City."[79]

PART THREE

Harlem Slum

CHAPTER 9

Harlem Tragedy:
An Emerging Slum

"I sit on my stoop on Seventh
Avenue and gaze at the sunkissed
folks strolling up and down and
think that surely Mississippi is
here in New York, in Harlem, yes,
right on Seventh Avenue."
—*The Messenger*, 1923

"I have been in places where cattle
and dogs sleep with masters, but
never before have I been in such a
filthy house."
—Judge William Blau's description of a Harlem tenement, 1922

I

The creation of a Negro community within one large and solid geographic area was unique in city history. New York had never been an "open city"—a city in which Negroes lived wherever they chose— but the former Negro sections were traditionally only a few blocks in length, often spread across the island and generally interspersed with residences of white working-class families. Harlem, however, was a Negro world unto itself. A scattered handful of "marooned white families . . . stubbornly remained" in the Negro section, a United States census-taker recorded, but the mid-belly of Harlem was predominantly Negro by 1920.[1]

And the ghetto rapidly expanded. Between the First World War and the Great Depression, Harlem underwent radical changes. When the twenties came to an end Negroes lived as far south as One Hundred and Tenth Street—the northern boundary of Central Park; practically all the older white residents had moved away; the Russian-Jewish and Italian sections of Harlem, founded a short generation earlier, were rapidly being depopulated; and Negro Harlem, within the space of ten years, became the most "incredible slum" in the entire city. In 1920 James Weldon Johnson was able to predict a glowing future for this Negro community: "Have you ever stopped to think what the future Harlem will be?" he wrote. "It will be the greatest Negro city in the world. . . . And what a fine part of New York City [the Negro] has come into possession of!"² By the late 1920's and early 1930's, however, Harlem's former "high-class" homes offered, in the words of a housing expert, "the best laboratory for slum clearance . . . in the entire city." "Harlem conditions," a *New York Times* reporter concluded, are "simply deplorable."³

II

The Harlem slum of the twenties was the product of a few major urban developments. One of the most important was the deluge of Negro migration to New York City then. The Negro press, now largely dependent on the migrant community for support, changed its former critical attitude of migration to one openly advocating urban settlement. (The exodus was so large, a Negro minister preached, that it must have been "inspired by Almighty God.")⁴ If one is looking for a dramatic turning point in the history of the urbanization of the Negro—"a race changing from farm life to city life"—it was certainly the decade of the twenties. Between 1910 and 1920 the Negro population of the city increased 66 per cent (91,709 to 152,467); from 1920 to 1930, it expanded 115 per cent (152,467 to 327,706). In the latter year less than 25 per cent of New York City's Negro population (79,264) was born in New York State. There were more Negroes in the city in 1930 than the combined Negro populations of Birmingham, Memphis and St. Louis. Similar population increases occurred in urban areas throughout the country.⁵

Negro migration in the twenties drew on areas of the South that had previously sent few people to New York City. The seaboard states of the Upper South—especially Virginia and the Carolinas—continued to be the main sources of New York's migrant Negro population, but people from Georgia and Florida and other Deep South states formerly under-represented also came in greater numbers: "Harlem became the symbol of liberty and the Promised Land to Negroes everywhere," the Reverend Dr. Powell wrote. "There was hardly a member of Abyssinian Church who could not count on one or more relatives among the new arrivals."[6] In 1930, some 55,000 foreign-born Negroes added to the growing diversity of the city's Negro population.

The following chart presents an exact description of the geographical origins of Negro migrants to New York City in 1930. I have selected states with 900 or more residents in the city:[7]

NEGRO IN-MIGRATION, NEW YORK CITY, 1930

Born in:

Virginia	44,471
South Carolina	33,765
North Carolina	26,120
Georgia	19,546
Florida	8,249
Maryland	6,656
Pennsylvania	6,226
New Jersey	5,275
District of Columbia	3,358
Alabama	3,205
Massachusetts	2,329
Louisiana	2,182
Ohio	1,721
Tennessee	1,651
Texas	1,592
Kentucky	1,216
Mississippi	969
Foreign-born	54,754

The rapid settlement of a heterogeneous Negro population coincided with another important population change—the migration of whites from all sections of Manhattan to other boroughs. For the first time since Dutch settlement Manhattan's population *declined* in the 1920's as first- and second-generation immigrants moved to nicer residential areas in the Bronx, Brooklyn and Queens. Many of the homes they left behind had deteriorated significantly. By 1930 a majority of New York City's foreign-born and second-generation residents lived outside Manhattan.[8] As whites moved out of Manhattan, Negroes moved in. The population of that borough declined 18 per cent in the 1920's as its Negro population increased 106 per cent. By 1930 Negroes represented 12 per cent of Manhattan's population—although they composed only 4.7 per cent of the population of the entire city.[9]

Harlem was the New York neighborhood most radically revamped by the population movements of the 1920's, although the Lower East Side also changed rapidly. Harlem underwent a revolution—what one contemporary accurately called a "stupendous upheaval." Between 1920 and 1930, 118,792 white people left the neighborhood and 87,417 Negroes arrived.[10] Second-generation Italians and Jews were responding to the same conditions of prosperity that promoted mobility in all the immigrant neighborhoods of Manhattan—they were not *only* moving away because Negroes settled near them. Conditions of life which satisfied immigrant parents were often unacceptable to children: "The tenements which housed their parents," immigration expert Edward Corsi wrote in 1930, "are being left behind by the children. . . ." "East Harlem used to have a great deal larger population," a survey of the Mayor's Committee on City Planning during the Great Depression concluded. "Like others of the older residential districts, it has suffered by the exodus of families to newer surroundings. . . ."[11]

The city's newest migrants moved into the Harlem flats vacated by Italians and Jews. Puerto Ricans came to live in East Harlem, created community organizations, and laid the foundations for "El Barrio" of today. By 1930 some 45,000 Puerto Ricans resided in New York City and most were heavily concentrated in East Harlem.[12] Negroes moved north along St. Nicholas Avenue—"On the Heights," they called it—and south into the heart of "Little Russia," the former Jewish section. "Just Opened for Colored" signs were common in the neighborhood. Mount Olivet Baptist Church occupied, and still occupies, the once exclusive Temple Israel of Harlem. Prince Hall Masons bought a building that "was formerly a home for aged Jews." Graham Court, a magnificent block-length apartment house on One Hundred and Sixteenth Street, with eight separate elevators and apartments of seven to ten rooms, was opened to Negroes in 1928.[13] By 1930, 164,566 Negroes, about 72 per cent of Manhattan's Negro population, lived in Harlem.[14] The Negro ghetto remained and expanded as the other ethnic ghettos disintegrated. The economic and residential mobility permitted white people in the city was, and would continue to be, largely denied Negroes. Most Negroes were "jammed together" in Harlem—even those who could afford to live elsewhere—with little possibility of escape.[15] "One notable difference appears between the immigrant and Negro populations," an important federal study of Negro housing concluded. "In the case of the former, there is the possibility of escape, with improvement in economic status, in the second generation, to more desirable sections of the city. In the case of Negroes, who remain a distinguishable group, the factor of race and certain definite racial attitudes favorable to segregation, interpose difficulties to . . . breaking physical restrictions in residence areas."[16] A rather ponderous paragraph, but a significant truth.

III

The settlement of West Indian Negroes in Harlem in the 1920's added another complicating dimension to the racial problems of this community—one that fostered discord rather than harmony among the city's Negroes. There were ten times as many foreign-born Negroes in New York City as in any other American urban area. In 1930, 54,754 foreign Negroes lived in the city—39,833 of whom resided in Manhattan. Miami, the next largest American city in terms of immigrant Negroes, was settled by only 5,512 people; Boston ranked third with 3,287 West Indians. About 25 per cent of Harlem's population in the twenties was foreign-born. Harlem was America's largest Negro melting pot.[17]

In the era of immigration restriction, West Indian Negroes came to America through what a contemporary called the "side door." The immigration laws of the 1920's seriously restricted the migration of Europeans and totally excluded Orientals but had little effect on peoples of the Caribbean. At first there were no restrictions on West Indian Negroes. After 1924, they could enter the country under quotas set aside for their mother countries. Since these quotas were never filled there was, in reality, a free flow of people from the islands to the United States in the 1920's.[18]

Although American Negroes tended to lump all the migrants together in a uniform image—"There is a general assumption," one migrant wrote, "that there is everything in common among West Indians"—it is important to recognize that Harlem's Negro immigrants represented a diverse group of peoples from dozens of different islands in the Caribbean.[19] Most Negro immigrants felt a strong attachment to their homeland. They demonstrated an "exaggerated" nationalism in America—a buffer against the strangeness of the new culture and the hostility they experienced—which was typical of white immigrant groups. It was common, for example, to find former British subjects at the office of the British consul protesting some difficulty they experienced in America.[20] Nationalistic organizations kept close check on American foreign policy in the Caribbean and often gave banquets for and listened to addresses by West Indian dignitaries. West Indian Negroes from all countries had the lowest rate of naturalization of all immigrant groups. The people white Americans and American Negroes called "West Indians" were really individuals from Jamaica, Trinidad, Barbados, Martinique, St. Vincent, St. Lucia, Dominica, British Guiana, St. Kitts, Nevis, Montserrat, Antigua, Virgin Islands, Bermuda, the Bahamas, and so on. Although the majority spoke English, some considered French their first tongue; others Spanish; a few Dutch. The fraternal and benevolent associations they founded were not inclusive organizations for all Negro immigrants, but exclusive ones—*landsmannschaften*—for people from specific islands. Danish settlers kept pictures of the King of Denmark in their homes; former British subjects held coronation pageants and balls ("Boxes, 12s. 6d.—Loges, 8s. 4d.") and flew the Union Jack in Harlem; Frenchmen had annual Bastille Day dances.[21]

Negro immigrants differed from each other in origin, yet in a broader sense they shared general experiences, desires and mores which set them apart *as a group* from their American brethren. Most came from societies in which class distinctions played a more important role in one's life than the color line—although the latter was certainly significant. Unaccustomed to common American racial slurs, they often refused to accept them without protest. The Pullman Company, for example, hesitated to employ West Indian Negroes, it was said, "because of their refusal to accept insults from passengers quietly."[22] Out of this heightened class consciousness came a small group of political and economic radicals in Harlem—"foreign-born agitators," local Negroes called them.[23] Many of Harlem's street-corner orators in the 1920's, though not all, were West Indian migrants. Hubert H. Harrison, a Virgin Islander, was among the most prominent. Harrison was a socialist, an expert in African history, a militant critic of American society and a proud defender of the "Negro's racial heritage." He conducted formal lectures in what he called the "Harlem School of Social Science," and others from street

corners—his "outdoor university." A Harlem church, the Hubert H.
Harrison Memorial Church, honors his memory. Others presented
talks on "Socialism vs. Capitalism," organized tenants' leagues, pub-
lished Marxist journals and tried to make Harlemites labor-conscious.
Richard B. Moore, Frank R. Crosswaith and the Reverend Ethelred
Brown—all Negro immigrants—were prominent local candidates for
Board of Aldermen, Assembly and Congress on Socialist and Com-
munist tickets—they usually polled an exceedingly small vote. Some
organized rent strikes, "rent parades," lobbied for social legislation at
City Hall and Albany and distributed radical literature in Harlem.
"There is no West Indian slave, no American slave," the short-lived
radical magazine *Challenge* commented. "You are all slaves, base,
ignoble slaves."[24]

This concern with "class" led to the emergence of a broader
tradition in America. What is striking about the Negro immigrant is
the way his response to American conditions, such as his exaggerated
sense of nationalism, was similar to the typical reactions of most
European immigrants. The Negro immigrant "did not suffer from the
local anesthesia of custom"[25] and he tried to create a meaningful
economic position for himself within American society. Menial labor
was, among most first-generation Negro immigrants, considered a
sign of social degradation and looked upon with "disgust." Most were
forced to accept such jobs initially, but were strongly motivated by
their traditions to improve themselves. As a group, West Indians
became noted for their ambition, thrift and business acumen. They
were called "pushy," "the Jews of the race," "crafty," "clannish."[26]
Negro journalist George S. Schuyler "admired their enterprise in
business, their pushfulness."[27] "The West Indians [are] legendary in
Harlem for their frugalness and thrift," one student noted. When a
West Indian "got ten cents above a beggar," a common local saying
ran, "he opened a business." Contemporary surveys of Negro business in Harlem and Columbus Hill demonstrate that a disproportionate number of small stores—the traditional "Race Enterprise"—
were owned by Negro immigrants. Dr. P. M. H. Savory, one of the
leading spokesmen of New York's foreign-born Negro community
from the 1920's to his death in June 1965, owned and published the
Amsterdam News. Many others achieved economic success within
the racial barrier.[28]

Another significant distinction between the foreign-born Negro and the American was their attitude toward family life. Slavery initially destroyed the entire concept of family for American Negroes and the slave heritage, bulwarked by economic conditions, continued into the twentieth century to make family instability a common factor in Negro life. This had not been true for most West Indians, and they arrived in America with the orthodox respect for family ties that was traditional of rural people. The West Indian family was patriarchal in structure—contrasted with the typically matriarchal American Negro home. The father, as key worker and wage earner in the islands, ruled the household with a solid hand. It was beneath his dignity to help with domestic chores. (This led American Negroes to brand West Indian men "cruel.")[29] Children were supposed to obey their parents rigidly—American Negroes considered them strait-laced; have long and formal courtships; and receive parental approval before marriage. Illicit sexual relations were considered the worst form of moral evil.[30] These traditions began to change in the second generation, but throughout the 1920's family solidarity was a pervasive force among New York's Negro immigrants.[31]

These differences in style of life were also evident in another important institution—the church. The majority of Harlemites were Baptists and Methodists; the immigrants were predominantly Episcopalian and Catholic.[32] The beautiful St. Martin's Episcopal Church was founded in Harlem in 1928 to minister to the needs of West Indian migrants. Services in immigrant churches were generally staid and quiet; Sunday a day of prayer, rest and visiting—as it had been on the islands. Observers were impressed with the differences between the emotionalism of a typical Harlem religious service and the moderation and restraint shown in churches of the foreign-born. Negro immigrants also objected to the general frivolity and "fast ways" that were part of a typical Sunday in Harlem.[33]

All these factors combined to make Harlem in the 1920's a battleground of intraracial antagonism. American Negro nativism spilled over to taint Harlemites' reactions to the West Indian. The Negro immigrant was ridiculed; his tropical clothing was mocked; children tossed stones at the people who looked so different; foreigners were taunted with such epithets as "monkey-chaser," "ringtale," "king Mon," "cockney." "When a monkey-chaser dies/Don't need no undertaker/Just throw him in de Harlem River/He'll float back to Jamaica," was a verse from a Harlem ditty of the twenties. West Indians came to Harlem, ran another common saying, "to teach, open a church, or start trouble." "Bitter resentment grew on both sides." Each group called the other "aggressive." "We have . . . in Harlem," NAACP director Walter White wrote, "this strange mixture of reactions not only to prejudice from without but to equally potent prejudices from within." "If you West Indians don't like how we do things in this country," an American Negro said tersely, "you should go back where you came from. . . ."[34]

The obvious hostility of American Negroes forced Negro immigrants to unite in defense organizations larger than their individual national groups. The West Indian Committee on America, the Foreign-Born Citizens' Alliance and the West Indian Reform Association were founded in the twenties to soften these intraracial tensions and promote "cordial relations between West Indians and colored Americans." Radio programs were devoted to discussions of "Intra-Race Relations in Harlem," and immigrants were urged to become naturalized citizens. American Negroes, in turn, were asked to tone down their "considerable prejudice against West Indians." A semblance of co-operation was achieved as mass meetings were held in Harlem churches. The hatreds of the 1920's did not die, however, until West Indian Negroes stopped migrating to New York. During the Depression more immigrants left New York than entered and intraracial tensions slowly eased. Young Harlemites today, even third-generation descendants of Negro immigrants, are often unaware of these old divisions. The unique type of intraracial hostility so prominent in the twenties has never reappeared. While it lasted, however, it served to weaken a Negro community in great need of unity. A divided Harlem confronted major social problems that desperately called for the co-operation of all.[35]

IV

The most profound change that Harlem experienced in the 1920's was its emergence as a slum. Largely within the space of a single decade Harlem was transformed from a potentially ideal community to a neighborhood with manifold social and economic problems called "deplorable," "unspeakable," "incredible." "The State would not allow cows to live in some of these apartments used by colored people . . . in Harlem," the chairman of a city housing reform committee said in 1927. The Harlem slum of today was created in the 1920's.[36]

The most important factor which led to the rapid deterioration of Harlem housing was the high cost of living in the community. Rents, traditionally high in Harlem, reached astounding proportions in the 1920's—they skyrocketed in response to the unprecedented demand created by heavy Negro migration and settlement within a restricted geographical area. "Crowded in a black ghetto," a sociologist wrote, "the Negro tenant is forced to pay exorbitant rentals because he cannot escape." In 1919 the average Harlemite paid somewhat above $21 or $22 a month for rent; by 1927 rentals had *doubled* and the "mean average market rent for Negro tenants in a typical block" was $41.77. In 1927 Harlem Negroes paid $8 more than the typical New Yorker for three-room apartments; $10 more for four rooms; and $7 more for five rooms, an Urban League survey noted.[37] Another report concluded that the typical white working-class family in New York City in the late twenties paid $6.67 per room, per month, while Harlem Negroes were charged $9.50.[38]

Realty values which had declined significantly prior to World War I *appreciated* in Harlem in the twenties.[39] Harlem experienced a slum boom. "The volume of business done in the section . . . during the last year is . . . unprecedented," *Harlem Magazine* announced in 1920. "Renting conditions have been very satisfactory to the owners and the demand for space . . . is getting keener every year [due] to the steady increase in the negro population," a *New York Times* reporter wrote in 1923. There was, in the language of a Harlem businessman, an "unprecedented demand for Harlem real estate."[40] For landlords—Negro and white (Negro tenants continually complained that Negro landlords fleeced them with equal facility as whites)—Harlem became a profitable slum.[41]

High rents and poor salaries necessarily led to congested and unsanitary conditions. The average Negro Harlemite in the 1920's, as in the 1890's, held some menial or unskilled position which paid low wages—work which was customarily "regarded as Negro jobs." There were generally two types of businesses in New York in terms of Negro hiring policy, E. Franklin Frazier wrote: "Those that employ Negroes in menial positions and those that employ no Negroes at all." Macy's, for example, hired Negroes as elevator operators, escalator attendants and cafeteria workers; Gimbels used none. "We have felt it inadvisable to [hire] colored people," a Metropolitan Life Insurance Company executive explained in 1930, "not because of any prejudice on the part of the company, but because . . . there would be very serious objection on the part of our white employees. . . ."[42] Throughout the city the vast majority of Negro men worked as longshoremen, elevator operators, porters, janitors, teamsters, chauffeurs, waiters and general laborers of all kinds. Negro women continued to work as domestics ("scrub women"), although in the 1920's an increasing number were employed as factory operatives in the garment industry and in laundries. Less than 20 per cent of Harlem's businesses were owned by Negroes.[43] The average Harlem family, according to President Hoover's Conference on Home Building and Home Ownership, earned $1,300 a year in the twenties; the typical white family in the city, $1,570. A variety of social investigations noted that working-class whites expended approximately 20 per cent of their income for rent, considered the proper amount by economists; Harlemites, 33 per cent and more.[44] An Urban League study of 2,160 Harlem families demonstrated that almost half (48 per cent) spent 40 or more per cent of their earnings on rent. A 1928 sample of tenement families found that Harlemites paid 45 per cent of their wages for housing. Similar conclusions were reached in a variety of local community studies.[45] Whatever the exact figure, few Negroes looked to the first of the month with expectancy.

Added to the combination of "high rents and low wages"[46] was the fact that Harlem's apartment houses and brownstones were originally built for people with a radically different family structure from that of the new residents. Seventy-five per cent of Harlem's tenements had been constructed before 1900.[47] The Negro community of the twenties, like all working-class peoples in times of great migration, continued to be most heavily populated by young adults—men and women between the ages of 15 and 44. Family life had not yet begun for many Negro Harlemites—as it had for older Americans and earlier immigrants who lived in the community previously. In 1930, 66.5 per cent of Harlem Negroes were between the ages of 15 and 44, contrasted with 56.5 per cent for the general population of Manhattan and 54.4 per cent for New York City at large. Harlemites who were married had few children. In 1930, 17.5 per cent of Harlem's population was under 14; the corresponding figure for New

York City was 24.5 per cent. The number of Harlemites under the age of 15 declined 14 per cent between 1920 and 1930, as whites left the neighborhood. There was a corresponding decrease of 19 per cent for those over 45 years of age.[48]

What all these statistics mean is simply that apartments of five, six, and seven rooms were suitable for older white residents with larger families and larger incomes—they obviously did not meet the needs of the Negro community in the 1920's. "The houses in the section of Harlem inhabited by the Negro were not only built for another race," E. Franklin Frazier noted, "but what is more important, for a group of different economic level, and consisting of families and households of an entirely different composition from those which now occupy these dwellings." "Unfortunately," Eugene Kinckle Jones of the Urban League stated, "the houses built before [the Negroes'] arrival were not designed to meet the needs . . . of Negroes." "The class of houses we are occupying today are not suited to our economic needs," John E. Nail said in 1921. Negro Harlemites desperately needed small apartments at low rentals: "One of the community's greatest needs [is] small apartments for small families with a reasonable rent limit. . . ."[49] Few realtors were philanthropic enough to invest their capital in new construction; older homes, properly subdivided, produced sufficient income. Only a handful of new houses were built in Harlem in the 1920's.[50]

A variety of makeshift solutions were found to make ends meet: "What you gonna do when the rent comes 'round," had been an old Negro song. The most common solution was to rent an apartment larger than one's needs and means and make up the difference by renting rooms to lodgers—"commercializing" one's home. In the twenties, approximately one white Manhattan family in nine (11.2 per cent) took in roomers, contrasted with one in four (26 per cent) for Negroes. Most lodgers were strangers people let into their homes because of economic necessity. It was difficult to separate "the respectable" from "the fast." "The most depraved Negroes lived side by side with those who were striving to live respectable lives," a contemporary complained. Urban reformers blamed many of Harlem's social problems on this "lodger evil."[51]

Every conceivable space within a home was utilized to maximum efficiency: "Sometimes even the bathtub is used to sleep on, two individuals taking turns!" Negro educator Roscoe Conkling Bruce wrote. Boardinghouses were established which rented beds by the week, day, night or hour. A large number of brownstones were converted to rooming houses: "Private residences at one time characteristic of this part of the city have been converted into tenements. . . ." One landlord transformed apartments in nine houses into one-room flats, a state commission investigating New York housing reported. Space which formerly grossed $40 a month now brought in $100 to $125. People were said to be living in "coal bins and cellars." In an extreme case, one social investigator discovered seven children sleeping on pallets on the floor of a two-room apartment. More common was the "Repeating" or "Hot Bed System"—as soon as one person awoke and left, his bed was taken over by another.[52]

An additional Harlem method devised to meet the housing crisis of the twenties was the "Rent Party." Tickets of admission were usually printed and sold for a modest price (25¢). All who wanted to come were invited to a party. Here is an example:[53]

> If you're looking for a good time,
>   don't look no more,
> Just ring my bell and I'll answer
>   the door.
> Southern Barbecue
> Given by Charley Johnson and Joe
> Hotboy, and How hot!

Chitterlings, pigs' feet, coleslaw and potato salad were sold. Money was raised in this way to pay the rent: "The rent party," *The New York Age* editorialized in 1926, "has become a recognized means of meeting the demands of extortionate landlords. . . ." The white world saw rent parties as picturesque affairs—in reality they were a product of economic exploitation and they often degenerated into rowdy, bawdy and violent evenings.[54]

A significant part of the deterioration of the neighborhood was caused by the migrants themselves. Some needed rudimentary training in the simplest processes of good health and sanitation (Booker T. Washington, it will be remembered, preached the "gospel of the toothbrush").[55] E. Franklin Frazier called many Negro Harlemites "ignorant and unsophisticated peasant people without experience [in] urban living. . . ." They often permitted homes and buildings to remain in a state of uncleanliness and disrepair. Landlords complained that apartments were looted and fixtures stolen, that courtyards and hallways were found laden with refuse. Clothes and bedding were hung out of windows; trash sometimes thrown down air shafts; dogs walked on rooftops; profanities shouted across streets; "ragtime" played throughout the night. "Ragtime is a sufficient infliction of itself," one wag complained, "but when it keeps up all night, it becomes unbearable." "Since the so-called 'Negro invasion,'" a colored woman noted, "the streets, the property and the character of everything have undergone a change, and if you are honest, you will frankly acknowledge it has not been for the . . . improvement of the locality. . . . Are we responsible for at least some of the race prejudice which has developed since the entry of Negroes in Harlem?" Negro journals criticized "boisterous" men who laughed "hysterically" and hung around street corners, and those who used "foul language on the streets." An editorial in the *Age,* one of many, attacked "Careless Harlem Tenants": "A great deal might be said about the necessity for training some of the tenants in the matter of common decency," it suggested. The absence of a sense of social and community responsibility, characteristic of urban life, obviously affected Negro Harlemites.[56]

All these factors combined to lead to the rapid decline of Harlem. The higher the rents, sociologists said, the greater the congestion: "Crowding is more prevalent in high-rent cities than in cities in which rent per room is more reasonable." In 1925, Manhattan's population density was 223 people per acre—in the Negro districts it was 336. Philadelphia, the second most congested Negro city in the country, had 111 Negroes to an acre of land; Chicago ranked third with 67. There were two streets in Harlem that were perhaps the most congested blocks in the entire world.[57]

People were packed together to the point of "indecency."[58] Some landlords, after opening houses to Negro tenants, lost interest in caring for their property and permitted it to run down—halls were left dark and dirty, broken pipes were permitted to rot, steam heat was cut off as heating apparatus wore out, dumb-waiters broke down and were boarded up, homes became vermin-infested. Tenants in one rat-infested building started what they called "a crusade against rats." They argued that the rats in their house were "better fed" and "better housed" than the people. Some common tenant complaints in the 1920's read: "No improvement in ten years"; "Rats, rat holes, and roaches"; "Very very cold"; "Not fit to live in"; "Air shaft smells";

"Ceilings in two rooms have fallen"; "My apartment is overrun with rats"; and so on.[59] There were more disputes between tenants and landlords in Harlem's local district court—the Seventh District Court —than in any municipal court in the five boroughs. Traditionally, municipal courts were known as "poor-men's courts"; Harlemites called the Seventh District Court the "rent court." Occasionally, socially conscious judges of this court made personal inspections of local tenements that were subjects of litigation. Without exception what they saw horrified them: "Conditions in negro tenements in Harlem are deplorable"; "Found few fit for human habitation"; "Negro tenants are being grossly imposed upon by their landlords"; "On the whole I found a need for great reformation"; were some of their comments. One municipal official accurately called the majority of Harlem's houses "diseased properties."[60]

V

And the disease did not confine itself to houses. To touch most areas of Harlem life in the 1920's is to touch tragedy. This was especially true of the health of the community. Theoretically, a section of the city inhabited by relatively young people should have ranked below the general population in mortality and sickness rates. Just the reverse was true. Undertaking was a most profitable Harlem business.[61]

From 1923 to 1927 an Atlanta University professor made an intensive study of Harlem health. His findings were shocking. During these years Harlem's death rate, for all causes, was 42 per cent in excess of that of the entire city. Twice as many Harlem mothers died in childbirth as did mothers in other districts, and almost twice as many Harlem children "passed" as did infants in the rest of New York. Infant mortality in Harlem, 1923–1927, was 111 per thousand live births; for the city, 64.5. Families wept at the processions of "so many little white caskets." Similar statistics are recorded for deaths from tuberculosis (two and a half to three times the city rate), pneumonia, heart disease, cancer and stillbirths.[62] An astounding number of Harlemites had venereal diseases. Negro children commonly suffered from rickets—a disease of malnutrition. More women than ever reported themselves "widows" to census-takers. Negro deaths by violence increased 60 per cent between 1900 and 1925.[63] With the single exception of the Lower West Side Health District,

Health center districts, 1930	Infant mortality per 1,000 live births	TB mortality per 100,000 population	Pulmonary TB new case rate per 100,000 population	Other infectious diseases, rate per 100,000 population	Venereal disease new case rate per 100,000 population	General mortality rate per 1,000 population
Manhattan						
Central Harlem	98	251	487	987	2,826	15.3
Lower East Side	62	116	302	1,160	892	14.0
Kips Bay–Lenox Hill	73	75	184	937	629	12.7
East Harlem	75	137	311	1,326	913	12.0
Lower West Side	83	156	391	1,201	1,318	16.7
Riverside	64	75	196	827	778	12.3
Washington Heights	52	72	203	937	668	10.5
Total	73	122	294	1,049	1,455	13.3

which included the old San Juan Hill neighborhood, Harlem was the most disease-ridden community in Manhattan.[64]

Whatever the causes of Harlem's health problems—and medical investigators continue to search for all the answers—a good deal can be laid at the door of slum environment. Urban reformers consistently showed a high correlation between poverty and congestion on the one hand and disease and death on the other. Mortality rates for infants whose mothers worked away from home, for example—and twice as many Negro women as white women in the city did—was higher than for children whose mothers remained at home; working-class families in old-law tenements (pre-1901) died at a higher-rate than those in newer houses; poverty led to the consumption of the cheapest foods, and this in turn fostered diseases of poor diet; working mothers died more readily in childbirth than unemployed women; and so on.[65] Added to all these considerations, however, was a deep strain of peasant ignorance and superstition embedded in the minds of thousands of migrants—foreign-born as well as native—who settled in Harlem. Quackery abounded in the community in the 1920's.[66]

Harlem had the reputation of a "wide-open city." Whatever you wanted, and in whatever quantity, so the impression went, could be bought there. This was certainly true for the variety of "spiritualists," "herb doctors," "African medicine men," "Indian doctors," "dispensers of snake oils," "layers-on-of-hands," "faith healers," "palmists," and phrenologists who performed a twentieth-century brand of necromancy there: "Harlem sick people are flocking to all sorts of Quacksters," an *Age* reporter noted. One man, "Professor Ajapa," sold a "herb juice" guaranteed "to cure consumption, rheumatism, and other troubles that several doctors have failed in." Powders could be purchased to keep one's wife home at night, make women fertile and men sexually appealing. "Black Herman the Magician" and "Sister P. Harreld" held séances and sold "blessed handkerchiefs," "potent powders," love charms, lodestones, amulets and "piles of roots." "Ignorance, cherished superstitions and false knowledge often govern Negroes in illness and hamper recoveries," a colored physician with the Board of Health wrote in 1926. Nine wood lice gathered in a little bag and tied around a baby's neck, some believed, would end teething. An egg fried brown on both sides and placed on a woman's abdomen would hasten labor. If a mother in the course of childbirth kicked a Bible from her bed to the floor, either she or her child would die. People had faith in the medicinal qualities of dried cobwebs, rabbit brains, "dirt-dauber tea," and something called "cockroach rum." In spite of efforts of physicians, health agencies and the Negro press to bring modern-day medical information to the community, quackery "continued to thrive with impunity in Harlem." It aggravated an already tragic situation.[67]

Accompanying the proliferation of healers, and rooted in the same rural consciousness which made quackery possible,[68] was the host of storefront churches founded in Harlem in the twenties. These were places that healed one's soul: "Jesus is the Doctor, Services on Sunday," read a sign which hung over one door. An investigator found 140 Negro churches in a 150-block area of Harlem in 1926. "Harlem is perhaps overchurched," W. E. B. DuBois said modestly. Only about a third—fifty-four—of Harlem's churches were housed in regular church buildings—and these included some of the most magnificent and costly church edifices in New York City. The rest held services in stores and homes and appealed to Harlem's least educated people. "Jack-leg preachers," "cotton-field preachers," as their critics called them, hung out their poorly printed signboards and "preached Jesus" to all who wanted to listen. One self-appointed pastor held meetings in the front room of his home and rented chairs fróm the local undertaker to seat his small congregation. In Harlem in the twenties one could receive the word of the Lord through such nondenominational sects as: "The Metaphysical Church of the Divine Investigation," "The Temple of the Gospel of the Kingdom," "The Church of the Temple of Love," "Holy Church of the Living God," "Temple of Luxor," "Holy Tabernacle of God," "Royal Fraternity Association," "Knights of the Rose and Cross," "Sons of God," "Sons of Christ," "Sons of Jehovah," "Sanctified Sons of the Holy Ghost," and the "Live-Ever-Die-Never" church. People not only had their worries removed in these places, a Negro clergyman wrote, but "their meager worldly goods as well."[69]

The ministers of these churches preached a fundamentalism which centered around the scheming ways of Satan, who was everywhere, and the terror and joy of divine retribution, with an emphasis on terror. One congregation expelled members who attended the theater or movies. "The devil runs every theatre," its pastor said. "He collects a tax on the souls of men and robs them of their seat in heaven." Services were fervent, loud and boisterous as members felt the spirit of the Lord and shouted and begged for His forgiveness. Tambourines sometimes kept up a rhythmic beat in the background and heightened the emotionalism to a state of frenzy. Neighbors of one storefront church sued the congregation for "conducting a public nuisance." The "weird sounds" which emanated from the building, they complained, seemed like a "jazz orchestra."[70]

> Are you ready-ee? Hah!
> For that great day, hah!
> When the moon shall drape her face in mourning, hah!
> And the sun drip down in blood, hah!
> When the stars, hah!
> Shall burst forth from their diamond sockets, hah!
> And the mountains shall skip like lambs, hah!
> Havoc will be there, my friends, hah!
> With her jaws wide open, hah!
> And the sinner-man, hah!
> And cry, Oh rocks! Hah!
> Hide me! Hah!
> Hide me from the face of an angry God, hah!
> Hide me, Ohhhhhh! . . .
> Can't hide, sinner, you can't hide.[71]

Contemporaries were uniformly critical of these evangelists—there were many Harlem "Prophets"—and most of these preachers were probably charlatans in some form. There was at least one exception, however. A new denomination, the Church of Christ, Apostolic Faith, was founded on the streets of Harlem by the Reverend Mr. R. C. Lawson in 1919. The Reverend Mr. Lawson, of New Iberia, Louisiana, "the only real Apostolic–Holy Ghost–Bible Preacher," presented what he called the "Full Gospel" on street corners of Harlem's worst blocks. He decried the lack of emotionalism in the more established urban churches—copying "the white man's style," he said—and offered recent migrants a touch of fire and brimstone and personal Christianity characteristic of religion in the rural South:

> I have found it, I have found it,
> the meaning of life, life in God,
> life flowing through me by the
> Holy Spirit, life abundant, peace,
> joy, life in its fullness.

Lawson started preaching on One Hundred and Thirty-third Street, east of Lenox Avenue. This area "was to Harlem what the Bowery is to the lower East Side," a Negro journalist recorded. From the streets, the Reverend Mr. Lawson moved into a small building and held services for those "fast drifting to a life of eternal darkness" every day and every night of the week. His Refuge Church of Christ became the founding church of the new denomination, and the Reverend Mr. Lawson its first bishop. By 1930 the Apostolic Church had some forty branches throughout the country and ran an orphanage, elementary school and "Bible Supply House"; it continues to prosper today. Annual conventions met in Refuge Church, "the most honored in the sisterhood of the Apostolic Church," and local leaders praised and publicized its good works for Harlem Negroes: "This church has had one of the most remarkable growths of any religious organizations in the country."[72]

Harlem was also a "wide-open city" in terms of vice and gambling.[73] The annual reports of the anti-vice Committee of Fourteen, founded in 1905, showed Harlem as the leading or near-leading prostitution center of Manhattan throughout the twenties. The Committee hired a Negro doctor, Ernest R. Alexander, to do a secret study of Harlem vice in 1928. His report emphasized the "openness of vice conditions in this district." Dr. Alexander personally found sixty-one houses of prostitution in the neighborhood—more than the combined totals of four other investigators hired at the same time to survey other districts. "There is a larger amount and more open immorality in Harlem than this community has known in years," Negro alderman George W. Harris noted in 1922. "It is a house of assignation . . . this black city," Eric D. Walrond wrote bitterly in the Negro journal *The Messenger*.[74]

> Her dark brown face
> Is like a withered flower
> On a broken stem.
> Those kind come cheap in Harlem,
> So they say.[75]

The Committee of Fourteen also disclosed that more than 90 per cent of these "daughters of joy" institutions were owned and managed by whites. Other evidence verifies this.[76]

Gambling also prevailed in the neighborhood: "Bootleggers, gamblers, and other panderers to vice have found it profitable to ply their vicious trades in this section." The poorest of the poor sought instant riches through the numbers racket. No sum was too small to bet—starting with pennies. "One can bet with plenty of takers on anything from a horse race to a mule race," the *Age* editorialized. Many Harlemites "would rather gamble than eat," it concluded. People selected numbers to coincide with birthdays, dreams, hymns or chapters and verses of Scripture in expectation that they would coincide with the clearing-house figures of the day. The odds were thousands to one against success, yet the smallest hope for a richer life was better than none and Negroes continued to play "policy" avidly. "The chief pastime of Harlem seems to be playing the numbers," George S. Schuyler wrote in 1925.[77]

"Buffet flats," "hooch joints," "barrel houses," and cabarets supplied Harlemites with illegal liquor, and occasionally other things, in the Prohibition era. Drugstores, cigar stores, sweetshops and delicatessens were used as "fronts" for speakeasies. "Harlem can boast of more drugstores than any similar area in the world," one Negro commented. "A plethora of delicatessen stores may be found in the Negro sections of New York, most of which are simply disguised bootlegging stores," a Harlemite concluded in 1924. "And so many confectioners! One never dreamed the Negroes were so much in need of sugar." "Speakeasies downtown are usually carefully camouflaged," a *New York Tribune* reporter noted. "In Harlem they can be spotted a hundred yards off."[78]

Poverty and family instability also led to a high incidence of juvenile delinquency. A community with fewer young teenagers should have shown a proportionally lower juvenile crime rate; as with Negro health, just the reverse was true. "The records of the Children's Court of New York for every year from 1914 to 1927 show a steady increase in the percentage of all crimes committed by Negro boys and girls," Owen R. Lovejoy of the Children's Aid Society reported. In 1914 Negro children represented 2.8 per cent of all cases before the juvenile court of New York City; in 1930 this figure rose to 11.7 per cent.[79]

Working mothers had little time to care for their children. Youngsters "with keys tied around their necks on a ribbon" wandered around the streets until families came home at night. A substantial portion were products of broken homes—families without a male head. One Harlem school principal testified that 699 of his 1,600 pupils came from families whose fathers were not living at home. Nor did the majority of Harlem schoolchildren ever have time to accustom themselves to the regularity of school life; many families were rootless. Three-fourths of all the Negro pupils registered in one Harlem school, for example, transferred to some other before the end of one school year; some schools actually experienced a 100 per cent turnover. Pupils from the South were seriously deficient in educational training: "They are at times 14 to 15 years of age and have not the schooling of boys of eight," a Harlem principal wrote. "We cannot give a boy back seven years of wasted life. . . ." The typical Harlem school of the twenties had double and sometimes triple sessions. The "usual class size" was forty to fifty and conditions were generally "immensely over-crowded": "The school plant as a whole is old, shabby, and far from modern." In some schools 25 per cent and more of the children were overage or considered retarded.

Negro children in Harlem often led disrupted and harsh lives from the earliest years of their existence: "Testimony has been given before us as to the moral conditions among children, even of tender age," a municipal agency investigating Harlem schools recorded, "which is not to be adequately described by the word 'horrifying.'" These conditions were obviously reflected in high rates of juvenile crime but more subtly, and worst of all, in a loss of respect for oneself and for life in general. Harlem youngsters developed "a sense of subordination, of insecurity, of lack of self-confidence and self-respect, the inability . . . to stand on their own feet and face the world with open eyes and feel that [they have] as good a right as anyone else."[80]

This then was the horror of slum life—the Harlem tragedy of the 1920's. "Court and police precinct records show," a municipal agency maintained, "that in arrests, convictions, misdemeanants, felons, female police problems and juvenile delinquencies, these areas are in the lead. . . ." It was no wonder that narcotics addiction became a serious problem then and that Harlem became "the center of the retail dope traffic of New York"; nor that local violence and hatred for the police were continually reported in the press.[81] The majority of Harlemites even during normal times lived "close to the subsistence level." Many were "under care" of charitable agencies in the period of relatively full employment. Those who needed money quickly and had no other recourse were forced to turn to loan sharks,

Negro and white, who charged 30 to 40 per cent interest: Harlem "has been infested by a lot of loan sharks," a municipal magistrate who dealt with such cases stated. In one form or another the sorrow and economic deprivation of the Depression had come to Harlem in the twenties: "The reason why the Depression didn't have the impact on the Negroes that it had on the whites," George S. Schuyler said, "was that the Negroes had been in the Depression all the time."[82]

CHAPTER 10 ⓘ

"Harlem Must Be Saved": The Perpetual Frontier

"The development of playgrounds has
lagged far behind the development of
poolrooms. . . ."
—Winfred B. Nathan, *Health Conditions in North Harlem* (1932)

"The agencies established are inadequate
to meet the needs of this teeming section."
—Owen R. Lovejoy, *The Negro Children of New York* (1932)

I

"Harlem must be saved," the Reverend Dr. Adam Clayton Powell, Sr., wrote in 1923. "It deserves the jealous protection of all good men."[1] But it was simpler to recognize Harlem's difficulties and reduce them to series of statistical reports than it was to resolve them. Social and economic disorders of such "stupendous proportions" taxed the ability of society to deal with them. The combined efforts of all the traditional welfare and charity organizations acted as little more than holding operations, and often not even this, in the struggle to alleviate the poverty, slum housing, crime, vice and poor health that seemed embedded in the community's life: "The development of playgrounds," a Negro educator observed, "has lagged far behind the development of poolrooms. . . ." When a social worker asked a group of unemployed young men to join a youth club, they asked her to "join their crap game."[2]

Nor was American society willing to concern itself with the often tragic lives of Harlem Negroes. Small groups of socially conscious people, Negro and white, devoted their energies to the attempt to soften the hardships of rapid Negro urbanization; the city as a whole, however, and American society generally, lived basically unaware that Harlem had any misfortunes at all. At the very time Harlem was transformed into the city's worst slum its image for most white

150

Americans, and some Negroes as well, was just the reverse—a gay place inhabited by "a singing race," one man thought. "The attitude of the average white New Yorker to Harlem is one of tolerant amusement," a journalist concluded. "He thinks of it as a region of prosperous night clubs; of happy-go-lucky Negroes dancing all night to jazz music. . . ." White slummers visited Harlem's speakeasies in the 1920's and concluded that "Cabaret life was the true essence of Harlem."[3] Had these people arrived at noon and inspected a rat-infested tenement, their image of the gay Negro might have been changed; yet American racial consciousness refused to recognize any but the supposedly joyous side of Negro culture. It was impossible to mobilize any massive support for racial reform in the 1920's because American society voluntarily blinded itself to the harsh realities of Negro existence.

II

Some forty or fifty social service agencies were active in Harlem in the 1920's.[4] The varieties of institutions founded in the Progressive Era continued their existence, accompanied the movement of Negroes to Harlem, and constantly expanded in size once they got there. Harlem's YMCA's and YWCA's, for example, became the largest Negro Y's in America in the twenties. The old Fifty-third Street YMCA "quietly passed" from the scene in 1919. New York's Visiting Nurse Service employed some twenty-five or thirty Negro nurses in Harlem in the 1920's. These women, supervised by a Negro social worker, made an amazing total of some 35,000 home visits annually. The White Rose Home, New York Colored Mission, Sojourner Truth and Katy Ferguson Homes "for lifting fallen young colored women," Hope Day Nursery, Utopia Neighborhood Club, Circle for Negro Relief—and many others—continually appealed to the public for larger contributions to meet the slum crisis of the twenties. "Harlem's Trouble Doctor," as Negroes called the local office of the Charity Organization Society, received an increasingly large number of applications for aid from Negroes. It was forced to open a second office in the neighborhood in the 1920's, and established closer liaison with the Negro community through a committee of colored volunteers. Varieties of local Negro groups were formed, like the North Harlem Community Council and the North Harlem Vocational Guidance Committee, which concentrated on improving local schools, housing and health. Weekly discussions covering every possible type of social problem met at the One Hundred and Thirty-fifth Street public library—the library which later became the famous Schomburg Collection. "Block Beautiful Associations" distributed posters urging residents to show greater pride in their neighborhood.[5]

One of the most publicized institutions founded in the 1920's was the Harlem Tuberculosis and Health Committee. The Committee, organized in 1922, was a branch of the New York Tuberculosis and Health Association. The "ravages of the white plague" killed such an inordinate number of black New Yorkers—it was, a Negro physician wrote, "Public Enemy Number One in Harlem"—that the parent association decided to establish a separate unit in the Negro ghetto. The Committee concentrated its major efforts on eradicating TB but conceived of its task broadly and eventually set up health clinics to cover everything from "social hygiene" and nutrition to prenatal care. When twelve Negro dentists volunteered their services, the Harlem Committee opened a much-needed and much-used free dental clinic.[6]

Committee doctors visited homes without charge in an effort to locate Harlemites with pretubercular conditions. Children from particularly dangerous situations—especially those suffering from malnutrition and others in extremely congested homes—were sent to the country for fresh air and wholesome food. Public lectures were given in churches, schools and fraternal organizations: "Why the Babies Die"; "What Harlem Can Do for Her Children"; "A Proper Diet"; "The Negro and Tuberculosis"; "The Care of the Baby"; "Quackery in Harlem"; "How Tuberculosis Spreads"; "The Value of Early Diagnosis." A Health Institute trained local general practitioners in the latest techniques of diagnosing and treating tubercular patients. Health exhibits, posters, movies ("Peter Meets the Menace" was one), public demonstrations ("Chew Chew the Health Clown" described the proper care and handling of the toothbrush), appeared throughout Harlem in annual "Save-A-Life" campaigns. The Committee also published a significant number of health pamphlets for local distribution. "The aim of our entire work is to make Harlem as healthy a community as possible," the Committee's chairman noted in 1927.[7]

And all this effort certainly did some good. The over-all rates of death from tuberculosis in Negro Harlem declined slightly each year in the 1920's—it is frightening to imagine how high they would have been without the Harlem Committee and other public medical agencies.[8] Yet tubercular deaths remained shockingly high nonetheless and showed a tendency to decline more slowly for Negroes than for whites. The gap separating the two groups widened rather than narrowed in these years. Between 1929 and 1933, for example, four times as many Negroes died of this disease in Harlem as did whites in other New York neighborhoods—earlier in the century the ratios were never higher than 2 to 1 or 3 to 1. Tuberculosis was Harlem's "Number One" killer throughout the Great Depression and remains a serious urban problem today.[9]

The failure of the Harlem Committee, for all its good will and effort, to root out TB more successfully was reflected in the similar inabilities of social workers to end unusually high rates of infant and maternal mortality, juvenile delinquency, illegitimacy, dope addiction and all the other yardsticks of urban maladjustment. It seemed the more reformers pushed against the rock of Harlem's troubles, the more it rolled back upon them.

At least two basic reasons explain the relative failure of social reform in Harlem in the 1920's. One was the constant state of flux in which the community lived. Those familiar with the urban settlement of other minority groups will recall that the peak years of immigration were always accompanied by the most difficult periods of social adjustment—high crime and disease rates, slum housing, juvenile crime and so on.[10] Lillian D. Wald's New York, Jane Addams' Chicago, Robert A. Woods's Boston or Paul U. Kellogg's Pittsburgh were far from pleasant places for European immigrants to live despite the important efforts of an entire generation of municipal reformers. The tensions and problems created by the rapid urbanization of rural people never eased significantly until the years of greatest migration ended.

Harlem, like many other urban Negro communities, underwent its most radical years of transformation and Negro settlement in the 1920's. Community efforts were simply overwhelmed by the magnitude of the population change that took place. The generation of Negro migrants that had come north since the 1890's and adjusted as best it could to urban living had to make room for the latest initiates from the South. Continual Negro migration acted, and continues to act, as a disruptive force and served to prevent the development of a more stable, secure and promising pattern of community life. The constant renewal of Negro population through migration made Harlem, in the words of a prominent social worker, a "perpetual frontier." In spite of all efforts, an urban reformer wrote, "the agencies established are inadequate to meet the needs of this teeming section."[11]

Neither was it possible to resolve the complex hardships of Harlem by isolating one problem from the maze of interrelated and inseparable difficulties Negroes experienced in the city. The Harlem Committee, for example, hoped to end TB through health education. Tuberculosis, however, was largely an urban disease that spread fastest under congested conditions. It simply could not be cured without a concerted attack on the over-all circumstances that made Harlem the most overcrowded neighborhood in the nation: "Socioeconomic problems involved in tuberculosis control . . . are no doubt the greatest," a local physician wrote, "and a satisfactory control will never be attained until they are solved. . . . It takes more than a Health Department, a hospital or a clinic to eradicate disease."[12] This was true of other areas of reform. The Children's Aid Society did some good by centering its efforts on building playgrounds in Harlem, but this was obviously no solution for the disorders that produced juvenile crime. Negro and white educators organized interesting programs of vocational training for Harlem's schools in the 1920's, but these could not open jobs for Negro youngsters in New York's predominantly lily-white corporations and unions.

What the situation demanded was a sympathetic full-scale attack on all the conditions that made Harlem the tragic community it was: "The task of alleviation in North Harlem is impossible without the active participation of the public."[13] A very small group of Negro socialists, those who met weekly in the offices of *The Messenger,* recognized this. A. Philip Randolph, Grace P. Campbell and Frank R. Crosswaith, for example, realized that social conditions in Harlem would never improve unless the economic base of the community was broadened. They created the Trade Union Committee for Organizing Negro Workers and had some success in opening jobs for Negroes in the clothing trades, but most major economic barriers remained intact. When they demanded a large-scale program of housing reform in the neighborhood, they were denounced as radicals.[14] American society was unwilling to make a full commitment to a program of racial justice that the situation called for. This, and the planlessness that historically typified American urban growth, especially in New York City, permitted Harlem to become the horrible slum it remains today.

III

The inadequacy of individual good will as a solution to Harlem's social problems was demonstrated in the history of the most ambitious project for community improvement undertaken in the 1920's— the Paul Laurence Dunbar Apartments. John D. Rockefeller, Jr., who gave millions of dollars for Negro social welfare and education throughout the country, was a regular contributor to Harlem agencies and charities. He gave $250,000 to help build the local YWCA; $72,000 for the New York City Welfare Council's anti-juvenile-delinquency program in Harlem; $37,500 to help pay the mortgage of a neighborhood youth club; $15,000 for the relief of Harlem unemployed.[15]

In 1925 the philanthropist was approached by the director of the New York Urban League, James H. Hubert, and a number of local leaders, and urged to lend his financial support to one of the community's greatest needs—a major program of housing reform: "A delegation of Harlemites conferred with Mr. Rockefeller . . . and urged that he lend his aid to solving the housing problems of the community," a Negro journal recorded. Rockefeller agreed that a "housing crisis" existed in the ghetto and immediately began to purchase land for a complex of new apartments. Negroes hailed the "New Philanthropy."[16]

The aim was excellence. Careful consideration was given every detail of planning to insure the eventual success of the project. Earlier model tenements, like those on San Juan Hill, sometimes failed when the neighborhoods surrounding them deteriorated so badly that decent people refused to live there.[17] The new Rockefeller project guaranteed against this by creating a neighborhood of its own in miniature—six apartment houses covering more than five acres of land, surrounded by parks, gardens and playgrounds. The majority of the 511 apartments ranged in size from two to five rooms, although some were larger, and thus met the requirements of the typically small Harlem family of the 1920's. To eliminate the "lodger evil," roomers were not permitted in the new Rockefeller houses. Because more Negro than white mothers in the city worked away from home, the Dunbar Apartments had its own nursery—equipped with Lilliputian furniture, Mother Goose friezes and a dozen cribs—where women could leave children for a modest fee. A clubroom was provided for teenagers.[18] One of the "best known Negroes in the country," Roscoe Conkling Bruce, was hired as resident manager of the houses. Bruce, son of the United States Senator from Mississippi during Reconstruction, Blanche K. Bruce, was a prominent educator in his own right. His name added prestige to the project within the Negro community. The architect's plan for the Dunbar Apartments was basically simple and functional. He used the best materials available to build apartments that were decent to live in, light and airy: "Every room has abundant access to sunlight and fresh air." The New York chapter of the American Institute of Architects awarded the Dunbar houses its first prize for design in 1927. The finished product was all that Rockefeller had hoped for, an architectural achievement of high order: "the most attractive model tenement in America," two experts in urban housing concluded. "The work speaks for itself," the journal *Architecture* commented, "and its eloquence should bring more of its kind to . . . other cities."[19]

Every physical aspect of the new project was obviously arranged with great care. The next step was to provide a reliable tenantry. Bruce and his wife personally interviewed every applicant for an apartment. Three references were taken from each prospective resident and these were carefully checked. "We let it be widely known," the manager wrote, "that the sporting fraternity, the daughters of joy, and the criminal element, [would] not be tolerated." When the houses were occupied in 1928 the tenants could best be described as middle-class Negroes—clerks, civil service employees, Pullman porters ("the aristocrats of Negro labor") and so on. The median wage of Dunbar residents was about $149 a month—some $40 a month higher than the income of the average Harlem family.[20]

The entire project may have seemed a "New Philanthropy" to contemporaries but it was cast conceptually in an earlier tradition of American tenement house reform—the nineteenth-century "limited-dividend" tradition of Brooklyn's pioneer builder of working-class homes, Alfred T. White, or the houses constructed in slum areas of New York City by the City and Suburban Homes Company. The Dunbar project certainly outdid its predecessors in size and beauty but it was, like them, what nineteenth-century reformers called "philanthropy on a business basis." Philanthropy, it was then argued, was most "gratifying" when it became a proper combination of good works and good business. The City and Suburban Homes Company, for example, hoped "to offer capital what is believed to be a safe and permanent five per cent investment, while furnishing wage-earners wholesome homes at current rates."[21] "The capitalist has here an altogether safe, gratifying, long-term investment," one man wrote of the Dunbar houses.[22]

Apartments were rented on a co-operative basis. Initially, each tenant made a down payment of $50 per room and then was charged a monthly assessment of $11.50 to $17.50 a room. When deductions were made for maintenance and the 5½ per cent interest on Rockefeller's investment, about 50 per cent was left in principal. At this rate, it was believed, every tenant would own his apartment in twenty-two years. Rockefeller was assured absolute control of the houses by holding the only preferred stock in the corporation. To encourage thrift furthermore, "to help the Negro help himself," as Rockefeller said, the Dunbar National Bank was opened as part of the housing complex in 1928.[23]

The high hopes surrounding the new undertaking lasted an exceedingly short time. The houses were completed on the eve of the Great Depression, and the Depression forced the management to modify its original plans radically. Within six months of the Dunbar's opening, a free placement service had to be established for tenants who lost their jobs. Shortly afterwards, arrangements were made to reduce the initial down payment for new tenants—it was eventually done away with altogether. Substantial reductions in rent were made in 1932 "to relieve those whose income had been cut due to the depression." The few larger apartments remained unoccupied because they were too expensive for most single families. The rule banning lodgers was modified to permit relatives to share these homes; in 1935 the six- and seven-room apartments were divided into two and three. So many tenants failed to meet their obligations by 1936 that Rockefeller foreclosed on the first mortgage he held. It was a business venture, he argued, and the business was singularly unsuccessful. Residents had their original investments returned and the Dunbar Apartments became Rockefeller's privately owned corporation. He sold the project to a group of realtors in 1937 and withdrew his support of the

Dunbar National Bank the next year. Harlem's "noble experiment," "the adventure in community building," had proved a failure.[24]

The Great Depression was the most obvious cause for the collapse of the Dunbar Apartments. Yet Rockefeller's plan for housing reform in Harlem had serious limitations from its inception. It provided middle-class housing at relatively high rentals to a population that was predominantly lower class. The Harlem families most desperately in need of new housing were bypassed by the Dunbar houses. It was a measure of the hopelessly weak economic position of the city Negro that even the small group of middle-class families chosen after the most careful processes of selection were unable to earn a steady income during the Depression. Hard times always seemed hardest on Negroes.

Nor was private "philanthropy on a business basis"—a nineteenth-century blend of Christian charity and free enterprise—an adequate social philosophy for the complex problems of twentieth-century urban life. Had the Dunbar Apartments succeeded they would have provided housing for 511 middle-class Negro families at the cost, to them, of $3.3 million. But there were more than 50,000 families in Harlem[25]—the large majority seriously in need of better homes and unable to afford even a modest investment to get them. A problem of this magnitude involved expenditures that were obviously beyond the resources of private charity or individual social reform, and beyond the interest of private capital.

The earliest public recognition of the failure of "limited-dividend" tenement house reform came with the New Deal's program of low-rent municipal housing as an obligation of government; when Rockefeller sold the Dunbar Apartments, the city's Harlem River Houses were nearing completion a few blocks away. This was certainly a more advanced concept than the earlier reliance on philanthropy, but society assumed its obligation hesitantly and, as the ghettos of the 1960's attest, inadequately.

CHAPTER 11

A Taste of Honey: Ward Politics

"Where are the leaders up there
[Harlem]? Who will point the way
for the thousands there?"
—*The New York Age,* 1910

"The New York Negro has learned to
play the game [of politics] in a
realistic fashion."
—Francis E. Rivers, Negro Assemblyman, 1930

I

Politics proved a more rewarding form of community activity. While the urbanization of the Negro obviously caused great difficulties, it also provided the base for significant political power—political power unprecedented in the history of the Negro in the North. As the Negro population increased in numbers, the cynical and apathetic attitudes that typified the reactions of white politicians in the late nineteenth century came to an end. The Negro did not become a major political force in New York City in the first thirty years of the new century, but there were signs of public recognition after 1900—and especially after the creation of Negro Harlem—that were never evident previously. Requests for offices which Negroes made in the 1880's and 1890's, and which were ridiculed or ignored then, were renewed and granted. Negro spokesmen arose at all levels of municipal politics and demanded greater recognition of the Negro community: "The Negro wants his manhood recognized and encouraged," one of them wrote.[1]

Politics is a practical business. Political recognition and patronage would be granted Negroes, Tammany sachem Richard Croker said in the 1890's, in "proportion to their works and numbers."[2] In the late nineteenth century, a small and disorganized Negro community was forced to accept the lowest offices that white politicos would offer.

Negroes received appointments as street cleaners, assistant janitors, laborers. An early Negro political leader held the office of "street inspector," and another Negro appointee was "Detailed Inspector of Garbage."[3] At election time, it was often said, Negro votes were sold for a few dollars: "The flagrant manner in which votes were bought . . . on election day," *The New York Age* editorialized in 1887, "was shameful."[4]

What further weakened the political position of the Negro in New York City in the late nineteenth century was an almost solid adherence to the Republican Party. Those few Negroes who questioned the political efficacy of supporting the party of the Union then were branded traitors: "Truly," a Republican politician wrote, "the black Dem. is a strange animal."[5] Negro Democrats were sometimes pelted with bricks and garbage, drenched with water and debris, attacked by mobs.[6] "The Tammany Hall Society of New York," a Negro said in 1890, "is the rankest nest of political crookedness anywhere . . . in the United States."[7] To vote Democrat was to label yourself a Judas.[8]

This almost religious devotion to the Republican Party minimized the importance of the already weak political position of the Negro. In 1897, for example, Negro Republicans in the city attempted to have James D. Carr appointed Assistant District Attorney. Carr, born in Baltimore in 1868, had outstanding qualifications for the position. He graduated Phi Beta Kappa from Rutgers University and received an LL.B. from Columbia University Law School in 1895.[9] His appointment was rejected, however. The "time had not come," he was told, "to appoint a negro to such . . . high office," and the District Attorney hired a colored messenger instead. The Colored Republican County Committee also endorsed a Negro for the office of coroner in 1897 but were again turned down: "I know the negroes better than they know themselves," Lemuel Eli Quigg, Republican county leader, told a Negro delegation. "You couldn't drive them out of the Republican Party with a sledgehammer."[10] "The Negro ballot has almost lost its potency," a Negro scholar concluded, "on account of the unconcerned cocksureness of one political party that the other side will not get the benefit of it."[11]

Those Negro Republicans who left the meeting with Quigg resolved to break with the party. They supported the Tammany candidate for mayor in 1897 and formed the earliest regular Negro

Democratic organization in the nation, the United Colored Democracy, in January 1898.[12] Members of the UCD were pariahs within the Negro community. They were socially ostracized and denounced. Edward E. Lee, "Chief" Lee, first Negro Democratic leader, was ridiculed by local Negro groups. For their decision to break with the Republican Party, however, the small group of Negro Democrats was given a measure of political patronage immediately. James D. Carr was appointed Assistant District Attorney, "Chief" Lee was made sheriff, and his successors held more important and lucrative jobs.[13]

Bipartisanship brought some minimal rewards in the 1890's but the United Colored Democracy remained an anomalous branch of the Democratic Party—it never became an integral part of the regular machinery of city politics. The Negro Democratic organization existed as a separate and segregated unit. The Negro boss theoretically supervised *all* the Negro wards in the city. His power rose and fell at the disposition of the white Democratic county leader or mayor, not at the will of his constituency. The UCD's structure *prevented* the emergence of grass-roots ward leaders and centered Negro Democratic influence in the hands of a single, often autocratic, boss. No similar political organization existed for any other minority group in New York City. In politics, as in other areas of urban life in the 1890's, the Negro was a second-class citizen.

II

The situation began to change in the early twentieth century when the first Negro politician of any significance in the entire history of the city arose in the Republican Party—Charles W. Anderson. Charlie, as his friends knew him, was a self-educated and self-made man. His only formal education was some tentative training—"he took some courses"—in high school and in business college.[14] Like so many prominent New York Negroes of his time, Anderson came to the metropolis to seek his fortune as a young man from a rural town. He was born in Oxford, Ohio, a year after the Civil War ended and came to Manhattan, at the age of twenty, in 1886. Anderson immediately became active in local Republican politics and stumped for the party in Negro wards in the late 1880's. In 1890 he was elected president of the Young Men's Colored Republican Club of New York County and rewarded for his services with a low-rung patronage position— gauger in a district office of the Internal Revenue Service. From then until his retirement in 1934, with the exception of a few months in. 1915, Anderson remained in public office. He became "the recognized colored Republican leader of New York"; "the race political leader."[15]

Charlie Anderson was an exceptionally bright, cultured, perceptive man and a gifted leader—"the unfailing observer," he was once called. His friend James Weldon Johnson recalled that Anderson was "much more than an ordinary orator," and could intelligently discuss English poetry and the state of world affairs. And Anderson, a member of the Metropolitan Museum of Art, preferred to talk over a glass of champagne. Shakespearean allusions are occasionally found in his speeches. Charles W. Anderson was obviously no hack politician.[16]

Anderson's letters are full of keen insights and predictions about contemporary politics—and he was rarely wrong. Throughout his life he paid the closest attention to detail. He could, for example, quote statistics on the exact number of registered voters in each assembly district or list the positions held by Negroes in the federal service and the salaries each job paid. In the first two decades of the twentieth century Anderson organized and supervised Negro Republican captains in every election district of Manhattan and was on the closest terms with most Negro religious and business leaders. He showed himself to be "a cool, calculating player in the game of politics." In 1908, for example, it was rumored that New York Negroes would not support William Howard Taft for President. Anderson issued orders to plaster windows in the Negro districts with pictures of Taft: "We are . . . putting lithographs in the windows of every colored man's house in the various black belts of the city," he wrote. "Any man passing through . . . will surely be convinced that the alleged disaffection of the negro voters is all moonshine." If you needed a job, wood in the winter, some contributions for Harlem charity or boxes of candy for a children's Christmas party, Charlie Anderson was the man to see. He worked quietly, efficiently—without the usual guffaw common to ward politics—and most often successfully, to get what he wanted. He was the complete politician.[17]

Political preferment was Anderson's natural reward. He quickly rose from gauger, to private secretary of New York State's Treasurer (1893–1895), to Chief Clerk in the State Treasury (1895–1898), to Supervisor of Accounts for the New York Racing Commission

(1898–1905). When Admiral Dewey returned from the Philippines and the Cuban fleet arrived in triumph at New York port after the Spanish-American War, Anderson was among the dignitaries to greet them. In 1905 he was appointed to what was undoubtedly the most responsible and important federal office held by any Negro politician in the early twentieth century: Collector of Internal Revenue for the Second New York District—the Wall Street District. Employees threatened to leave when they heard of their new Negro boss, but most remained on the job. "Strangely enough, the bottom did not drop out of Manhattan and the sun did not refuse to shine," *The New York Age* scoffed. "None of the employees left their employment and bolted for the door. They stuck to their desks *and* to their salaries." The young man from the small Ohio town had come a long way in fifteen years. "I doubt when we both left Ohio," a successful friend of his wrote, "that either of us believed that you would be in a position to collect, and I with a pressing need of paying, income tax. . . ."[18]

Anderson was certainly qualified for the post and his administration was noted for its honesty and thoroughness: "Capacity, courtesy . . . and high efficiency have been the qualities most remarked in his conduct of [the] office. . . ." He handled without a flaw the complicated new procedures made necessary by the passage of the income tax amendment in 1913. On his own initiative, he accepted checks rather than cash from local corporations during the Recession of 1907 and thus helped ease what he called the "financial stringency": "I accepted checks in payment of internal revenue tax, and I believe, [I] was the only collector in the country to do so," he told Booker T. Washington. "This materially assisted in relieving the situation here, and helped the merchants greatly. . . ." When the economic crisis ended, thankful businessmen offered him a personal gift. It would have been unethical for a collector to accept, so Anderson rejected the offer: "I have never permitted a private interest to interfere in the remotest way with my performance of any public duty," he said on a later occasion. Instead, he suggested that any money raised be sent to Tuskegee as a contribution to Negro education. Shortly afterwards Washington received a gift of $900, presented in Anderson's honor, from the Collector's clients.[19]

Charles W. Anderson had risen to his unique position in New York politics as a result of his own energy and ability, but his appointment as Collector in Theodore Roosevelt's administration was made through the all-pervasive political influence of Booker T. Washington.[20] Anderson was a devoted supporter of Washington and perhaps Washington's most trusted lieutenant. He guarded his mentor's interests with a religious fervor: "I am not easily frightened," he once wrote, "and when I believe in a man, no opposition . . . can swerve me by as much as a hair's breadth." "Always remember," he said at another time, "that absolute loyalty is more desired in a lieutenant than brains, experience or power. . . . Without this, all [else is] worse than useless." When Washington died, Anderson wrote of "how dearly I loved him." "It is a priceless thing to remember such loyal and disinterested friendship," Washington's personal secretary, Emmett J. Scott, replied.[21]

Anderson could be ruthless in guarding Washington's interests or doing Washington's bidding. He kept constant check on the activities of Negro Democrats, the followers of W. E. B. DuBois, and all persons who even remotely threatened Washington's authority or name. Anderson's voluminous correspondence with Washington constantly warns him of "men who play double," "the enemy," and urges their ouster. "It is high time that these crooks should be exposed," he wrote of two Negro Democrats. "What do you think about it?" If anyone in public office stepped out of line, he tried to use his influence in New York City or Washington to have him quieted or removed.[22]

A glaring case in point was that of the militant Negro Socialist and black nationalist Hubert H. Harrison. Harrison worked in the New York City post office early in the century and, in 1911, published some disparaging remarks about Booker T. Washington's leadership. Charlie Anderson dealt with him swiftly and efficiently. With obvious pride, he explained the situation to Washington: "Do you remember Hubert H. Harrison? He is the man who wrote two nasty letters against you in the New York 'Sun.' He is a clerk in the Post Office. The Postmaster is my personal friend. . . . Can you see the hand? I think you can. Please destroy this, that it may not fall under another eye. . . . If he escapes me, he is a dandy." Six weeks later Washington received the following note: "I am sure you will regret to learn that Mr. Hubert H. Harrison has been dismissed from his position as clerk in the New York Post Office." As long as he lived Harrison wondered whose influence had been used to arrange his dismissal.[23]

Anderson participated actively in the often bitter internecine warfare that split Negro leadership in the early twentieth century between the supporters of the Niagara Movement—W. E. B. DuBois, William Monroe Trotter, J. Max Barber and many others—and the followers of Booker T. Washington. To him, the Niagara people were visionaries who demanded full racial equality too quickly in a society unwilling to grant it. Anderson hoped for future gains but was willing to settle for something concrete in the present: "We do not belong to that group to whom nothing is desirable but the impossible," he once commented. "Some of us are trying to provide opportunities for members of the race. . . ."[24]

When one considers the long range interests of the Negro people in full equality, Anderson's views were certainly questionable. They did, however, prove an important immediate boon to Harlemites and to New York's Negro community generally. To Charlie Anderson, improving the race most often meant using his influence to find more and better-paying jobs for New York's Negro community. Anderson's correspondence dealing with questions of political patronage alone was voluminous. He found positions for Negroes as mechanical draftsmen, state examiners of auto chauffeurs, deputy collectors and gaugers in the Internal Revenue Service, customhouse inspectors and clerks ("I pulled off another colored inspector of Customs"), messengers, post office employees, immigration inspectors ("directed from Washington, at my request"), attorneys to examine election frauds ("This will throw a few hundred dollars . . . his way"), referees in foreclosure suits, assistant superintendents in the post office ("the first time it has been done in this state"), assistant district attorneys ("my man McDougald"), deputy United States marshals, stenographers ("she realizes $200 per year more than the white stenographers in the office"). When Judge Lorenz Zeller, a former counsel for the Brewers' Association, came before the city's Bar seeking approval for a higher position, Anderson scotched his hopes. He presented the Bar Association with documentary evidence that Zeller, as judge, refused to find bartenders guilty of violating the State's Civil Rights Act for failing to serve Negroes. As a result of Anderson's disclosures Zeller's candidacy was disapproved.[25] In 1914 Charles S. Whitman, whom Anderson first met as New York County District Attorney, was elected Republican governor of the state. Charlie used his influence with Whitman to win more jobs for Negroes, including one for himself later on, and arranged to have state legislative documents printed in the Negro press.[26] Samuel J. Battle applied to the New York police force for an appointment as patrolman. Battle, a giant of a man in perfect condition, was somehow unable to pass the department's physical examination. He asked the editor of the *Age*, Fred R. Moore, for assistance, and Moore spoke to Anderson. Charlie went to see the mayor, who immediately arranged for a new examination. In 1911 Samuel J. Battle was appointed the first Negro policeman on the New York City force. (People were taken on guided tours to see the strange phenomenon— a Negro policeman patrolling his beat. Battle recalled children taunting him: "There goes the nigger cop, there goes the nigger cop!" they shouted.) More Negroes received appointments to municipal and federal positions through Anderson's intercession than at any previous time in city history.[27]

Charles W. Anderson was a fine politician and a recognized votegetter, but his position as Collector primarily rested on Booker T. Washington's influence in the Republican Party. When Woodrow Wilson was elected President, Anderson, along with almost every other Negro federal office-holder, lost his job. After Washington's death in 1915, Anderson's political future seemed uncertain.[28]

That his power was not solely the gift of Washington was demonstrated in his public career after 1915. Charlie Anderson was unemployed only a few months. W. E. B. DuBois, obviously not on the closest terms with Anderson, was so impressed with his public record that he recommended his appointment as Minister to Haiti in the new Democratic administration. (DuBois supported Wilson in 1912.) "I do not know that Anderson would accept," DuBois wrote, "but it would be a graceful thing if he is offered this position after his remarkable service as Internal Revenue Collector."[29] Anderson did not get this job, but he received another offer from Albany. Governor Whitman, he was told, "wanted him placed." The governor appointed him Supervisory Agent of the State Agriculture Department in New York City—a well-paying patronage position. From his new post Anderson directed all state marketing operations and inspectors within the city.[30]

His career continued to blossom. In the presidential election of 1916 Anderson, as Chairman of the Colored Advisory Committee, directed the Republican Party's national campaign among Negroes. Gubernatorial, congressional and mayoralty candidates sought his support at election time. As an influential member of Harlem's Republican organization in the Nineteenth Assembly District he helped nominate, manage campaigns for and elect assemblymen and aldermen—white and Negro. He represented the ward as delegate to Republican state and national conventions and, in 1920, toured Negro communities throughout the Northeast in the interests of the national ticket. (In a speech at Newport, Rhode Island, he declared the easiest way to convert a Negro Democrat was to take "him on a little excursion through certain Southern States.") As a member of the Mayor's Committee on Receptions to Distinguished Guests, Anderson greeted the many dignitaries who visited the city, and he also attended all major local political functions. In 1923 a new federal Internal Revenue district was created in New York City—the Third District, which included Harlem. Anderson, the obvious man for the post, was appointed Collector. Although no manuscript records survive to tell the inside story of Anderson's influence on this job, the newspapers reported a surprising number of Harlem ward-heelers employed in the Internal Revenue Service. A Nineteenth AD election district captain was Charlie's secretary. An attendant in Harlem's public bathhouse, active in local politics, found himself promoted to Deputy Collector. The same old magic was apparently working again.[81]

A number of factors helped Charlie Anderson remain in political power. His earlier career provided him with influential friends, like Whitman, and an unimpeachable reputation for loyalty—"a party man"—honesty and efficiency. More important, however, was the fact that Anderson's career luckily extended into a new era of Negro urban politics. The doors of political preferment did not open to Negroes until their numbers and voting strength had increased considerably through migration; and especially after their concentration in Harlem. By the second decade of the twentieth century, Harlem's Negro community was large enough for all politicians to see. Anderson reaped the benefits of the growing importance of the Negro vote within the city. His appointment as Collector in the new revenue district was the "biggest job held by a Negro," but it was only one of many opportunities that brought greater political recognition to the colored community. The Republican boss of New York County, Samuel S. Koenig, apparently pushed hard for Anderson's appointment, and when it was made, Koenig said "it was with the definite idea of securing recognition for colored voters to which they are justly entitled."[32]

Anderson directed the Third District until his retirement in 1934— he died four years later. His importance in Harlem politics was restricted after 1927, however, when he became seriously ill and could no longer continue to work actively: "Nowadays he is rarely seen." Subordinates, it was reported, assumed the more burdensome duties of the collectorship until his retirement. Up to the time of his illness he was certainly a dynamic political figure. He was the first leader in city history to push open the doors of political opportunity for Negroes; and he had the good fortune to see other forces keep them open—wide enough, in fact, to provide room for himself at a crucial time in his political career. The rise of Charlie Anderson in many ways typified the political awakening of Negro New York: "I regarded him as being, beyond any doubt, the very ablest Negro politician," James Weldon Johnson wrote. "You just can't think of Republicanism in New York," a Negro newspaper editorialized, "without remembering Charlie Anderson."[33]

III

The unprecedented concentration of Negroes in Harlem permitted the entire community to take a more active role in politics. Unfortunately for Negro politicians, an accident of political geography divided the Negro vote between two assembly districts, the Nineteenth and Twenty-first. The Negro ghetto was one solid residential unit, but the Negro vote was split between districts which included substantial numbers of whites—Jews in the Nineteenth and Irish in the Twenty-first, although other ethnic groups were represented in smaller numbers. In 1930, after a decade of mass migration, Negroes composed 70 per cent of the population in each district.[34] This unintentional gerrymander tended to somewhat limit the political power of Negroes and forced them to share influence with white politicians and district leaders. Despite this, however, Negroes made significant political advances in Harlem in the 1920's. Too long, it was argued, had the Negro been treated as a pawn in the city politics; too often had Negroes been forced to accept "crumbs from the patronage table": such "fine, lucrative and honorable positions of spittoon cleaning and floor sweeping." The time has come, a Negro leader wrote, for "Official Recognition of the Negro's Interest."[35]

Negroes were aided in their struggle for power by the operation of an active two-party system in Harlem, especially in the 1920's. The United Colored Democracy continued its existence as a special Negro organization within the city's Democratic Party. Its leader after 1915, Harvard-educated Ferdinand Q. Morton, worked sympathetically with the white Democratic bosses of Harlem through the early 1930's. In exchange for his assistance Morton was recognized as the most powerful Negro Democrat in the city and was given almost dictatorial control of Negro patronage. Although Harlem Negroes unwaveringly supported Republican presidential candidates until 1932,[36] and usually cast their votes for Republican governors,[37] they showed greater political independence in local politics after the First World War.[38] In 1921, for example, Democratic mayoralty candidate John F. Hylan, known as an honest leader among Negroes, polled an amazing (for a Democrat) 73.6 per cent of Negro Harlem's vote. Negro Democrats represented Harlem in the state assembly and on the city's Board of Aldermen at varying times throughout the twenties. In 1922 Harlemites, for the only time, supported Al Smith for governor—he won in a landslide that year. Although the Republican tradition remained the stronger, Harlem became the first Negro community in the nation to lend significant support to the Democratic Party. "The Negro in Harlem," James Weldon Johnson commented in 1924, "has in very large degree emancipated himself from [single-party domination], and become an intelligent voter."[39]

And the Negro community reaped the benefits of its emerging political independence. No longer would "cocksure" Republican politicians say, as they had in the 1890's, that the Negro vote could not be driven from the party of Lincoln "with a sledgehammer." "Your race has too long segregated itself politically," Mayor Hylan wrote a Harlem supporter in 1921. "I can think of nothing which will contribute more effectively towards [your] progress . . . than this removal of the barriers behind which [you] so long remained in political isolation." Shortly after his victory in 1921, Hylan proved his point by selecting Ferdinand Q. Morton, who actively campaigned for him, to a lucrative and important city office, Chairman of the Municipal Civil Service Commission: "the first appointment in the history of our city of a colored man to head this or any other department."[40] Hylan's successor, James J. Walker, reappointed Morton to this municipal cabinet-rank position. After prodding from

Morton, Republican aldermen, the NAACP and the North Harlem Medical Society, five Negro physicians were appointed for the first time to the regular staff of Harlem Hospital in 1925, and a training school for Negro nurses was established there. A sweeping reorganization of the hospital took place in 1930, in Jimmy Walker's administration, and Harlem Hospital was opened without restriction to Negro doctors. In 1932 more than seventy Negro interns and physicians worked there. This was, an NAACP memorandum concluded, "the most decisive step ever taken anywhere in the United States for recognition of . . . colored doctors and nurses."[41] Both Hylan and Walker, New York's only mayors in the 1920's, were regular visitors to Harlem; attended plays in Negro theaters; greeted conventioning Negro organizations; lectured before fraternal and church groups: "No Discrimination in the Administration of the Government of New York City"; "Mayor's Attitude on Ku Klux Klan"; "Discrimination Against Negroes." They dedicated new Negro parks, playgrounds and churches and had some of the more objectionable features cut out of the film *Birth of a Nation* before it was shown in the city. Al Smith campaigned in Harlem each time he ran for office: "Call on me and I will help, either in word or deed," Smith said. "What the negro is entitled to and should receive is a square deal and equal opportunities in civic life," Hylan told Urban League director James H. Hubert. "These are rights guaranteed to him under the constitution." Never before had Democratic politicians shown as much interest in the Negro's welfare—and his vote.[42]

The most significant political advance made by the Negro community was the election of Harlemites to legislative offices. In 1917, for the first time in city history, a Negro was nominated by a regular district organization for the state assembly. (Negro independents ran in Harlem, and lost, in 1913 and 1915.) The Republicans of Harlem's Nineteenth AD selected Edward Austin Johnson for the office. They chose a well-qualified man, a politician whose career symbolized a major transition in American Negro and urban history: the loss of Negro political power in the South, and its reacquisition in northern metropolitan centers.

Johnson, born in Raleigh, North Carolina, in 1860, received his earliest education from books sent south in barrels by sympathetic northerners after the Civil War. He became a lawyer, Professor of Law and Dean at Shaw University in Raleigh. As an active southern

Negro Republican of the late nineteenth century, he served as alderman, assistant district attorney and delegate to three national Republican conventions.[43] He was also well-known as the author of books on Negro history and a rather unique, poorly written utopian novel, *Light Ahead for the Negro* (1904). This novel visualized racial harmony in a future South. In "Phoenix," Georgia, 2206, Johnson foresaw a "high-minded" and "sympathetic" South; a South in which "the spirit of helpfulness to Negroes [became] so popular that it permeated all classes"; a section in which "the subdued look of the old-time Negro" had disappeared forever. "I silently prayed," he concluded, "God bless the New South!" But the Phoenix was a mythical bird and in the harsher reality of his present, shortly after completing *Light Ahead,* Negroes were practically disfranchised in North Carolina and men like Johnson stripped of political power. Rather than accept a proscribed life, Johnson, like his fellow North Carolinian George Henry White, migrated from his home state. He came to New York City in 1907, practiced law and bought some property in Harlem. When he was elected in 1917 he became the first Negro to sit in the state legislature.[44] Five other Negroes, four Republicans and one Democrat, followed him to the state assembly from the Nineteenth and Twenty-first AD's in the 1920's. In 1919 Republican Charles H. Roberts became New York City's first Negro alderman. Other Negroes were elected in the next decade. A clergyman noted, "Political opportunity has knocked on the door of the Harlem Negro."[45]

These men acted as spokesmen for their community. Through their initiative, in a political structure now willing to recognize Negro demands, Harlem Negroes received the "solid benefits which accrued" from "an awakening political consciousness."[46] Johnson as assemblyman, for example, drafted and helped pass a new civil rights law for New York State in 1918. It extended the "equal accommodations" privileges of earlier acts to include every conceivable type of public business—skating rinks, billiard parlors, bowling alleys, ice cream parlors. The white press congratulated Johnson on the quality and thoroughness of his legislation. He also arranged to have a state employment office opened in Harlem: "an additional public employment office . . . which . . . would best serve the interest of the negro population."[47] In 1916 Harlem's National Guard unit, the "Fighting Fifteenth" (later the 369th), was outfitted. Negroes had unsuccessfully requested a military organization for themselves since the Spanish-American War. Harlem's "Hell Fighters" made a distinguished record in France during World War I: the entire outfit was awarded the *Croix de guerre* for bravery by the French government, and the "Fifteenth" spent more days in combat (191) than any other American unit. A "Happy Harlem," a "proud Harlem," greeted the soldiers on their return, and the "Fifteenth's" exploits became part of the ghetto's folklore. In the 1920's the largest National Guard armory in the state was constructed in Harlem for New York's "Black Watch." Everyone claimed to be responsible for the legislation which organized the "Fifteenth" and built its new armory: Republicans and Democrats, mayors, aldermen, assemblymen, congressmen, white and Negro politicians. Whatever the exact truth, the most important point is that the legislation passed and politicians were interested enough to try to claim some part in it.[48]

Other acts beneficial to the Negro community were sponsored by Harlem's representatives. After a decade of pressure, two Negro Republicans in the state assembly, with the "particularly arduous" and "helpful" efforts of the white county chairman, forced the passage of an act which divided Harlem's Seventh District Municipal Court into a new administrative entity—the Tenth District. This *intentional* gerrymander guaranteed the election of two Negro judges —another city first—to the municipal bench in 1930. "The lines of the district were deliberately redrawn . . . to assure the elections of two colored judges," Francis E. Rivers, who drafted the bill, wrote. Republican sponsors of the bill were dismayed when two Negro Democrats were elected to fill the posts. A Harlem assemblyman was also responsible for introducing a state housing act—which passed— that protected tenants from "unjust" and "unreasonable" evictions or rent increases, and from landlords who failed to make necessary repairs. Harlem's aldermen, Republicans and Democrats, arranged to have playgrounds, parks and "bathhouses for the poor" built in the neighborhood in the 1920's. A once politically voiceless people had begun to find leaders who worked for the "realization of the hopes of the race." "The New York Negro," a colored assemblyman noted, "has learned to play the game [of politics] in a realistic fashion."[49]

But political leadership often inherently involves questions of personal ambition and power that sometimes conflict with, rather than supplement, the interests of a community. Competition for power among individual Negroes sometimes impeded the progress of the entire group. The accepted structure of the United Colored Democracy, for example, precluded any struggle for leadership in the Democratic ward organizations of Harlem. Ferdinand Q. Morton was recognized by all Democratic mayors and county chairmen as the sole spokesman of Negro Democracy. He used his authority to quiet local demands for the election of Negro Democratic leaders in the Nineteenth and Twenty-first AD's; this could only weaken his seemingly absolute control of "Black Tammany." Dissident Democrats complained that he was "haughty," "secretive," "exclusive," and acted as an "overlord." "Morton is utterly without the social qualities which make a leader easily accessible to his constituents and responsive to their needs," one of them commented. Others called him "arrogant," "cynical" and "vindictive." The UCD—"a segregated party in the County of New York for colored voters, headed by a leadership over which the colored voters have no control nor power of removal"— might have been acceptable to an earlier generation, a Negro Democrat said, but it "has outlived its usefulness" in the 1920's.

As long as Democratic mayors used Morton as the vehicle of city patronage, local Negro Democrats were unable to do more than voice their complaints and pray for change—he who held the jobs controlled the party. In fact, those who shouted defiance too often and too loud found themselves unemployed. A clerk in Harlem's municipal court, a superintendent of Harlem's state employment office and a New York County deputy sheriff were suddenly dismissed for "incompetency" after criticizing Morton's leadership or refusing to contribute ten per cent of their salaries to the UCD. Morton remained the virtual dictator of Negro Democracy until Republican Fiorello H. La Guardia was elected mayor in 1933. The liberal mayor cut the taproot of Morton's strength—patronage—and this caused the UCD to "cease functioning." La Guardia agreed to reappoint Morton Civil Service Commissioner on condition that he break with the Democratic Party. The Negro boss, who always regarded politics "as a selfish, desperate game," saved himself and left the Democratic Party: "Mr. Morton gave up his Tammany affiliations and announced he had joined the American Labor Party, with which the Mayor is affiliated," the *Age* recorded. In the twilight of his career Morton continued to practice the dictum he always relied upon as the only true source of political power: "We should take this political situation as a cold-blooded business proposition," he once said. "We should treat it as an honest-to-goodness shopping trip. Politics . . . is but a theoretical bargain counter, to buy wares and get the best we can in bargains. . . . " As Morton closed a deal for himself, Harlem Democrats, freed from his control, took over local district organizations from the old white bosses—the Nineteenth AD in 1935; the Twenty-first AD in 1939.[50]

Negro Republicans traditionally operated within the confines of regular party structure. Their struggle to elect Negro district leaders was thus less difficult than it had been for Democrats, but dissension was evident in Republican ranks too. Although Negro Republicans composed the majority of voters in the Nineteenth and Twenty-first AD's through most of the 1920's, and also the majority of county committeemen in each district—whose votes determine district leadership—it took an unusual effort to unseat the "real Harlemites," the men "born and raised in this section," who had control of the party when whites represented a majority in the neighborhood.

Leaders were powerful men. They alone distributed the patronage of the party—and this included enticing and sometimes lucrative positions. When necessary, it was reported, they could run "well-oiled" campaigns. Politics was a key source of mobility in every lower-class community and the influence of the district leader could mean the making or breaking of a young career. It was he, for example, who largely determined nominees for local office; and nomination or election to the state legislature or Board of Aldermen often carried unanticipated dividends with it. Take the case of Mvles A. Paige. Paige, born in Montgomery, Alabama, graduated from Columbia University Law School in 1924 and was admitted to the Bar the next year. He was selected to run for the State Senate in August 1926. On September 5, Corporal Myles A. Paige went to summer camp with Harlem's 369th Infantry. Within a week the twenty-nine-year-old corporal had somehow been promoted second lieutenant; a week later, first lieutenant; and three days after that, captain and company commander. He must have performed unusual heroics in those two and a half weeks. Paige later became a municipal judge.[51]

District leaders had a wide source of influence and many local Negro politicians—lawyers, government clerks, election district captains, deputy sheriffs, secretaries to judges, election inspectors, Prohibition agents, postal employees, deputy collectors of Internal Revenue, varieties of municipal workers—hesitated to question their authority. When dissatisfied Negro Republicans demanded that white leaders step down—"Get rid of Conklin," "Grenthal must go"—the whites refused, and used a barrage of threats, dismissals and bribes to keep their positions as long as possible. In the midst of one battle, Robert S. Conklin, boss of the Twenty-first AD, sent letters to district captains telling them to support him or "get out." He "was fighting for his political life," he said. Prior to 1929 all efforts to elect Negro Republican leaders in the Nineteenth and Twenty-first AD's were defeated when a majority of colored committeemen joined with the white minority to vote against Negro insurgents: "As usual," the *Age* commented after one of these fights, "Negroes were pitted against each other. . . ."[52]

The breakthrough came in 1929 after a resolute effort on the part of Negro politicians, clergy and press. Abraham Grenthal, Republican leader of the Nineteenth AD and assemblyman 1924–1928, was the target of attack. Grenthal lived in the Jewish section of lower Harlem. He had attended the neighborhood public schools, City College, and graduated from New York Law School in 1914. As an active club politician, he was appointed election district captain, and rose from there to leader. He seemed to have been a conscientious ward boss who voiced the demands of his Negro constituency as well as his white. As assemblyman, for example, he fought for low-income housing legislation and rent control; he introduced bills to allow bootblacks to keep their stands open on Sundays, and to have a monument built honoring the 369th; he lectured on local problems in Negro churches. The Jewish leader even dressed as Santa Claus to distribute mittens and stockings to Harlem's poor in the winter. That he was popular in the community was demonstrated by his re-election to the assembly on five successive occasions—even against the opposition of Negro Democrats.[53]

The demand that Grenthal resign, then, rested not so much on his past record as on the fact that Negroes were the new majority in Harlem and wanted the political leadership their numbers warranted. Negroes urged Grenthal to "gracefully withdraw." "The time is ripe for the assertion of racial independence," a Negro politician said. "The idea of white men picking leaders for Negroes will no longer be tolerated." "There is an overwhelming sentiment among members of

my group that one of their number should be the leader and another a
member of the Assembly of the 19th District," Fred R. Moore told
the white politician. "All racial groups throughout the city advance a
similar argument—the Italian, the Jew, etc. It is the only way by
which [minority] groups get elective representation."[54]

But politicians rarely "gracefully withdraw" from power, and
Grenthal refused. Fred R. Moore, then alderman of the district,
organized a slate of independent Republicans—including a Negro
district leader—to run against Grenthal and the regular party's
candidates for state and city offices in the 1929 primaries. He kept
the contest on the front page of his newspaper, equated a vote for
Grenthal with race disloyalty and arranged for Negroes of local and
national prominence—Chicago's congressman Oscar DePriest, A. M.
E. Bishop Reverdy C. Ransom, the Reverend Dr. Adam Clayton
Powell, Sr.—to speak in Harlem for the insurgents' cause: "The fight
is on and we are in it heart and soul." *Advance,* a Harlem church
newspaper, printed scathing attacks on Grenthal's leadership and
predicted his defeat in the primaries: "He has had his political day in
the 19th," an *Advance* editorial maintained. "His winding sheets
have been made. The hearse is backed up ready to receive his
expiring corpse. His requiem will be said in the Primaries."[55]

And it was. The concerted effort was successful. The insurgent
ticket defeated Grenthal's by large majorities and subsequently went
on to win in the 1929 election. Lieutenant Colonel Charles W.
Fillmore, officer in the 369th and auditor in the New York State Tax
Bureau, became the first Negro district leader in city history. At
about the same time a quiet agreement for "dual leadership" was
reached in the Twenty-first AD. The white section of the district, the
"Hill," continued to be represented by the white leader, Robert S.
Conklin; the Negro part of the neighborhood, the "Valley," was
turned over to Negro architect and politician Charles W. B. Mitchell.
"Harlem Has Redeemed Itself," the headlines of the Negro press
shouted. "It has freed itself of alien leadership. . . ."[56]

The Negro community obviously made significant political advances, but higher elective offices remained closed to this generation
of Harlemites. The fact that Harlem contained more people in less
space than any other area in the nation gave Negroes local political
recognition, but paradoxically, it also prevented the election of a
Negro congressman. No effort was spared to elect a Harlemite to the

House of Representatives. In 1924 the Republican Party avoided a threatened Negro revolt in Harlem by nominating and actively supporting Charles H. Roberts for congress. (The former white Republican candidate was encouraged to step down with a nomination to a judicial post.) Roberts was defeated then, and so were two other Negro congressional candidates in later elections—Edward A. Johnson in 1928, and Hubert T. Delany in 1929. The basic problem was not lack of Negro support, as more Negroes registered and voted in these campaigns than in others, but the difficulty caused by political geography. The Nineteenth and Twenty-first AD's were part of a larger congressional district—the Twenty-first CD—which included three solidly white and traditionally Democratic assembly districts. The importance of the Negro vote, although substantial enough to warrant nominations, was restricted by its very concentration. Chicago Negroes, partially because their population was spread across a wider geographic and political area, were able to elect a Negro congressman in 1928. The Nineteenth and Twenty-first AD's contained 25 per cent of the vote of the congressional district, and though these sections voted heavily for Negro congressmen each time they ran, their numbers were insufficient to offset the white Democratic vote in surrounding neighborhoods. Democrats, hesitant to chance defeat in a "safe" district, refused to run a Negro candidate. It was not until Harlem's political boundaries were redrawn, in 1944, that New York elected its first Negro member of the House of Representatives—the present occupant, Adam Clayton Powell, Jr.[57]

Although the Negro's political progress in New York City was not an unqualified success, there obviously was greater advance in this sphere of community activity than in all others. While the social and economic position of the city's Negroes tended to remain stable or, with the Great Depression, even retrogressed, there was significant political mobility. In the 1890's Negroes were an almost powerless minority group; the least influential minority group in the metropolis. Their role, if any, was on the farthest periphery of municipal affairs. Within the next generation, the generation that settled in Harlem, Negroes became an integral part of city government and politics— and politics proved a wedge for economic advancement. In the 1890's there were *no* Negro policemen and firemen; in the 1920's these departments not only hired Negro applicants but promoted them to supervisory positions. Similar strides were made in municipal hospitals, the Board of Education, the sanitation department, the Board of Health, city courts and public agencies generally. Negroes tasted the sweetness of political power for the first time, and this power grew as their population expanded. At the turn of the century they argued their cause from a position of weakness: "The black, poor, weak, helpless [citizen]," a Negro lawyer said plaintively at the time of the 1900 riot, should be treated as the equal of "the most influential official. . . . Life is as dear to us as it is to . . . the most exalted."[58] Within the next generation the indifference that characterized the reactions of municipal officials in the 1890's ended and they openly competed for and courted Negro support. Political problems obviously remained to be dealt with in the future, but the apathy of the 1890's was never repeated. The question: "Where are the leaders up there [Harlem]? Who will point the way for the thousands there?" had, in some small measure, been answered."

Epilogue:
Symbols of the Jazz Age—
The New Negro and
Harlem Discovered

"You don't know, you don't know my mind,
When you see me laughin', I'm laughin'
to keep from cryin'. . . ."
—Negro folksong

"Within the past ten years Harlem has
acquired a world-wide reputation.
. . . It is . . . known as being exotic,
colourful, and sensuous; a place
where life wakes up at night."
—James Weldon Johnson, *Black Manhattan* (1930)

I

The dominant patterns of Harlem life were largely set in the 1920's, and have remained remarkably unchanged ever since. The intensity of most Harlem social problems has gradually diminished in the last generation, but two surveys of the community in the 1960's, *Youth in the Ghetto* and *A Harlem Almanac*, depict a neighborhood strikingly similar to the ghetto of the twenties.[1] The present generation has inherited the unsolved problems of the past.

If the 1920's added anything to our knowledge of social conditions in Harlem, it presented a distorted and negative image of reality. The Negro community was "discovered" in the twenties, and its reputation was not that of a tragic slum, but a "place of laughing, swaying, and dancing"; and this image spread not only throughout the nation but throughout the world. European visitors considered a trip to Harlem a "must" on their itineraries of American sights, and European journals carried articles on the community's "exotic" night spots.[2] "Within the past ten years," James Weldon Johnson noted in

179

1930, "Harlem has acquired a world-wide reputation." It would be difficult to find a better example of the confusions, distortions, half-truths and quarter-truths that are the foundations of racial and ethnic stereotypes than the white world's image of Harlem in the 1920's.

The portrayal of Harlem that developed in the twenties was *primarily* a product of broader changes in American society. The 1920's, as is well known, was a remarkable age in American intellectual history. A cultural rebellion of the first order erupted from beneath the complacency and conservatism that were dominant characteristics of American society and politics then. It was the time writers, artists, scholars, aesthetes and bohemians became aware of the standardization of life that resulted from mass production and large-scale, efficient industrialization—the "Machine Civilization," that "profound national impulse [that] drives the hundred millions steadily toward uniformity."[3] These intellectuals declared war on tenets of American thought and faith that had remained sacrosanct for three hundred years. As a by-product of their attack on traditional American middle-class values, which were constantly called "Puritanical," literary rebels and others discovered the Negro, America's "outcast," and created a semimythical dreamland which they came to idealize— "storied Harlem."[4]

In some part, this growing national awareness was caused by significant changes within Negro society. There seemed to be a new militancy in the Negro world during and after World War I—reflected in Harlem's well-known Silent Parade to protest the 1917 East St. Louis race riots, in the racial program and consciousness of Marcus Garvey, in A. Philip Randolph's struggling movement to found the Brotherhood of Sleeping Car Porters and Maids, in the numerous little leftist groups active in Harlem, in the national campaign to promote federal antilynching legislation. Yet American society did not really take these movements seriously in the 1920's— Garvey was considered a comical figure; an antilynching law was never enacted; riots continued; Randolph's union made little headway before the Great Depression; the leftists were largely ignored or considered crackpots.[5]

The twenties also saw the rise of a noteworthy group of Negro writers and scholars, and America gave *them* considerable recognition. Some of the novels, plays, poems, books and articles of Countée Cullen, James Weldon Johnson, George S. Schuyler, Claude McKay,

Wallace Thurman, Zora Neale Hurston, Jessie Fauset, Rudolph Fisher, Jean Toomer, Charles S. Johnson, E. Franklin Frazier and others were good enough in their own right to justify public acclaim. The poetry of Langston Hughes continues to be widely read. Harlem was the center of this "New Negro Renaissance" and, like an "ebony flute," it lured Negro writers to it: "Harlem was like a great magnet for the Negro intellectual, pulling him from everywhere," Langston Hughes wrote.[6] Claude McKay came to Harlem from Jamaica, after two years at an agricultural college in Kansas; Jean Toomer originally came from an Alabama plantation; Langston Hughes arrived in 1921 after a sojourn in Mexico. "I can never put on paper the thrill of the underground ride to Harlem," Hughes recalled. "I went up the steps and out into the bright September sunlight. Harlem! I stood there, dropped my bags, took a deep breath and felt happy again."[7] Wherever they wandered in the twenties, and many went to Paris or Africa for a time ("The cream of Harlem was in Paris"), the Negro literati always returned *Home to Harlem* (to use the title of a McKay novel). Little theater, art and political-discussion groups flourished in the community. Negro literary and political magazines made their appearance: *Fire, The Messenger, Voice of the Negro, The Negro Champion, Harlem.* The One Hundred and Thirty-fifth Street library became Harlem's cultural center. "The Schomburg Collection," George S. Schuyler remembered, "used to be a great gathering place for all the people of the Renaissance."[8] In the 1920's one could hear lectures there by such prominent people as Franz Boas, W. E. B. DuBois, Carl Van Doren, James Weldon Johnson, Carter G. Woodson, Kelly Miller, Melville J. Herskovits, R. R. Moton and Arthur A. Schomburg. Harlem became what contemporaries called the "Mecca of the New Negro."[9]

Some observers, Negro and white, looked to this outburst of literary and artistic expression as a significant step toward a more general acceptance of Negroes by American society. Alain Locke, gifted writer and Howard University professor, argued that social equality would result from the recognition of the Negro as an "artist class." "It seems that the interest in the cultural expression of Negro life . . . heralds an almost revolutionary revaluation of the Negro," he wrote in 1927. It was "an augury of a new democracy in American culture."[10] Heywood Broun, well-known journalist and critic, addressed the New York Urban League at a Harlem church.

He believed "a supremely great negro artist, [an artist] who could catch the imagination of the world, would do more than any other agency to remove the disabilities against which the negro race now labors." "This great artist may come at any time," Broun concluded, and he asked his audience to remain silent for ten seconds to imagine the coming of the savior-genius.[11] This same theme of a broad cultural acceptance evolving from the recognition of the "New Negro" as "a creator" dominates the writings of James Weldon Johnson in the twenties. Johnson and others somehow believed that American racism was a process that could be reasoned with; a phenomenon that would crumble when whites recognized that Negroes had extraordinary artistic talents. "I am coming to believe," Johnson wrote his close friend Carl Van Vechten, "that nothing can go farther to destroy race prejudice than the recognition of the Negro as a creator and contributor to American civilization."[12] "Harlemites thought the millennium had come," Langston Hughes remembered. "They thought the race problem had at last been solved though Art. . . ."[13]

There was an element of realism in the romantic hopes of Johnson, Broun and Locke. For white Americans to grant that the Negro was capable of making *any* contribution to American culture was in itself a new idea—"that the Negro is a creator as well as creature . . . a giver as well as . . . receiver."[14] A new and more liberal vision of democracy developed among social scientists in the twenties. Scholars like Robert E. Park, Herbert A. Miller, Franz Boas, Melville J. Herskovits, Charles S. Johnson, Bruno Lasker, E. Franklin Frazier and Horace M. Kallen attacked traditional American attitudes toward assimilation and "Americanization." A more vital and beautiful democracy would arise, they argued, by permitting ethnic groups to maintain their individuality, rather than conceiving them as swallowed up, or melted down, in the one dominant American culture. Each group, given freedom of expression and development, would then make valuable contributions to American society. Diversity, cultural pluralism, should be fostered and encouraged, they wrote, not stifled.[15]

A spate of articles and books published in the twenties seriously analyzed and attempted to understand the Negro's place in the nation. The dozens of volumes about Negroes written by pseudo-scientists and racists at the turn of the century were replaced by works which attempted to cut through racial stereotypes ("generalized theories about racial qualities") and tried to find some viable program of "interracial cooperation." "The American Negro can no longer be dismissed as an unimportant element in the population of the United States," one man concluded. Bruno Lasker's *And Who is My Neighbor?* and *All Colors* were among the earliest serious studies of American interracial attitudes.[16] *The Annals* of the American Academy of Political and Social Science printed a thick volume of studies on Negroes by the nation's leading scholars.[17] *The World Tomorrow,* a fascinating Christian-Pacifist journal, devoted two full issues to similar articles in the 1920's.[18] Most of the major periodicals of the decade contained many serious and important studies of Negro life. The artistic and human value of Negro spirituals, folk songs, folk legends and music was first seriously recognized in the twenties (many considered them America's most important contributions to world culture); Darius Milhaud, after listening to Negro music in Lenox Avenue cafés, composed pieces which made use of jazz rhythms and instruments; *In Abraham's Bosom,* one of Paul Green's many plays of southern Negro life, won the Pulitzer Prize in 1927; Eugene O'Neill and Robert E. Sherwood constructed plays and novels around Negro characters and themes.[19] As important as this new recognition was, however, it was a minor trend in American thought. The generation that advocated cultural pluralism was also the generation that revived the Ku Klux Klan, and permanently restricted foreign immigration into the United States.

Had intellectuals like Johnson and Locke looked more critically at the stereotype of the "New Negro" that developed in the writings of most white commentators of the twenties, they would have further questioned the extent of interracial understanding that existed then. White literary rebels created a "vogue in things Negro," "an enthusiasm for Negro life and art" that bordered on being a cult.[20] They saw Negroes not as people but as symbols of everything America was not. The concept of the existence of a "New Negro" and the publicity given to it in the 1920's was primarily the result of this new awareness and interest in Negro society by what one writer called the "New White Man."[21] The generation that discovered "newness" all around itself—New Humanism, New Thought, New Women, New Criticism, New Psychology, New Masses, New Poetry, New Science, New Era, New Words, New Morality and so on—also found a "New Negro"; and the concept became a cultural weapon: "Another

Bombshell Fired into the Heart of Bourgeois Culture." "Negro stock is going up," novelist Rudolph Fisher wrote, "and everybody's buying."[22]

In the literature of the twenties, Negroes were conceived as "expressive" ("a singing race") in a society burdened with "unnatural inhibitions"; their lives were "primitive" and "exotic" (these two words appear repeatedly) in a "dull," "weary," and "monotonous" age; they could laugh and love freely in a "land flowing with Socony and Bryan and pristine Rotary purity." Negroes were presented as people who lived an "entire lifetime of laughs and thrills, [of] excitement and fun"—they had an "innate gayety of soul." "Ecstasy," Joseph Wood Krutch noted in *The Nation*, "seems . . . to be his [the Negro's] natural state."[23] The stereotype of the Negro that existed in American society in the nineteenth century, and which I described earlier, was largely untouched by the new interest in Negro life. It continued in such "all-talking melodramas" as "Lucky Sambo," "Hearts in Dixie," and "Hallelujah," or in the new radio hit "Amos and Andy." In the twenties, however, the ludicrous image of the Negro as "darky" became a subordinate theme, eclipsed by the conception of the Negro as sensuous and rhythmic African. Negroes were still thought to be alienated from traditional American virtues and values, as they had been since colonial times, but this was now considered a great asset. "To Americans," a perceptive contemporary wrote in 1929, "the Negro is not a human being but a concept."[24]

II

This was the background against which white America and the world came to know Harlem: "with our eyes focused on the Harlem scene we may dramatically glimpse the New Negro." A large Negro community had gathered in Harlem prior to World War I, but aside from small numbers of dedicated social workers, American society seemed willing to overlook its existence. In the twenties, however, Harlem was made a national symbol—a symbol of the "New Negro"; a symbol of the Jazz Age. It was seen as the antithesis of Main Street, Zenith and Gopher Prairie. Whatever seemed thrilling, bizarre or sensuous about Harlem life became a part of the community's image; whatever was sad or tragic about it, ignored. "White folks discovered black magic there," Claude McKay said.[25]

Harlem of the twenties was presented as a "great playground,"

America's answer to Paris.[26] The institution that best describes this aspect of Harlem's image was the white slumming party: "it became quite a rage . . . to go to night clubs in Harlem," Carl Van Vechten recalled.[27] Cabarets were filled nightly with handsomely dressed white slummers who danced the Charleston or Black Bottom, listened to jazz or watched risqué revues. Some night spots, like the Cotton Club (which had "the hottest show in town") and Connie's Inn (which competed for the honor), catered exclusively to whites. They were, a journalist commented, dives "where white people from downtown could be entertained by colored girls."[28] If one were looking "to go on moral vacation," or wished to soften "the asperities of a Puritan conscience," Harlem's cabarets promised to do the job. The following is an advertisement, written especially for "white consumption," and distributed by a man who supplied "Slumming Hostesses" to "inquisitive Nordics" (each card was said to have a suggestive picture on it):[29]

Here in the world's greatest city it would both amuse and also interest you to see the real inside of the New Negro Race of Harlem. You have heard it discussed, but there are very few who really know. . . . I am in a position to carry you through Harlem as you would go slumming through Chinatown. My guides are honest and have been instructed to give the best service. . . . Your season is not completed with thrills until you have visited Harlem.

"White people," the *Age* commented, "are taking a morbid interest in the night life of [Harlem]."[30]

And the interest continued to grow throughout the decade. Carl Van Vechten's novel of Harlem life, *Nigger Heaven* (1926), sold 100,000 copies "almost immediately," and brought its author a substantial fortune. It was translated into French, Swedish, Russian and Japanese.[31] Van Vechten's book contained some interesting commentaries on the structure and problems of Negro society—the role of the middle class; "passing"; prejudice; color-consciousness—but its plot was contrived, sensationalistic and melodramatic; replete with orgies, drugs and seduction; a hodgepodge of *True Confessions* and the front pages of a tabloid. Its characters were unbelievable as people.[32] "The squalor of Negro life, the vice of Negro life," Van Vechten said, "offer a wealth of novel, exotic, picturesque materials to the artist." *Nigger Heaven* was "recognized in every quarter . . . as *the* portrayal of contemporary life in Harlem," its publisher said (and it undoubtedly was).[33] The white world looked curiously at the success of Marcus Garvey, whose movement basically reflected a profound Negro desire for racial pride and respect in a society that denied them, and concluded that Negroes in Harlem "have parades almost every day."[34] White intellectuals and bohemians knew Harlem through the cabarets, or at the famous parties in the salon of the "joy-goddess of Harlem," A'Lelia Walker's "Dark Tower": "dedicated to the aesthetes, young writers, sculptors, painters—a rendezvous where they may feel at home."[35] Bessie Smith, the great blues singer, toured America with her "Harlem Frolic" company. Josephine Baker ("Josephine of the Jazz Age") wowed them in Harlem as a young chorus girl, and went on to international acclaim in Europe. "From a world of stone with metal decoys/Drab stone streets and drab stone masses/New York's mold for the great middle-classes, Africa passes/With syncopated talking the Congo arouses."[36]

White audiences, like gluttons at a feast, vicariously tasted the "high yallers," "tantalizin' tans," and "hot chocolates" that strutted around in the Blackbird Revues, or in such plays as *Lulu Belle* (1926) and *Harlem* (1928)—and made them top box-office successes. *Black Boy* and *Deep River,* dramas which emphasized a more serious side of Negro life, were failures.[37] "Ten years ago," one Negro reviewer of *Lulu Belle* commented, "this play would have been unprofitable. Twenty years ago it would have caused a riot."[38] The following is a handbill distributed to advertise the play *Harlem,* "A Thrilling Play of the Black Belt":[39]

> Harlem! . . . The City that Never Sleeps! . . .
> A Strange, Exotic Island in the Heart of
> New York! . . . Rent Parties! . . . Number
> Runners! . . . Chippies! . . . Jazz Love! . . .
> Primitive Passion!

"How soon this common theme shall reach the nauseating state," a caustic critic remarked, "is not easy to tell."[40]

The Great Depression brought an abrupt end to the concept of a "New Negro" and the image of Harlem as an erotic utopia. A nation sobered by bread lines no longer searched for a dreamland inhabited by people who danced and loved and laughed for an "entire lifetime." America found the "New Negro" less enticing in the 1930's. Connie's Inn, the Lafayette Theatre and other places of entertainment went out of business. Leading figures of the Renaissance: Wallace Thur-

man, Richard B. Harrison, A'Lelia Walker, Rudolph Fisher, Charles
S. Gilpin, Florence Mills and Arthur A. Schomburg died in the late
twenties or thirties. Miss Walker's famous Villa Lewaro, another
gathering place of the Renaissance, was sold at public auction. Most
of the Negro literati, though not all, stopped writing or, if they
continued to do so, found a less responsive American audience for
their works.[41] All the Negro literary magazines folded.

And, as the exotic vision of the twenties passed, a new image of
Harlem emerged—a Harlem already known to stolid census-takers,
city health officers and social workers. "The rosy enthusiasms and
hopes of 1925," Alain Locke said ten years later, "were . . . cruelly
deceptive mirages." The ghetto was revealed in the thirties as "a
nasty, sordid corner into which black folk are herded"— *"a Harlem
that the social worker knew all along but had not been able to
dramatize. . . . There is no cure or saving magic in poetry and art
for . . . precarious marginal employment, high mortality rates, civic
neglect,"* Locke concluded.[42] It was this Harlem, the neighborhood
not visible "from the raucous interior of a smoke-filled, jazz-drunken
cabaret," the Harlem hidden by the "bright surface . . . of . . .
night clubs, cabaret tours and . . . arty magazines," that was devastated by the Depression; and has remained a community with an
inordinate share of sorrow and deprivation ever since. "The depression brought everybody down a peg or two," Langston Hughes wrote.
"And the Negroes had but few pegs to fall." The myth-world of the
twenties had ended.[43]

Retrospect:
The Enduring Ghetto*

This essay will discuss what I consider the most important generalization that emerges from a study of Negro life in New York City from the early nineteenth century to the present.[1] At first glance the worlds seem hardly comparable. The most obvious distinctions appear to be the radical changes in Negro status and in race relations that have taken place between the Jacksonian era and the America of Watts, Newark and Detroit. It is my thesis, however, that despite seeming transformations, some of which I shall describe, the essential structure and nature of the Negro ghetto has remained remarkably durable since the demise of slavery in the North. There is an unending and tragic sameness about black life in the metropolis over the two centuries.

Some of the most obvious differences should be noted within this dominant pattern of continuity. The most striking relate to the size and origins of the Negro population. When slavery ended in New York in 1827, some 13,000 black people, the majority of whom had been born within the state, resided in Manhattan. They represented 1.5 percent of the city's population on the eve of the Civil War, when, at the same time, more than half the residents of the metropolis were foreign born. The Negro population remained relatively stable from the 1850's through the 1870's as the city literally became "Gotham," with Manhattan's population exceeding a million in 1875. Between 1860 and 1890 Negroes never represented more than 1.6 percent of the city's increasingly heterogeneous popula-

*The term "ghetto" is most commonly applied to racially restrictive housing patterns. It is meant to have broader connotations in this essay: as an impressionistic and interpretive phrase which meaningfully summarizes the social, economic and psychological positions of black people in the city in the nineteenth and twentieth centuries and also symbolizes the tone of urban race relations in these years.

tion.[2] They were indeed "invisible" to all but a small group of abolitionists in the antebellum period and the handful of religious and charity workers in the late nineteenth century.

Mass migration after the 1890's reshaped the Negro community. By 1900, for the first time in the city's history, more than half the black population had migrated from other states. In 1920 more Negroes lived in New York City than in any other American urban area. The present black community, exceeding a million, represents the largest concentration of blacks in any metropolitan area in American history. The status of a formerly "invisible" minority ("It is a . . . whole stratum of society . . . of whose very existence most of us are wholly unaware") has been transformed into one of the principal concerns of contemporary society. The burgeoning growth of the Negro population has also laid the foundations for the important shift in ghetto militancy and mood that have characterized America's urban areas since Harlem's riot of 1964. And it has also permitted the emergence of a modicum of black political power—a force that was almost totally absent from nineteenth-century life.[3]

Another difference, one most commonly pointed to, deals with the physical location of the black population. There were no Harlems in the nineteenth century. Although Negroes were usually more concentrated in one single area than in others—early in the century in Five Points, later in the Tenderloin and San Juan Hill districts—these neighborhoods were small enough to be bordered by and interspersed with streets occupied by whites. Occasionally, especially among the lower classes, some whites lived in the same tenements as Negroes.[4] A more general dispersion was caused by the number of Negro domestics who resided in the homes of their white employers. When the Quakers of Philadelphia attempted to estimate the size of the black population in 1837 and 1847, for example, they found it necessary to add 4,000 to 5,000 people to their calculations to account for "servants living in."[5] In 1835, six Manhattan wards had more than 1,000 Negro residents; in 1860 and 1875 four wards had a similar number of inhabitants; in 1890 there were again six wards of heavy Negro concentration, each inhabited by 2,000 to 4,000 black people.[6]

Dr. Robert C. Weaver has used this apparent dispersion of Negro residences in the nineteenth-century city to argue that black people were "concentrated but not always separated" then. "Few Americans realize that widespread, enforced residential segregation on the basis of color is relatively new in the North," Weaver writes. ". . . Negroes, themselves, though better informed than the general public, sometimes forget that their ancestors and older friends were not always hemmed into too little space. . . . The Negro ghetto in northern cities is of recent origin."[7] The implications of Weaver's interpretation are obvious (and are analogous to other well-known historical restoration themes dealing with slavery and race relations): If America once permitted greater residential mobility to Negroes, present advocates of racially-free occupancy in the city are attempting to reclaim an older tradition that was lost under the pressure of the great migrations of the twentieth century; they are not establishing a new one. History in this view becomes a useful weapon for the socially conscious city planner, a tool for the housing reformer. The danger, however, is that in attempting to destroy the racial myths of our past new ones, in turn, may be advanced.

No one can question the basic facts of nineteenth-century human geography, but one may ask about their meaning. Did the wider dispersion of Negro residences imply a more enlightened racial view of housing then? Was there any substantive difference between a small group of densely populated ghettos and one, two or three large ones? Were the smaller ghettos of the nineteenth century more livable, healthful and wholesome than those of the twentieth? Might black youngsters in the nineteenth century have had a more hopeful vision of their future than those in recent times?

Whatever evidence we have points to an emphatic "no" for all of these questions. The sections of the city where the races had closest contact were also those traditionally subject to periodic violence. The brutal frenzy, mutilations, lynchings and burnings that accompanied the draft riots of 1863 occurred in the sections of lower and midtown Manhattan where Negroes and whites—especially but not only the Irish—lived in close proximity to one another. The Tenderloin and San Juan Hill sections were the centers of a serious race riot in 1900 and a lesser confrontation in 1905. San Juan Hill itself was named as a parody on the interracial conflicts that took place on a steep upgrade leading to the Negro section.[8] The checkerboard housing patterns that permitted a closer contact of people were as likely to breed trouble as brotherhood. They were not symbols of viably integrated communities.

And conditions within the ghettos for other than the small black middle class were as appalling in the nineteenth century as they have remained in the twentieth. Charles Dickens visited some lower-class Negro homes in Five Points in 1842 and described them as "leprous houses," "hideous tenements," "cramped hutches." They lacked minimal comforts, were dingy, dark, and surrounded by alleys "paved with mud knee-deep." "Where dogs would howl to lie, women and men . . . slink off to sleep, forcing the dislodged rats to move away," Dickens wrote.[9] Other contemporaries found lower-class Negroes living in cellars, rickety shanties and in the "Old Brewery"—a beer factory ingeniously transformed into a tenement house. What was probably America's first model tenement was constructed for the city's black population in 1855; an obvious sign of their need for improved housing then.[10] A Committee of Merchants formed to aid victims of the draft riots found one old man lying in a small room. It was, they recorded, "the kitchen, sitting-room, bedroom and garret of four grown persons and five children." The committee, which provided financial assistance to practically every black family in Manhattan in 1863 (aid was received by 12,782 Negroes), referred to typical Negro homes as "humble tenements."[11]

The lengthiest description of an antebellum Northern ghetto that has yet come to light depicts a Negro slum of Philadelphia in 1847. An investigating group of Quakers, careful to point out that this was the *worst* Negro neighborhood in the city, was shocked by the "dismal abodes of human wretchedness" they uncovered. The following is a section of their report:

We followed through a dirty passage, so narrow, a stout man would have found it tight work to have threaded it. Looking before us, the yard seemed unusually dark. This we found was occasioned by a long range of two story pens, with a projecting boarded walk above the lower tier, for the inhabitants of the second story to get to the doors of their apartments. This covered nearly all the narrow yard, and served to exclude light from the dwellings below. We looked in every one of these dismal abodes of human wretchedness. Here were dark, damp holes, six feet square, without a bed in any of them, and generally without furniture, occupied by one or two families: apartments where privacy of any kind was unknown—where comfort never appeared. We endeavoured with the aid of as much light as at mid-day could find access through the open door, to see into the dark corners of these contracted abodes; and as we became impressed with their utter desolateness, the absence of bedding, and of ought to rest on but a bit of old matting on a wet floor, we felt sick and oppressed. Disagreeable odours of many kinds were ever arising; and with no ventilation but the open door, and the foot square hole in the front of the pen, we could scarcely think it possible that life could be supported, when winter compelled them to have fire in charcoal furnaces. . . . Some of these six by six holes, had six and even eight persons in them, but more generally two to four. . . . It is not in the power of language to convey an adequate impression of the scene of this property.[12]

Similar reports have issued from the offices of investigating agencies ever since. Social reformers in the 1880's and 1890's, for instance, concluded that New York City Negroes paid more money for housing and received less adequate accommodations in return than any other ethnic group in the metropolis. "The present housing conditions of the vast majority of colored families in New York can only be characterized as disgraceful," a late-nineteenth-century survey maintained.[13] Black sociologists Ira De Augustine Reid and E. Franklin Frazier found the same to be true in the 1920's; contemporary students have uncovered similar conditions today.[14] Statisticians in 1960 could not find a single census tract in Harlem in which more than 45 percent of the housing was considered adequate. In one tract 91 percent of the homes were classified as slums.[15] And, although some people were shocked to learn of Harlem's current population density,[16] it should be recognized that New York's predominantly Negro neighborhoods have been the most congested residential areas of the city at least since the early twentieth century. The studies have droned on but the conditions have endured.

Nor have there been marked differences in the economic status of Negro New Yorkers over the two centuries. To come to a fair estimate of antebellum economic conditions in the city, one must first evaluate the rhetoric that pervaded the debate over slavery and freedom in the 1830's, 1840's and 1850's. Defenders of slavery were anxious to prove that Negroes could not survive as free men. As one contemporary put it, racists "attempted to prove that freedom made the black man insane, blind . . . deaf and dumb. . . ."[17] Black and white abolitionists, on the other hand, regularly responded to the attack by emphasizing the benefits of freedom and the great progress that had been made by free Negroes in the North, in spite of handicaps. They customarily compiled biographical sketches of successful black businessmen and professionals or totaled the *aggregate* wealth of the

Negro community to illustrate that economic progress had been made in the North.[18] Neither side presented a representative view of the economic status of the free Negro majority.

Although some free Negroes were permitted to work as craftsmen, and a small, militant, middle class of teachers, businessmen, caterers and journalists existed in New York City and in other Northern cities,[19] the majority of the antebellum Negro population lived in poverty and worked as domestics ("day's work women"), unskilled laborers, or in some service occupation. In 1855, the New York State Census recorded a hundred or more city Negroes engaged in the following occupations: dressmakers, cooks, waiters, laundresses, laborers, porters, and coachmen. The largest occupational grouping, the only one in which more than a thousand Negroes were employed, was domestic service. There were one Negro lawyer and six Negro physicians in Manhattan's black population of 11,840. At no time between 1825 and 1865 did more than 2 percent of the city's Negro population own the $250 worth of property that would have qualified them to vote; in 1855, 91 percent paid no taxes.[20] This is obviously a description of a predominantly lower-class community: a "hard working, honest, humble people," "the great body are of the laboring class."[21]

Individuals who somehow acquired skills were often not permitted to use them or, if allowed to do so, often remained mired in the same type of job throughout their entire careers. The traditional routes to upwardly mobile economic positions were generally blocked by race prejudice; what the leading black abolitionist and emigrationist Samuel Ringgold Ward called "the ever-present, ever-crushing Negro-hate." Ward, who grew up in New York City in the Jacksonian era, illustrated this theme in his autobiography by describing the career of W. L. Jeffers, a black clerk. "I never knew but one colored clerk in a mercantile house," Ward recalled. "Mr. W. L. Jeffers was the lowest clerk in a house well known in Broad Street, New York; but he never was advanced a single grade, while numerous white lads have since passed up by him, and over him, to be members of the firm. Poor Jeffers, till the day of his death, was but one remove above the porter."[22] Black abolitionists repeatedly offered similar illustrations at antislavery meetings and black protest conventions and urged white allies to help them break through these economic barriers.

Data over the last hundred years obviously vary. In the last quarter century there has been a meaningful increase in the number of Negro women who work in clerical positions in the city, a reflection of some general progress of the black middle class in the nation.[23] When such advances are measured against areas of increasing technological unemployment, economic stagnation and economic retrogression, however, their significance is muted. Over the decades one finds an essentially similar pattern: a relatively small, though presently growing, urban Negro middle class, and an overwhelmingly working-class or semi-skilled Negro majority employed in marginal occupations. In unending repetition the largest number of city Negroes work as domestics, janitors, porters, servants, cooks, waiters, chauffeurs, longshoremen, laundry operatives, messengers, elevator operators, general factory help of some kind and lower-level clerks. The traditional Negro entrepreneur has been and still is the owner of a small store in the ghetto who supplies the community with a few standard services: grocers, hair stylists, undertakers, restaurant and bar owners. Two-thirds of the men and three-fourths of the women in Central Harlem today continue to work in service and unskilled positions. Only 7 percent of Harlem men are employed in professional or managerial occupations, and half of the community's families earn less than $4,000 annually. "The roots of the pathology of ghetto communities lie in the menial, low-income jobs held by most ghetto residents," Kenneth B. Clark writes of present-day Harlem. "The Negro has been left out of the swelling prosperity and social progress of the nation as a whole. He is in danger of becoming a permanent economic proletariat."[24] Professor Clark's analysis in the 1960's echoes the views of New York City's newspaper the *Colored American* in the 1830's, those of black abolitionists Theodore S. Wright, Charles L. Reason, Frederick Douglass, Charles Lenox Remond, W. C. Nell and dozens of others in the 1840's and 1850's, the published reports of the New York Colored Mission in the 1870's, 1880's and 1890's, and the innumerable articles and treatises that have analyzed the status of the city's Negro population throughout the twentieth century. All complained of the poverty, discouragement and loss of pride that resulted from enforced Negro economic and social immobility over the centuries. As a New Yorker wrote in 1830: "We adopt a system towards them, which is directly calculated to debase and brutalize the human character; and then condemn them for the . . . desolation which this system produced."[25]

And the same might be said about popular racial attitudes of the white majority over the two centuries, although the question is quite complex and deserves intensive analysis. Many immigrant groups that settled in the metropolis acquired a racist position in the very process of assimilation; one way to adopt the values of the dominant culture, one way to become "American," was to be anti-Negro. The dignified and sensitive black abolitionist, Charles Lenox Remond, pointed to this phenomenon in 1854. On a stroll through State Street in Boston he ran into a hail of vile epithets tossed at him by Boston's Irish immigrants who, among other things, told him to leave the country. "I cannot but settle down in the conviction, that were it not for this spirit of negro hate, we should not hear them say these things," Remond commented.[26]

Such ethnic-racial antagonisms have always been most intense when they coincided with concrete situations—economic competition on the docks in the 1850's and 1860's, residential succession in Harlem in the early twentieth century, the recent fight over a New York City Civilian Review Board—but they have never been absent from city life. Black leaders in all generations noted this ethnic and racial pecking order and wrote about it with bitterness. "It is quite remarkable how easily . . . foreigners catch on to the notion . . . to treat Afro-Americans disdainfully and contemptuously," the Negro *New York Age* commented in 1905. "Pat O'Flannagan does not have the least thing in the world against Jim from Dixie," a black school principal said at the first meeting of the NAACP, "but it didn't take Pat long after passing the Statue of Liberty to learn that it is popular to give Jim a whack."[27] A *Newsweek* survey in the summer of 1966 uncovered an inordinate amount of blue-collar racism in Northern areas throughout the country. It disclosed a surprising number of people who continue to believe in the ancient racial myths and stereotypes.[28]

The endurance of a popular folklore of racism, especially among working-class ethnic groups, has itself been countered by a tradition of nativism in the black community. Negroes in the city and elsewhere—conservatives, moderates, radicals—have often been disheartened by the eventual acceptance accorded white immigrant groups over the years while Negroes, as native Americans, have remained alienated. Bishop Richard Allen, a prominent early-nineteenth-century Negro clergyman, pointed to this problem as early as 1827. Rejecting the lures of the American Colonization Society, Allen said: "Why should they send us into a far country to die? See the thousands of foreigners emigrating to America every year: and if there be ground sufficient for them to cultivate, and bread for them to eat, why would they wish to send the *first tillers* of the land away?"[29] A prominent New York Negro physician and Liberty Party politician, James McCune Smith, wrote an essay on "The German Invasion" in 1859. "And we, sharp witted American sovereigns, will not wake up to the importance and thoroughness of this German invasion," Smith said, "until some 4th day of March, a man shall uncover his head on the Capitol steps and deliver an Inaugural in good *High Dutch* . . . and merchant marts on Broadway, shall hang out signs declaring "English spoken here.""[30]

Black novelist and Garrisonian, William Wells Brown, described the hostility he felt when he returned from an extended visit to England in the 1850's. Two foreigners, "mere adventurers," readily boarded the bus at the dock but "I was told that 'niggers' were not allowed to ride." "They were foreigners, and I am American," Brown wrote, "and when they landed in this country, they were boasting that they had arrived at a land of liberty, where they could enjoy religious and political freedom. I, too, might have rejoiced, had I not been a colored man, at my return to my native land. But I knew what treatment I had to expect from my countrymen—that it would not be even such as was meted out to those foreigners. . . ."[31]

Disparaging remarks about immigrants traditionally ran through speeches delivered at the many state and national black conventions of the antebellum years. They are especially evident in discussions of the suffrage. A New York City minister denounced restrictions on the Negro vote while the franchise was "granted to European paupers, blacklegs and burglars!!!"[32] Frederick Douglass said that if the Negro knew "as much sober as an Irishman knows when drunk, he knows enough to vote." An 1864 Negro convention issued an "Address to the People of the United States" which stressed the importance of the vote as the key protective weapon in a democracy. "In a republican country where general suffrage is the rule, without the ballot personal liberty and . . . other . . . rights become mere privileges held at the option of others," their statement insisted. "What gives the newly arrived immigrants special consequence?; not their virtue, because they are often depraved; not their knowledge, because they are often ignorant; not their wealth, because they are often poor."[33]

Shortly before his death Malcolm X demonstrated that this abrasive theme has endured in black thought. "If you and I were Americans, there'd be no problem," Malcolm said. "Those Hunkies that just got off the boat, they're already Americans; Polacks are already Americans; the Italian refugees are already Americans. Everything that came out of Europe . . . is already an American. And as long as you and I have been here, we aren't Americans yet."[34] The anti-Semitism that has recently flourished in America's ghettos is most obviously directed at Jewish businessmen in these neighborhoods but, in perspective, seems also rooted in a historical tradition of more ancient vintage.

This is not to suggest that there have been *no* changes in racial attitudes or conditions in the North over these many years,[35] but it is to say that whatever positive modifications occurred were short-lived or secondary in importance to the broader truth: the continuance of an enervating and destructive racism; the institutionalization, in thought and action, of second-class citizenship for black people. In the 1870's and 1880's, a barrage of legislative reforms cracked patterns of racial discrimination which had remained intact since the city was settled by the Dutch. Negroes were legally guaranteed equal access to public transportation facilities, theaters, restaurants and cemeteries. The officially segregated public schools were transformed into ward schools and Negro teachers after the 1890's were permitted to take jobs throughout the city. Especially since World War II New York has been the most progressive state in the nation in legislating against job and housing discrimination. Social workers and urban reformers from the Progressive era to the present have attempted to alleviate the myriad social and medical problems that inundate the ghetto.

But none of these actions effected meaningful changes in the fundamental economic and social proscriptions that continued to endure and that prevented full Negro equality in the city. The point may be illustrated by a look at the schools. What value was an education, segregated or integrated, to a youngster whose economic vistas were limited to jobs for "beggarly paid menials?"[36] There was no doubt of the mental capacities of Negro students in the Jacksonian period. Those who attended African Free School No. 2, for example, were taught map drawing, astronomy, logarithms and navigation in addition to the standard subjects. Examinations were public, and given by specialists in the various fields. Some Negro students demonstrated their abilities by scoring impressively on these tests.[37]

Yet many were too poor to come to school at all. Some lacked proper clothing and were apparently ashamed to register.[38] Others, forced to work at very young ages, remained in school only long enough to "attain a knowledge of mere monosyllable spelling and reading."[39] Negro parents sometimes removed youngsters and put them to work. "It is a common complaint of colored teachers," a Negro New Yorker commented in 1859, "that their pupils are taken from school at the very time when their studies became most useful and attractive."[40] About half the black youngsters in New York City and in Philadelphia in the pre-Civil War era had no formal education.[41] A well-known nineteenth-century Negro educator, Charles B. Ray, also complained that the city's black school facilities were "painfully neglected," "old and dilapidated." "Caste Schools," they were called.[42]

And those who managed to complete a public-school education regularly entered a hostile world which refused to recognize and employ their talents. "After a boy has spent five or six years in the school," a teacher observed in 1830, "and . . . is spoken of in terms of high approbation by respectable visitors . . . he leaves school, with every avenue closed against him, which is open to the white boy for honorable and respectable rank in society, doomed to encounter as much prejudice and contempt, as if he were not only destitute of that education . . . but as if he were *incapable* of receiving it."[43] The black Reverend Theodore S. Wright made the same point a few years later. The most gifted children, he said, could find no place willing to use their skills: "He can't work. Let him be ever so skilled as a mechanic, up starts prejudice, and says 'I won't work in the shop if you do.' Here he is scourged by prejudice and has to go back, and sink down to some of the employments which white men leave for the most degraded."[44]

What followed then, as now, was the debasing cycle of low economic status, low self-esteem, limited aspiration, self-destructive or publicly destructive behavior. Parents employed as menials could offer their children little hope for a brighter future. "Instead of seeing their parents in honor and office with power to command and be obeyed," a sensitive observer recorded in the 1850's, the Negro child "sees them at the command of others. Instead of the deferential greeting, and the respected salutation, he hears his father nicknamed 'Dick,' 'Jake,' or 'Ole uncle,' or perhaps 'Cuffy,' or 'Old nigger'; his mother he hears addressed as 'Moll Dinah,' 'Suke,' or 'Black Bets.' Thus in early childhood the circumstances that surround his parents, and the treatment they receive from [the] community all tend to diminish his respect and reverence for them, hence to depreciate his respect for himself." It was not surprising to overhear a five- or six-year-old girl in 1859 saying to herself: "O dear, I do wish I was white."[45]

Similar problems are encountered in the late nineteenth and twentieth centuries. Black educator William Lewis Bulkley, who entered the city school system in the 1890's and made a distinguished career for himself, said his students left school "to open doors, run bells or hustle hash" for the rest of their lives. "On every hand avenues of employment are shut tight, discouragement begins and [Negro children] leave school to work at any menial employment that offers itself," Bulkley wrote.[46] Social worker Frances Blascoer made a comprehensive study of Negro school children in 1915 and found the same to be true then. "There was a general belief among school principals, social workers and colored clergymen that the restriction of industrial opportunities because of their race was sapping the ambition of the colored boys and girls," Blascoer wrote.[47] School administrators throughout the twentieth century hesitated to raise the aspirations of black youngsters in fear, they said, that it would only lead to frustrations after graduation. In 1937 an educator bluntly told an investigating commission of the state legislature: "Let's not mince words; let's be practical about this matter—the Negro is not employed in certain trades, so why permit him to waste his time taking such courses."[48] Malcolm X, one of the smartest students in his Lansing school, once told his English teacher he'd like to become a lawyer. He was immediately advised to be more "realistic" in his aspirations and since his woodworking was admired by all he was told to take up carpentry.[49]

The continuing crisis of ghetto education has received unprecedented attention in the last decade. Studies of the 1950's and 1960's demonstrate that about half the Harlem youngsters who go to high school drop out before completing their degrees. Most who graduate receive "general" diplomas—little more than a recognition of attendance—and their economic status differs not at all from that of the others who dropped out.[50] James B. Conant, shocked by what he discovered, maintained that such conditions threatened the future of America: "Potentialities for trouble—indeed possibilities of disaster—are surely there," he said.[51] What is new in this situation is not that it exists, but that Conant and others are willing to see it for the first time. "Our Children Have Been Dying" for generations.[52]

Other comparable examples may be studied (and it is the primary intention of this essay to spur such interests)—those relating to health, family structure and social disorganization, to cite a few—but my guess is that the thesis would remain unchanged. Despite occasional periods of racial reform, little has ever been done that permanently improved the fundamental conditions of life of most Negroes in Northern cities, nor if New York City is a representative model has any ideology or program radically improved the tone of race relations in the North. What has in our time been called the social pathology of the ghetto[53] is evident throughout our history; the wounds of centuries have not healed because they've rarely been treated. By all standard measurements of human troubles in the city, the ghetto has always been with us—it has tragically endured.

Bibliographical Essay

The following is a select bibliographical essay of the works I found most valuable in the preparation of this book, and others that may be useful to scholars.

General Historical Studies of Negro New York

There are only two published books which attempt to survey the history of Negroes in New York City from colonial times to the early twentieth century: James Weldon Johnson's *Black Manhattan* (New York, 1930), and Mary White Ovington's *Half A Man: The Status of the Negro in New York* (New York, 1911). Johnson's study is primarily a popular and impressionistic history—he did not intend it to be otherwise. I found it most valuable for Johnson's sketches and recollections of Negroes in the theater and arts in the early twentieth century. *Half A Man* was written in the years 1904–1910. Although Miss Ovington tries to summarize the early history of Negro New York, she is most successful in describing life in the Tenderloin and San Juan Hill in the first decade of the twentieth century. The first chapter of her *The Walls Came Tumbling Down* (New York, 1947) is largely a repetition of the material she published in *Half A Man,* but it does include some new and interesting facts. George Edmund Haynes's *The Negro At Work in New York City: A Study in Economic Progress* (New York, 1912) originated as a Columbia University doctoral dissertation. Haynes later became a Negro leader of national prominence. His information on nineteenth-century economic life is sketchy, but his detailed material on Negro employment and small business in the early twentieth century, often derived from personal investigation and interviews, is enlightening.

The best over-all history of Negro New York is an unpublished study completed during the Great Depression under the auspices of the WPA. The three drafts of this social history are located in the Schomburg Collection. Each of the research papers written for the project is also at the Schomburg. I benefited from these throughout my research but used the utmost caution in double-checking the information they contained. Few were totally free of error, and many were simply exercises in research and writing. Seth M. Scheiner has recently published *Negro Mecca* (New York, 1965), a revision of his 1963 New York University dissertation.

Statistical Sources

It is possible to obtain the most exact information relating to Negroes in New York City, and elsewhere, through various publications of the United States Bureau of the Census. *Negro Population in the United States, 1790–1915* (Washington, D.C., 1918) and *Negroes in the United States, 1920–1932* (Washington, D.C., 1935) are the two most important general works. I have thoroughly surveyed each census volume on *Population, Occupations* and *Vital Statistics* for the years 1890–1930. These compilations not only provide a breakdown of Negro population by state, city and ward, but also present exact data on the numbers of Negroes employed in every occupation in each borough in New York City. A special volume on New York City, the results of an intensive investigation in the 1880's, was published with the *Eleventh Census, 1890: Vital Statistics of New York City and Brooklyn* (Washington, D.C., 1894). *Statistics of Women at Work, 1900* (Washington, D.C., 1907) also contains important information on Negro life.

Unfortunately, the published New York State Censuses of 1905 and 1915 omit data on the racial composition of the population. In the nineteenth century, however, the state census did record such information. Franklin B. Hough's *Statistics of Population of the City and County of New York. . . .* (New York, 1866), derived from the state census of 1865, is a handy abstract of statistical information on the Negro in the city from the seventeenth century to the Civil War. Walter Laidlaw's *Population of the City of New York, 1890–1930* (New York, 1932) and his massive *Statistical Sources for Demographic Studies of Greater New York, 1910* (New York, 1913), 2 Vols., are guides to twentieth-century conditions.

A number of reports of municipal agencies and local reform and social work organizations provided specific information which could not be obtained from other works. Annual Negro mortality and birth statistics are published in the *Annual Report of the New York City Health Department*. Articles on the health problems of the Negro community regularly appeared in the *Monthly Bulletin* of the Department of Health. One of the most important sources of municipal statistics is the *First Report of the Tenement House Commission of New York City* (New York, 1902), Vol. II. The Commission compiled data on the number of families on each block in Manhattan in 1902. Every block is numbered, and can be located on maps printed in this volume. The ethnic composition of every Manhattan street—by numbers of families—can be derived from this source. Statistics on Negro population, wages, rent, the cost of living generally, and many other things may be found in The Federation of

Churches and Christian Workers of New York City, *First, Second, Third and Fourth Sociological Canvasses* [each a separate volume] (New York, 1896–1899); Louise Bolard More, *Wage-Earners' Budgets: A Study of Standards and Cost of Living in New York City* (New York, 1907); and Robert Coit Chapin, *The Standard of Living Among Workingmen's Families in New York City* (New York, 1909).

Negro Migration and Settlement

Negro migration to the North prior to the First World War has largely been overlooked by historians and social scientists. World War I is usually considered the starting point of significant Negro migration to northern urban areas. Thomas J. Woofter, however, in his *Negro Problems in Cities* (New York, 1928), links Negro migration to the general trend of rural movement to urban centers since 1900. Woofter's *Negro Migration: Changes in Rural Organization and Population of the Cotton Belt* (New York, 1920) primarily deals with migration within Georgia. I was made aware of the earlier movement of Negroes northward through the maps in C. Warren Thornthwaite, *Internal Migration in the United States* (Philadelphia, 1934). Contemporary recognition of the movement of southern Negroes during and after World War I led to a voluminous literature on the subject. Louise Venable Kennedy's and Frank Ross's book-length bibliography, *Bibliography of Negro Migration* (New York, 1926), is an extraordinary source that lists the major contemporary studies and articles on migration. This book was completed as part of a general survey of Negro migration undertaken at Columbia University in the 1920's. Three other volumes were produced as a result of this project: Louise Venable Kennedy, *The Negro Peasant Turns Cityward: Effects of Recent Migrations to Northern Centers* (New York, 1930); Edward E. Lewis, *The Mobility of the Negro: A Study in the American Labor Supply* (New York, 1931); and Clyde Vernon Kiser, *Sea Island to City: A Study of St. Helena Islanders in Harlem and Other Urban Centers* (New York, 1932). Carter G. Woodson's *A Century of Negro Migration* (Washington, D.C., 1918), is now outdated. There is interesting information in Arna W. Bontemps and Jack Conroy, *They Seek A City* (New York, 1945). Charles S. Johnson traces the increase in Negro migration to the decline of European immigration in "Substitution of Negro Labor for European Immigrant Labor," *Proceedings of the National Conference of Social Work* (New York, 1926), 317–327. The standard work on West Indian immigration is Ira De Augustine Reid, *The Negro Immigrant: His Background, Characteristics and Social Adjustment, 1899–1937* (New York, 1939).

Difficulties confronted by the earliest generation of southern Negroes in New York City are studied in the following: Paul Laurence Dunbar, *The Sport of the Gods* (New York, 1902); the entire issues of *Charities,* XV (October 7, 1905), and *The Annals,* XXVII (May 1906); George Edmund Haynes, "The Movement of Negroes from the Country to the

City," *The Southern Workman*, XLII (April 1913), 230–236. A few contemporary masters' essays in sociology proved exceptionally helpful: William Fielding Ogburn, "The Richmond Negro in New York City: His Social Mind As Seen in His Pleasures" (1909); Robert Zachariah Johnstone, "The Negro in New York—His Social Attainments and Prospects" (1911); Seymour Paul, "A Group of Virginia Negroes in New York City" (1912); and Ernest Jasper Hopper, "A Northern Negro Group" (1912). All were written at Columbia University.

C. Vann Woodward's *The Strange Career of Jim Crow* (New York, 1955) is the starting point for any analysis of southern reaction to the Negro in the late nineteenth and early twentieth centuries. It is a groundbreaking work, but the thesis is somewhat overstated. Excellent articles on the subject are: Guion Griffis Johnson, "The Ideology of White Supremacy, 1876–1910," in Fletcher Melvin Green, ed., *Essays in Southern History* (Chapel Hill, 1949), 124–156; Bert James Loewenberg, "Efforts of the South to Encourage Immigration, 1865–1900," *South Atlantic Quarterly*, XXXIII (October 1934), 363–385; and Rowland T. Berthoff, "Southern Attitudes Toward Immigration, 1865–1914," *Journal of Southern History*, XVII (August 1951), 328–360.

Of the dozens of racist volumes produced at the turn of the century, the following are representative and gory: Charles Carroll, *The Negro A Beast, or, In the Image of God* (St. Louis, Mo., 1900); William P. Calhoun, *The Caucasian and the Negro in the United States. They Must Separate. If Not, Then Extermination . . .* (Columbia, S.C., 1902); Robert Wilson Shufeldt, *The Negro: A Menace to American Civilization* (Boston, 1907); Carlyle McKinley, *An Appeal to Pharaoh: The Negro Problem and Its Radical Solution* (Columbia, S.C., 1907); William P. Pickett, *The Negro Problem: Abraham Lincoln's Solution* (New York, 1909). Popular attitudes of southern white farmers toward the Negro, 1899–1901, are preserved in hundreds of pages of testimony in *Report of the Industrial Commission on Agriculture and Agricultural Labor* (Washington, D.C., 1901), Vol. X.

Negro New York—Pre-Harlem

There are a few published articles on the Negro population of New York City in the nineteenth century: Arnett G. Lindsay, "The Economic Condition of the Negroes of New York Prior to 1861," *Journal of Negro History*, VI (April 1921), 190–199; Aaron Hamlet Payne, "The Negro in New York Prior to 1860," *The Howard Review*, I (June 1923), 1–64; Leo H. Hirsch, Jr., "New York and the Negro, from 1783 to 1865," *Journal of Negro History*, XVI (October 1931), 382–471; Monroe N. Work, "The Life of Charles B. Ray," *ibid.*, IV (October 1919), 361–371; Herman D. Bloch, "The New York City Negro and Occupational Eviction, 1860–1910," *International Review of Social History*, V (1960), 26–38, and Bloch, "The New York Negro's Battle for Political Rights, 1777–

1865," *ibid.*, IX (1964), 65–80; Seth M. Scheiner, "The New York City Negro and the Tenement," *New York History*, XLV (October 1964), 304–315. Biographical sketches of prominent nineteenth-century New York Negroes are in the WPA research papers. Leon F. Litwak's *North of Slavery: The Negro in the Free States, 1790–1860* (Chicago, 1961) is primarily a study of interracial relations and institutional prejudice, but it does contain some interesting descriptive material on Negroes in northern cities.

A more thorough understanding of nineteenth-century Negro life may be derived from masters' essays and doctoral dissertations. Leslie H. Fishel, Jr., "The North and the Negro, 1865–1900: A Study in Race Discrimination" (Ph.D. dissertation, Harvard University, 1954), and August Meier, "Negro Racial Thought in the Age of Booker T. Washington, Circa 1880–1915" (Ph.D. dissertation, Columbia University, 1957), are works of high quality and thoroughness. Meier's excellent dissertation was published in somewhat abbreviated form as *Negro Thought in America, 1880–1915: Racial Ideologies in the Age of Booker T. Washington* (Ann Arbor, 1963). The following Columbia University masters' essays all contain solid information: John P. Clyde, "The Negro in New York City" (1899); Lucille Genevieve Lomax, "A Social History of the Negro Population in the Section of New York City known as Greenwich Village" (1930); Philmore L. Groisser, "The Free Negro in New York State, 1850–1860" (1939); and Joan Cohen, "The Social Conditions of the Negro in New York City, 1830–1865" (1951). Robert S. Dixon's "Education of the Negro in the City of New York, 1853–1900" (M.A. thesis, City College, 1935) has useful data.

There are a few primary sources which describe nineteenth-century Negro life in New York City. Among the most important are: Charles C. Andrews, *The History of the New-York African Free Schools* . . . (New York, 1830), and the extant copies of the New York Negro newspaper *The Colored American* for 1837 and 1838. Both are at the New-York Historical Society. The Schomburg Collection has microfilms of *The New York Globe* (1883–1885), *The New York Freeman* (1885–1887), and *The New York Age* (1887–1891, and scattered issues in the 1890's).

Two manuscript collections at the Schomburg, the John Edward Bruce and the Reverend Dr. Alexander Crummell Manuscripts, contain some relevant data. Waring Cuney, "Interview with Jerome B. Peterson: An Account of Wealthy Negroes, 1880–1890" (WPA research paper); "Wealthy Negroes," *The New York Times*, July 14, 1895, and "New York's Rich Negroes," *The Sun*, January 18, 1903, present biographical sketches of colored businessmen and professionals. All of Jacob Riis's books on New York City mention Negroes, as does his "The Black Half," *The Crisis*, V (April 1913), 298–299. Perceptive commentaries by W. E. B. DuBois may be found in a series of articles he wrote in 1901: *The New York Times*, November 17, 24, December 1, 8, 15, 1901. The reminiscences of Samuel R. Scottron were published in "The Industrial and Professional Pursuits of Colored People of Old New York," *The*

Colored American Magazine, XIII (October 1907), 265–267, and in many issues of *The New York Age* in 1905. Samuel J. Battle, the first Negro policeman in Manhattan, describes Negro life in the Tenderloin and San Juan Hill in "The Reminiscences of Samuel J. Battle" (Oral History Research Office, Columbia University, 1960). Some personal papers of John B. Nail, the Negro café owner, are preserved in the James Weldon Johnson Collection, Yale University. (Mrs. James Weldon Johnson, Grace Nail Johnson, is Nail's daughter.) Other material is recorded in James Weldon Johnson, *The Autobiography of an Ex-Coloured Man* (New York, 1960); Reverend Dr. Adam Clayton Powell, Sr., *Against the Tide: An Autobiography* (New York, 1938); Bishop Alexander Walters, *My Life and Work* (New York, 1917); Bishop Reverdy C. Ransom, *The Pilgrimage of Harriet Ransom's Son* (Nashville, 1950?); and James Weldon Johnson, *Along This Way* (New York, 1933).

Interracial Relations

The softening of institutionalized racial prejudices in New York City and in the North in the late nineteenth century is documented in Fishel's "The North and the Negro, 1865–1900." Magnificent collections of plays and vaudeville shows, from which I attempted to draw a characterization of the stereotype of the Negro at the turn of the century, are in the Schomburg Collection, and in the Atkinson Collection at the University of Chicago. The same image emerges in stories about Negroes in the white press, and in the newspaper clippings compiled in scrapbooks at the Gumby Collection, Columbia University. Manuscripts relating to the race riot of 1900—letters of protest, transcripts of the trials of policemen, the police commissioners' report to the mayor—are in the Van Wyck Papers, Municipal Archives. The case of "The People vs. Arthur J. Harris," including summaries of the testimony of witnesses, is on file at the Municipal Court Building. A few papers of the Citizens' Protective League are among the Miscellaneous Manuscripts, Schomburg Collection. [Frank Moss], *Story of the Riot: Persecution of Negroes by Roughs and Policemen in the City of New York, August, 1900* (New York, 1900), contains the notarized statements of eighty Negroes beaten during the riot.

As racial antagonism increased in New York City, municipal reformers attempted to improve the position of the Negro. Practically all the social service agencies that came into existence by 1915 are discussed in Frances Blascoer's *Colored School Children in New York* (New York, 1915). The *Annual Reports* of the New York Colored Mission are in the Schomburg Collection, and the Certificate of Incorporation of that society is in the New York City Hall of Records—along with the papers of incorporation of most other social service agencies. A director of the Urban League, L. Hollingsworth Wood, wrote on the organization in "The New York Colored Mission—Good Samaritan Inn," *Opportunity,* V (March 1927), 82–83. A biographical sketch of Victoria Earle Matthews and a summary of her work at the White Rose Home appeared in her obituary, *The New York Age*, March 14, 1907. Also see Mary L. Lewis, "The White Rose Industrial Association," *The Messenger*, VII (April 1925). On Frances A. Kellor and the National League for the Protection of Colored Women see: Kellor, *Out of Work: A Study of Employment Agencies. . . .* (New York, 1904); Kellor, "Assisted Emigration from the South: The Women," *Charities*, XV (October 7, 1905), 12–13; "Conditions Existing in the City of New York prior to May 1st 1904, Which Led to the Creation of this Office," a statement by the Commissioner of Licenses, in the Municipal Archives; and E. M. Rhodes, "The Protection of Girls Who Travel: A National Movement," *The Colored American Magazine*, XIII (August 1907), 114–115. Mary White Ovington's "Reminiscences" were published in the Baltimore *Afro-American*, September 1932–February 1933. Other information on her activities may be found in *Half A Man; The Walls Came Tumbling Down; How the NAACP Began* (New York, 1914); "The National Association for the Advancement of Colored People," *Journal of Negro History*, IX (April 1924), 107–116; "Beginnings of the NAACP," *The Crisis*, XXXII (June 1926), 76–77. Miss Ovington's secretary, Mrs. Richetta G. Wallace, was helpful in supplying details about her life that were unclear in the sources. Manuscript material on the CIICN is in the J. G. Phelps Stokes Collection, Columbia University. "The Reminiscences of William J. Schieffelin," president of the CIICN and supporter of Booker T. Washington, are in the Columbia University Oral History Research Office. It would have been impossible to re-create the life of William Lewis Bulkley without the assistance of the New York City Board of Education. I was permitted to see Bulkley's files, which contained valuable biographical information as well as an outline of his public school career. The archivist of Syracuse University sent me photostatic copies of Bulkley's graduate school records.

The political power of the Negro community increased as the population expanded. White politicians and municipal officials began to court Negro support and accede to demands that Negroes made for political recognition and patronage. The voluminous correspondence of Charles W. Anderson and Booker T. Washington, covering the years 1904–1915, often deals with questions of patronage and local Negro politics. It is a key manuscript source. These letters are in the Washington Papers, Library of Congress. The mayoralty papers of John F. Hylan, James J. Walker and Fiorello H. La Guardia are the major sources for a study of the changed attitudes of white politicians. Also see the Oral History reminiscences at Columbia University of Martin C. Ansorge (1949) and Samuel S. Koenig (1950). The *Official Canvass of Votes*, published each year in the *City Record*, records votes by election districts. The Schomburg Collection has files of newspaper clippings on Anderson's and Morton's careers, as it does for many other prominent Negroes. Other than this, it is necessary to turn to articles which appeared in *The New York Age* over decades to reconstruct the political history of Negro New York. On the rise of the

Negro National Guard Unit see: Arthur W. Little, *From Harlem to the Rhine: The Story of New York's Colored Volunteers* (New York, 1936); Emmett J. Scott, *Scott's Official History of the American Negro in the World War* (Chicago, 1919); Addie W. Hunton and Kathryn M. Johnson, *Two Colored Women with the American Expeditionary Forces* (Brooklyn, 1920); and Wilmer F. Lucas, "The 369th Infantry, New York National Guard," *The Crisis*, XXXVII (April 1930), 120–123. Unfortunately, the papers of Charles S. Whitman, the New York governor so active in Negro affairs, have not been preserved in the state archives.

White Harlem

There is no general history of New York City that would stand the test of modern scholarship. The nineteenth-century multi-volumed tomes, such as James Grant Wilson's *The Memorial History of the City of New-York* (New York, 1893), 4 Vols., are the works of antiquarians. They peripherally discuss Harlem in the colonial period, devote many pages to the Revolutionary Battle of Harlem Heights, but never re-create or develop an organized history of this section of Manhattan. James Riker, *Revised History of Harlem (City of New York): Its Origin and Early Annals* (New York, 1904), is the most significant secondary source. Its main concern is the history of Harlem in the seventeenth century. The 1904 edition (the first edition appeared in 1881) contains some 400 pages of genealogical data. Riker's diffuse footnotes often include information on Harlem in the nineteenth century, and I found them as valuable as the text. Colonel Alonzo B. Caldwell, *A Lecture: The History of Harlem* (New York, 1882), and Herbert Manchester, *The Story of Harlem and the Empire Savings Bank, 1889–1929* (New York, 1929), were helpful pamphlets.

To find out about white Harlem in the late nineteenth and early twentieth centuries, it was necessary to turn almost exclusively to primary sources. A number of local magazines and newspapers have survived. The New-York Historical Society has a file of the biweekly *Harlem Local Reporter* which is practically complete for the 1890's. This newspaper, along with the *Harlem Monthly Magazine* (1893, 1902), *Harlem Life* (1899–1900), *Harlem Magazine* (1912–1933), and the *Harlem Home News* (1911–1913), provides the best information on the history of the white population of Harlem.

Reminiscences of white Harlem by old residents contain fascinating information. Frederick A. Birmingham's *It Was Fun While It Lasted* (Philadelphia, 1960) is the only book-length memoir. The following were the most significant pamphlets and articles: Ella Bunner Graff, *Reminiscences of Old Harlem* (n.p., 1933); Richard Webber, Jr., "Historical Sketch of Harlem," *Harlem Magazine*, I (October 1912), 16–17; "Old-Timers' Tales of Harlem's Growth," *ibid.*, III (December 1914), 16–22; Samuel M. Brown, "Harlem's Early Transit Facilities," *ibid.*, IV (September 1915), 11; Michael C. O'Brien, "Memories of Hooker's Building," *ibid.*, IV (May 1916), 11, 17; Charles H. Fuller, "Harlem—from 'Cradle Days' to Now," *ibid.*, XV (October 1925), 6–7, 24; Berta Gilbert, "Morgenthau Reminisces About Harlem," *ibid.*, XX (May 1931), 4, 15–16; Elmer Rice, "A New York Childhood," *The New Yorker*, IV (September 22, 1928), 36–40; "The Reminiscences of John T. Hettrick" (Oral History Research Office, Columbia University, 1949).

Land and property speculation played an important part in the history of Harlem from the 1870's through the 1920's. The "Harlem Commons Syndicate" is an unpublished collection of newspaper clippings, letters, wills and other items relating to Harlem property. It, along with Walter H. Shupe's *First Annual Statement of the Harlem Commons Syndicate* (New York, 1884), and *Deduction of the Harlaem Commons* (New York, 1872), are at the New-York Historical Society. The New-York Historical Society also has a number of boxes of material on Harlem land transfers. Sections of Abraham Cahan's *The Rise of David Levinsky* (New York, 1960) magnificently re-create the mood of the turn-of-the-century real estate craze. The best source of information on speculation in Harlem land is the weekly *Real Estate Record and Builders' Guide*. It is possible to check each transfer of property in New York City through its columns, and every issue is voluminous. The *Record and Guide* also published *A History of Real Estate, Building, and Architecture in New York City During the Last Quarter of a Century* (New York, 1898). For an example of one speculator who made great profit in Harlem and built an opera house there, see Vincent Sheean, *Oscar Hammerstein I: The Life and Exploits of an Impresario* (New York, 1956). Henry Pennington Toler's *Arise Take Thy Journey* (New York, 1903) and Carl Horton Pierce's *New Harlem Past and Present: The Story of an Amazing Civic Wrong Now At Last To Be Righted* (New York, 1903) were written by men who tried to prove that descendants of colonial landholders still had legal claim to Harlem land.

The publications of many local institutions have survived—political clubs, social and charitable organizations, churches. See: Reverend Edgar Tilton, Jr., *The Reformed Low Dutch Church of Harlem: Historical Sketch* (New York, 1910); Collegiate Reformed Church of Harlem, *Two Hundred and Fiftieth Anniversary* (New York, 1910); William B. Silber, *A History of St. James Methodist Episcopal Church at Harlem, New York City, 1830–1880* (New York, 1882); Harlem Independent Schützen Corps, *Golden Jubilee, 1880–1930* (New York, 1930); *Harlem Library Bulletin* (1902–1905); Harlem Relief Society of the City of New York, *Annual Reports* (1893–1920); and the various publications of the Harlem Democratic and Republican clubs, the Harlem Regatta Association, and the Harlem Board of Commerce.

Organized opposition to Negro settlement may be traced through articles which appeared in *Harlem Magazine*, *The Crisis* and *The New York Age*, and the *Harlem Home News*. Some of the restrictive housing covenants were filed at the New York City Hall of Records. I knew of the existence of one covenant through press reports and located it and others by systematically checking the real estate records for each Harlem block. The city classifies each street by a specific number. With this number it is possible to locate separate "Libers" which record property transactions in New York City from colonial times to the present. The following "Libers," each in Section 7 at the Hall of Records, contained restrictive agreements: 127, pp. 365–368; 128, pp. 145–150; 151, pp. 134–146; 152, pp. 297–301; 159, pp. 7–15. *Harlem Survey* (New York, 1917?), published by the Harlem Board of Commerce, is a valuable document that depicts the radical ethnic changes that had taken place in Harlem by the First World War.

Negro Harlem

A substantial literature on the ghetto has accumulated in the last three years. A good starting point is Ernest Kaiser's bibliographical essay "The Literature of Harlem," *Freedomways*, III (Summer 1963), 276–291. This entire issue of *Freedomways* is devoted to Harlem and has appeared, in somewhat different form, as John Henrik Clarke, ed., *Harlem: A Community in Transition* (New York, 1965). Two exceptionally valuable studies are HARYOU, *Youth in the Ghetto: A Study of the Consequences of Powerlessness and a Blueprint for Change* (New York, 1964), and Columbia University Bureau of Applied Social Research, *A Harlem Almanac* (New York, 1964).

Claude McKay's *Harlem: Negro Metropolis* (New York, 1940) is primarily a popular history of Harlem in the 1930's. Myrtle Evangeline Pollard, "Harlem As Is: The Negro Business and Economic Community. . . ." (M.A. thesis, City College, 1937), also deals with the 1930's. It is a lengthy study, but rambling and disorganized. Information on the founding of Negro Harlem may be obtained from James Weldon Johnson's *Black Manhattan* (New York, 1930), and Robert C. Weaver's *Negro Ghetto* (New York, 1948).

The early history of Negro Harlem may best be studied through the thousands of articles and items that appeared in *The New York Age* (1905–1940) and *The Crisis* (1911–1940). Other helpful data were printed in *The Colored American Magazine* (1900–1909), *The Southern Workman* (1900–1920), *The Messenger* (1919–1929), and *Opportunity* (1923–1940).

Philip A. Payton, Jr.'s role in the founding of Negro Harlem has luckily been preserved in the Booker T. Washington Papers, Library of Congress. Emmett J. Scott, Washington's secretary, was a director of the Afro-American Realty Company and received regular reports of the corporation's activities from Fred R. Moore. Without their correspondence, it would have been impossible to uncover reliable information on the Realty Company. The "Certificate of Incorporation of the Afro-American Realty Company, June 15, 1904" is on file in the Hall of Records. "Crowder vs. Philip A. Payton, Jr. and the Afro-American Realty Company" (1907), the stockholders' suit against Payton, also threw valuable light on the company's operations. The plaintiff's charges, orders for the arrest of Payton, the final decision of the court and a copy of the original *Prospectus* of the corporation (New York, 1904) were all preserved with the papers of the case at the Hall of Records.

Most of the prominent people active in Harlem· in the earliest years of Negro settlement are dead. The exact dates of their deaths may be checked in the annual *Negro Year Books*. A few contemporary records and statements are extant, however. An important interview with Payton was recorded in *The New York Age*, December 5, 1912. John M. Royall's description of the real estate boom, its collapse, and the subsequent movement of Negroes into Harlem is found in the *Age*, June 11, 1914. The role of the Reverend Dr. Hutchens C. Bishop in buying property for St. Philip's Protestant Episcopal Church is reviewed by his son in Waring Cuney, "Notes from an Interview with Reverend Shelton Bishop" (WPA research paper). A few letters of John E. Nail are in the James Weldon Johnson Collection, Yale University. The "John E. Nail Scrapbook," also at Yale, includes newspaper clippings of the Nail and Parker realty company, notices of Nail's death and material on Harlem in the Depression. Nail was also interviewed by a WPA researcher and described Negro Harlem in the first decade of the twentieth century in Odetta Harper, "Interview with John E. Nail." Powell's *Against the Tide* includes interesting recollections of Harlem, as does Battle's "Reminiscences."

Contemporary surveys and articles on Harlem proved to be of the utmost importance in tracing the emergence of the community as a slum. The most valuable were: National League on Urban Conditions Among Negroes, *Housing Conditions Among Negroes in Harlem, New York City* (New York, 1915); Benjamin H. Locke's "The Community Life of a Harlem Group of Negroes" (M.A. thesis, Columbia University, 1913); the New York Urban League's "Twenty-Four Hundred Negro Families in Harlem: An Interpretation of the Living Conditions of Small Wage-Earners" (typescript, Schomburg Collection, 1927); "Harlem: Mecca of the New Negro," *The Survey*, LIII (March 1, 1925), 629–724; E. F. Dycoff, "A Negro City in New York," *The Outlook*, CVIII (December 23, 1914), 949–954; Harlem Board of Commerce, *Harlem Survey* (New York, 1917?); Rollin Lynde Hartt, "'I'd Like to Show You Harlem!'" *The Independent*, CV (April 2, 1921), 334–335; Eric D. Walrond, "The Black City," *The Messenger*, VI (January 1924), 13–14; Chester T. Crowell, "The World's Largest Negro City," *The Saturday Evening Post*, CXCVIII (August 8, 1925), 8–9, 93–94, 97; "The Negro City," *The American Review of Reviews*, LXXIII (March 1926), 323–324; Owen R. Lovejoy, "Justice for the Negro Child," *Opportunity*, VII (June 1929), 174–176; E. Franklin Frazier, "Negro Harlem: An Ecological Study," *The American Journal of Sociology*, XLIII (July 1937), 72–88; The Mayor's Commission on Conditions in Harlem, "The Negro in Harlem: A Report on Social and Economic Conditions Responsible for the Outbreak of March 19, 1935" (La Guardia Papers). Files on Negro life through the 1940's are included in the La Guardia Collection. James Ford, *et al., Slums and Housing: With Special Reference to New York City* (Cambridge, Mass., 1936), 2 Vols.; *Annual Reports of City and Suburban Homes Company* (1896–1930); Winfred B. Nathan, *Health Conditions in North Harlem, 1923–1927* (New York, 1932); Owen R. Lovejoy, *The Negro Children of New York* (New York, 1932); The President's Conference on Home Building and Home Ownership, *Report of the Committee on Negro Housing* (Washington, D.C., 1932); and Committee of Fourteen, *Annual Reports* (1905–1929), are exceptionally enlightening.

The revolutionary recognition of the Negro and Harlem in the twenties may best be traced through the periodicals. Practically all the major magazines, from the *Ladies' Home Journal* to *The American Mercury*, printed stories and articles on Negro life. The white journals that carried the most material on the Negro were: *The World Tomorrow, The Nation, The New Republic* and *The American Mercury*. The major theme I attempted to develop in the "Epilogue" is clearly typified by the following articles: Konrad Bercovici, "The Black Blocks of Manhattan," *Harper's Monthly Magazine*, CXLIX (October 1924), 613–623; Clement Wood, "Hosea Before the Rotary Club," *The World Tomorrow*, VIII (July 1925), 209–210; George S. Schuyler, "Blessed are the Sons of Ham," *The Nation*, CXXIV (March 23, 1927), 313–315; Joseph Wood Krutch, "Black Ecstasy," *ibid.*, CXXV (October 26, 1927), 456–458; and Hermann Keyserling, "What the Negro Means to America," *The Atlantic Monthly*, CXLIV (October 1929), 444–447. Diana N. Lockard's "The Negro on the Stage in the Nineteen Twenties" (M.A. thesis, Columbia University, 1960) analyzes the image of the Negro as "savage" in the drama. Perceptive contemporary criticisms of the distorted view of Negro life that emerged when the "Negro was in vogue" are Wallace Thurman's "Nephews of Uncle Remus," *The Independent*, CXIX (September 24, 1927), 296–298; and George Chester Morse's superb "The Fictitious Negro," *The Outlook and Independent*, CLII (August 21, 1929), 648–649.

The most valuable manuscript sources for a study of the Negro Renaissance are the papers of Carl Van Vechten, James Weldon Johnson and Langston Hughes in the James Weldon Johnson Memorial Collection, Yale University. Two excellent autobiographies by Negro writers discuss Harlem in the twenties: Langston Hughes, *The Big Sea* (New York, 1940); and Claude McKay, *A Long Way From Home* (New York, 1937). Wallace Thurman's *Infants of the Spring* (New York, 1932) is a novel about the Renaissance. The novels written by Negroes in the twenties are full of information on Harlem life, as are "The Reminiscences of Carl Van Vechten" (1960); "The Reminiscences of George S. Schuyler" (1960); and "The Reminiscences of Benjamin McLaurin" (1960). All these are in Columbia University's immensely valuable Oral History Collection. Alain Locke's *The New Negro: An Interpretation* (New York, 1925) is a classic statement of the views of the 1920's.

Notes

NOTES TO CHAPTER 1

1. Booker T. Washington and Robert E. Park, *The Man Farthest Down: A Record of Observation and Study in Europe* (New York, 1912), *passim*.

2. Bureau of the Census, *Negro Population in the United States, 1790–1915* (Washington, D.C., 1918), pp. 43–45; *Twelfth Census, 1900: Population* (Washington, D.C., 1901), I, 869, II, 193; Kelly Miller, "The Economic Handicap of the Negro in the North," *The Annals of the American Academy of Political and Social Science*, XXVII (May 1906), 547.

3. Mary White Ovington, *Half a Man: The Status of the Negro in New York* (New York, 1911), p. 148.

4. Bureau of the Census, *Statistics of Women at Work, 1900* (Washington, D.C., 1907), p. 146; W. E. B. DuBois, "The Black North," *The New York Times*, November 17, 1901; Federation of Churches and Christian Workers in New York City, *Second Sociological Canvass* (New York, 1897), p. 40.

5. *Twelfth Census: Occupations*, pp. 634–641.

6. Booker T. Washington, *The Negro in Business* (Boston, 1907), pp. 104–109; Samuel R. Scottron, "The Industrial and Professional Pursuits of Colored People of Old New York," *The Colored American Magazine*, XIII (October 1907), 265–266; *The New York Age*, July 27, 1905; *The New York Globe*, March 29, 1884; *The New York Times*, January 30, 1901; "The Negro Artisan," *Atlanta University Publications, No. 7* (Atlanta, 1902), p. 134.

7. Waring Cuney, "Interview with Jerome B. Peterson: An Account of Wealthy Negroes, 1880–1890" (WPA research paper, Schomburg Collection); Ovington, *Half A Man*, p. 29.

8. "Wealthy Negroes," *The New York Times*, July 14, 1895; "The Negro American Artisan," *Atlanta University Publications, No. 17* (Atlanta, 1912), p. 132.

9. Henry Collins Brown, *In the Golden Nineties* (New York, 1928), p. 84.

10. Ovington, *Half A Man*, p. 78.

11. Robert Ernst, *Immigrant Life in New York City, 1825–1863* (New York, 1949), pp. 66–67, 214–217.

12. *Ibid.*, p. 104.

13. James W. C. Pennington, *The Fugitive Blacksmith* (New York, 1849), p. 55.

14. Quoted in Lucille Genevieve Lomax, "A Social History of the Negro

Population Living in the Section of New York City known as Greenwich Village" (M.A. thesis, Columbia University, 1930), pp. 79–81.

15. "Our Friends Discourage Us," *The Colored American*, August 12, 1837; "Importance of the Mechanic Arts to Colored Youth," *ibid.*, December 22, 1838; Arnett G. Lindsay, "The Economic Condition of the Negroes of New York Prior to 1861," *Journal of Negro History*, VI (April 1921), 195.

16. "The Negro Artisan," pp. 29–30.

17. Quoted in Philmore L. Groisser, "The Free Negro in New York State, 1850–1860" (M.A. thesis, Columbia University, 1939), pp. 102–114.

18. Lomax, "A Social History," pp. 81–84.

19. The following are the exact numbers of Negroes in New York City who owned enough property to qualify for the franchise, 1825–1865. Adapted from Franklin B. Hough, *Statistics of Population of the City and County of New York. . . .* (New York, 1866), p. 240.

	Total Negro Population of New York City	Qualified to Vote
1825	12,559	68
1835	15,061	84
1845	12,913	255
1855	11,840	100
1865	9,943	44

20. Ernst, *Immigrant Life*, p. 67.

21. Hough, *Statistics of Population*, p. 230; *Negro Population, 1790–1915*, p. 64.

22. Bureau of the Census, *Vital Statistics of New York City and Brooklyn, 1890* (Washington, D.C., 1894), pp. 7 and *passim;* City of New York, *Annual Reports of the Department of Health* and *Monthly Bulletins of the Department of Health; Twelfth Census, 1900: Vital Statistics,* III, 458–464; R. R. Wright Jr., "The Migration of Negroes to the North," *The Annals of the Academy of Political and Social Science,* XXVII (May 1906), 563.

23. *Vital Statistics of New York City*, pp. 14, 441; New York Colored Mission, *Annual Report for 1905* (New York, 1906), p. 11; *The New York Age*, January 22, 1922.

24. For contemporary recognition of these medical problems and their continuing influence on Negro life see: "Mortality Among Negroes in Cities," *Atlanta University Publications, No. 1* (Atlanta, 1903); "Social and Physical Conditions of Negroes in Cities," *Atlanta University Publications, No. 2* (Atlanta, 1897); The New York Association for Improving the Condition of the Poor, *Health Work for Mothers and Children in a Colored Community* (New York, 1924); Ransom S. Hooker, *Maternal Mortality in New York City: A Study of all Puerperal Deaths, 1930–1932* (New York, 1933), pp. 57, 77, 91, 163–165; Jean Downes, *An Experiment in the Control of Tuberculosis Among Negroes* (New York, 1950); Janet B. Hardy and Miriam E. Brailey, *Tuberculosis in White and Negro Children* (Cambridge, Massachusetts, 1958), 2 Vols.

25. Mary White Ovington, *The Walls Came Tumbling Down* (New York, 1947), p. 51.

26. *The New York Globe,* February 16, 1884.

27. *Ibid.,* January 6, 1883.

28. The following sketches of Negro neighborhoods in the early nineteenth

century are primarily intended to describe them. Little information about them is extant and to find the exact causes for the decline of Five Points and the succession of Greenwich Village as Negro sections would involve a more detailed study of fugitive sources than I have been able to make.

29. Joan Cohen, "The Social Conditions of the Negro in New York City, 1830–1865" (M.A. thesis, Columbia University, 1951), pp. 6–12; Herbert Marshall and Mildred Stock, *Ira Aldridge: The Negro Tragedian* (London, 1958), p. 32; *The New York Freeman*, February 19, 1887; *The Colored American*, March 25, 1837; Caroline F. Ware, *Greenwich Village, 1920–1930; A Comment on American Civilization in the Post-War Years* (Boston, 1935), p. 12.

30. Charles Dickens, *American Notes* (London, 1900), pp. 102–105; Ernst, *Immigrant Life*, p. 39.

31. Charles C. Andrews, *The History of the New-York African Free Schools. . . .* (New York, 1830), pp. 57, 121–122.

32. Five Points House of Industry, *Monthly Record*, II (May 1858), 54–55.

33. "The Dens of Death," *New York Daily Tribune*, June 5, 1850; G. G. Foster, *New York by Gas-Light: With Here and There a Streak of Sunshine* (New York, 1850), pp. 56–57.

34. Ernst, *Immigrant Life*, p. 39; Groisser, "Free Negro," p. 88; Kate Holladay Claghorn, "The Foreign Immigrant in New York City," *Reports of the Industrial Commission on Immigration . . . and on Education* (Washington, D.C., 1911), XV, 453.

35. For a photograph of the Workingmen's House and the Negroes of the district see James Ford, *et al.*, *Slums and Housing: With Special Reference to New York City* (Cambridge, Mass., 1936), II, 673.

36. Marshall and Stock, *Ira Aldridge*, pp. 28–47.

37. Wesley Curtwright, "Rise of Negro Churches in New York, 1827–1860" (WPA research paper, Schomburg Collection), p. 1; *The New York Age*, December 9, 1909, March 30, 1911, April 17, 1913; Monroe N. Work, "The Life of Charles B. Ray," *Journal of Negro History*, IV (October 1919), 361–371.

38. *The New York Age*, May 29, 1913; *The Crisis*, IX (February 1915), 166–167.

39. Andrews, *African Free Schools*, pp. 23–24.

40. *The New York Freeman*, January 31, 1885; "History of Our Schools in New York," *The New York Age*, July 13, 1905; Wesley Curtwright, "Life of James McCune Smith"; Simon Williamson, "The Life and Work of Henry Highland Garnet" (WPA research papers, Schomburg Collection); *Calendar of the Manuscripts in the Schomburg Collection of Negro Literature* (New York, 1943?), pp. 51–55. On the Downing family see Lorenzo T. Greene, "Protest Against Separate Schools in Rhode Island, 1859," *The Midwest Journal*, I (Summer 1949), 102–103; and *The Crisis*, XII (June 1916), 61.

41. Rev. Dr. Alexander Crummell, "Lecture Sermon on John Peterson, for 50 years a Teacher in An African School. . . ." Crummell Manuscripts, Schomburg Collection.

42. *The New York Age*, March 22, 1890; "For He Was a Good Man" (1886), Crummell Papers.

43. Five Points House of Industry, *Monthly Record*, IV (May 1860), 12–14.

44. *The New York Freeman*, February 19, 1887.

45. New York City Board of Health, *Annual Report, 1893* (New York, 1894), p. 164.

46. Charles W. Gardner, *The Doctor and the Devil: A Startling Exposé of Municipal Corruption* (New York, 1894), pp. 52, 57.

47. Henry Collins Brown, *In the Golden Nineties* (New York, 1928), p. 348.

48. Jacob A. Riis, *How the Other Half Lives: Studies Among the Tenements of New York* (New York, 1957), p. 117.

49. Lomax, "A Social History," pp. 91 ff; Jacob Riis, "The Black Half," *The Crisis*, V (April 1913), 298–299.

50. *The New York Age*, July 27, 1905.

51. Riis, *How the Other Half Lives*, p. 112.

52. John P. Clyde, "The Negro in New York City" (M.A. thesis, Columbia University, 1899), p. 3.

53. Bureau of the Census, *Eleventh Census, 1890: Population* (Washington, D.C., 1894), I, 564.

54. "Bruce Grits Column" (n.d.), Bruce Manuscripts, Schomburg Collection.

55. William McAdoo, *Guarding a Great City* (New York, 1906), pp. 91, 93 ff.

56. Ovington, *The Walls Came Tumbling Down*, p. 40; *The New York Age*, December 26, 1912; "Oldest New York's Past and Present Racial and Religious Conditions," *Federation*, III (December 1904), 4; George Edmund Haynes, *The Negro at Work in New York City: A Study in Economic Progress*, in Columbia University *Studies in History, Economics and Public Law*, XLIX (New York, 1912), p. 51.

57. "The Reminiscences of Samuel J. Battle" (Oral History Research Office, Columbia University, 1960), p. 22; Ovington, *The Walls Came Tumbling Down*, p. 35; William Fielding Ogburn, "The Richmond Negro in New York City: His Social Mind as Seen in His Pleasures" (M.A. thesis, Columbia University, 1909), p. 48; Niles Carpenter, *The Sociology of City Life* (New York, 1932), p. 78; *The New York Age*, January 13, 1916.

58. The Federation of Churches and Christian Workers in New York City, *Second Sociological Canvass* (New York, 1897), p. 85; *The New York Freeman*, March 7, 1885; Riis, *How the Other Half Lives*, pp. 113–114.

59. These were Mount Olivet Baptist, St. Mark's Methodist Episcopal, St. James Presbyterian, Union Baptist, St. Cyprian's Episcopal and St. Benedict the Moor's Roman Catholic.

60. Ovington, *The Walls Came Tumbling Down*, p. 40; Ogburn, "The Richmond Negro," pp. 49–52.

61. M. R. Werner, *It Happened In New York* (New York, 1957), pp. 36–116; Reverend Dr. Charles H. Parkhurst, *Our Fight With Tammany* (New York, 1895), *passim; New York Daily Tribune*, August 25, 1900; *The New York Times*, January 8, 1898, March 19, 1900, March 31, 1900; *The New York Age*, April 5, 1906, March 21, 1907; "The Terrible Tenderloin," *ibid.*, March 29, 1906.

62. Richard J. Latimer, "History of Negro Saloons" (WPA research paper, Schomburg Collection); James Weldon Johnson, *Along This Way* (New York, 1933), pp. 175–176; Riis, *How the Other Half Lives*, p. 117. At one place the management provided dusters for clients who bet themselves down to their bare essentials. James Weldon Johnson, *The Autobiography of an Ex-Coloured Man* (New York, 1960), pp. 96–97.

63. Reverend Charles S. Morris, "The Terrible Tenderloin," *The New York Age*, February 22, March 29, 1906.

64. Powell successfully campaigned to clean up West Fortieth Street. "The

last woman carried out of the block to serve four months in Blackwell's Island for prostitution was a member of the Abyssinian Church and one of the loudest shouters of the Sunday Morning Prayer Band," he remembered. Reverend Dr. Adam Clayton Powell, Sr., *Against the Tide: An Autobiography* (New York, 1938), pp. 49–57. See also Reverend Charles S. Morris to J. G. Phelps Stokes, December 6, 1902 (Stokes Manuscripts, Columbia University, Box 18).

65. Battle, "Reminiscences," p. 35.

66. "The Reminiscences of John T. Hettrick" (Oral History Research Office, Columbia University, 1949), pp. 46–47, 73; Wirt Howe, *New York at the Turn of the Century, 1899–1916* (Toronto, 1946), p. 27.

67. Bishop Reverdy C. Ransom, *The Pilgrimage of Harriet Ransom's Son* (Nashville, 1950?), p. 202.

68. St. Benedict's was partially founded on a legacy to Negro Roman Catholics bequeathed by Father Thomas Farrell. Father Farrell was a pastor of a church in Greenwich Village during the Civil War and a strong supporter of the Union. When the war began he nailed an American flag to the roof of his church and vowed to leave the country if the South won. St. Benedict's was opened in November 1883 on Bleecker Street and moved to West Fifty-third Street in 1898. It remains there today. *The New York Age*, February 20, 1913; "St. Benedict the Moor" (WPA research paper, Schomburg Collection); *The New York Globe*, July 28, 1883, November 10, 1883, March 8, 1884.

69. *New York Daily Tribune*, August 29, 1900.

70. A Negro YMCA had been established in 1867 but it was unsuccessful. Mount Olivet Baptist Church, *Mortgage Liquidation Journal* (New York, 1946), p. 9; Silas Xavier Floyd, *Life of Charles T. Walker, D.D.* (Nashville, 1902), pp. 104, 108–109; *The New York Age*, May 9, 1912, May 22, 1913. The title "Colored Men's YMCA" comes from a letterhead in the J. G. Phelps Stokes Manuscripts, Columbia University, Box 18.

71. Johnson, *Along This Way*, pp. 152, 170–183.

72. Haynes, *The Negro at Work*, pp. 80–81; Ernest Jasper Hopper, "A Northern Negro Group" (M.A. thesis, Columbia University, 1912), pp. 22–23, 34–35.

73. The Federation of Churches and Christian Workers in New York City, *First Sociological Canvass* (New York, 1896), pp. 88–90, 92, 97, 102–105; *Second Sociological Canvass*, pp. 16–17, 20–21, 25–27, 67–70, 73, 76, 85, 93–95; Frances Blascoer, *Colored School Children in New York* (New York, 1915); Robert Coit Chapin, *The Standard of Living Among Workingmen's Families in New York City* (New York, 1909), *passim;* Louis Bolard More, *Wage-Earners' Budgets: A Study of Standards and Cost of Living in New York City* (New York, 1907), *passim;* Tom McConnon, *Angels in Hell's Kitchen* (New York, 1959), p. 35; Ovington, *Half A Man*, p. 36.

74. W. E. B. DuBois, *The Souls of Black Folk: Essays and Sketches* (New York, 1953), p. 161.

NOTES TO CHAPTER 2

1. *The New York Age*, August 1, 1912.

2. There are two problems that confront anyone attempting to determine the increase in New York City's Negro population, 1890–1910. In 1890 the Census reported statistics for "Colored" people, including Chinese, Japanese and Indians. Another problem is the consolidation of counties into Greater New York

in 1898. "New York City" meant Manhattan and the Bronx in 1890, but Manhattan, Bronx, Queens, Richmond and Brooklyn in 1900 and 1910. I have corrected the statistics of 1890 for these two problems so that a more accurate comparison of population growth can be made. In doing so I have subtracted 5,000 (which is approximately accurate) from the 1890 figure to allow for Oriental population:

	1890	1900	1910
Manhattan	25,674	36,246	60,534
Bronx		2,370	4,117
Brooklyn	10,946	18,367	22,708
Queens	3,582	2,611	3,198
Richmond	981	1,072	1,152
	41,183		
	−5,000		
Approximately	36,183	60,666	91,709

United States Census Office, *Eleventh Census, 1890: Population* (Washington, D.C., 1895), I, 509, 543–545; *Twelfth Census, 1900: Population* (Washington, D.C., 1901), I, CXX, 631; *Thirteenth Census, 1910: Population* (Washington, D.C., 1913), I, 178.

3. William L. Bulkley, "Race Prejudice as Viewed from an Economic Standpoint," *Proceedings of the National Negro Conference* (New York, 1909?), p. 90.

4. Mary White Ovington, *Half A Man: The Status of the Negro in New York* (New York, 1911), p. 48.

5. Sources of New York State In-Migrant Population, 1910.

Born in:

Virginia	29,157
North Carolina	10,283
South Carolina	6,698
Georgia	3,792
Florida	1,257

There are no published statistics that give the exact states of birth for the Negro population of New York City in these years. These statistics are for the state as a whole. New York City was the center of the migrant population, however, and it is safe to assume that these figures would be even more heavily weighted on the side of southern migration there. They do present the general trend of migration to New York City typical of pre-World War I years. United States Census, *Negro Population in the United States, 1790–1915* (Washington, D.C., 1918), pp. 77, 78. In 1890, of the 68,543 Negroes in New York State, 40,177 were born there. United States Census, *Eleventh Census, 1890: Population* (Washington, D.C., 1895), I, 576–579.

6. *The New York Age*, June 5, 1913.

7. *Negro Population, 1790–1915*, p. 68.

8. The exact figure is 198,679. *Idem.* These statistics omit the migration of 1910–1914, which was considerable.

9. United States Census, *Thirteenth Census, 1910: Population* (Washington, D.C., 1913), IV, 707–709.

10. C. Warren Thornthwaite, *Internal Migration in the United States* (Philadelphia, 1934), p. 12 and map opposite p. 12.

11. George Edmund Haynes, *The Negro at Work in New York City: A Study in Economic Progress*, in Columbia University *Studies in History, Economics and Public Law*, XLIX (New York, 1912), p. 17.

12. Frederick J. Brown, *The Northward Movement of the Colored Population: A Statistical Study* (Baltimore, 1897).

13. W. E. B. DuBois, "The Negro in Farmville, Virginia: A Social Study," United States Department of Labor, *Bulletin No. 14* (Washington, D.C., 1895), p. 5.

14. W. E. B. DuBois, *The Philadelphia Negro: A Social Study*, in University of Pennsylvania Series in *Political Economy and Public Law*, XIV (Philadelphia, 1899), pp. 79–80.

15. W. E. B. DuBois, "The Black Vote of Philadelphia," *Charities: A Review of Local and General Philanthopy*, XV (October 7, 1905), 31.

16. John P. Clyde, "The Negro in New York City" (M.A. thesis, Columbia University, 1899), p. 3.

17. "The Condition of Negroes in Various Cities," United States Department of Labor *Bulletin*, II (May 1897), 257–369.

18. Carl Kelsey, "Some Causes of Negro Emigration: The Men," *Charities*, XV (October 7, 1905), 16.

19. *Ibid.* In 1906 *The Annals of the American Academy of Political and Social Science* also studied "The Industrial Conditions of the Negro in the North," XXVII (May 1906); and in 1913 "The Negro's Progress in Fifty Years," a book-length survey, in XLIX (September 1913).

20. *The New York Age*, June 10, 1907, July 4, 1912, November 16, 1911.

21. *The New York Times*, March 18, 1901.

22. Carter G. Woodson, *A Century of Negro Migration* (Washington, D.C., 1918), pp. 159–166.

23. "Hope something has been done regarding Pinchback." Booker T. Washington to Charles W. Anderson, July 4, 1905; Anderson to Washington, July 17, 1909, July 20, 1909, January 11, 1910, August 1, 1910. Washington Papers, Library of Congress.

24. *The New York Age*, October 6, 1910, May 22, 1913.

25. *Ibid.*, November 21, 1907; *New York Daily Tribune*, September 5, 1900; August Meier, "Negro Racial Thought in the Age of Booker T. Washington, Circa 1880–1915" (Ph.D. dissertation, Columbia University, 1957), p. 807.

26. DuBois, *Philadelphia Negro*, pp. 44–45.

27. Lillian Brandt, "The Make-Up of Negro City Groups," *Charities*, XV (October 7, 1905), 7–11.

28. Helen A. Tucker, "Negro Craftsmen in New York," *The Southern Workman*, XXXVI (October 1907), 545–551.

29. Haynes, *Negro At Work*, pp. 58–61.

30. W. E. B. DuBois, "The Northern Negro Problem," *The New York Age*, October 3, 1907; R. R. Wright, Jr., "The Migration of Negroes to the North," *The Annals*, XLIX (September 1913), 570.

31. *The New York Age*, April 6, 1905.

32. Paul Oliver, *Blues Fell This Morning: The Meaning of the Blues* (London, 1960), p. 23.

33. *The New York Freeman,* September 19, 1885.

34. *The New York Age,* September 22, 1910; William Fielding Ogburn, "The Richmond Negro in New York City: His Social Mind as Seen in His Pleasures" (M.A. thesis, Columbia University, 1909), p. 33.

35. *Report of the Industrial Commission on Agriculture and Agricultural Labor.* . . . (Washington, D.C., 1901), X, 351; R. R. Wright, Jr., "The Migration of Negroes," 564. *Report of Industrial Commission* hereafter cited as *USIC,* X.

36. R. R. Wright, Jr., "The Migration of Negroes," 566; Haynes, *Negro At Work,* pp. 31–32.

37. Seymour Paul, "A Group of Virginia Negroes in New York City" (M.A. thesis, Columbia University, 1912), p. 41.

38. C. Vann Woodward, *The Strange Career of Jim Crow* (New York, 1955), chapter II; C. Vann Woodward, *Origins of the New South, passim;* Woodson, *A Century of Negro Migration,* p. 161; NAACP, *Thirty Years of Lynching in the United States, 1889–1918* (New York, 1919); James Elbert Cutler, *Lynch Law: An Investigation into the History of Lynching in the United States* (New York, 1905), p. 161; Paul, "A Group of Virginia Negroes," p. 12; Ida B. Wells, *A Red Record: Tabulated Statistics and Alleged Causes of Lynching in the United States* (Chicago, 1895).

39. Meier, "Negro Racial Thought," pp. 157–158, 916.

40. There actually were some Negroes who did go to Africa in these years. An Abraham Lincoln African Aid and Colonization Society was established in Oklahoma in 1909. "Chief Sam" (Alfred Charles Sam), a bogus African chief, outfitted a steamer which left Galveston in 1914. T. McCants Stewart, Negro clergyman and lawyer of New York, finally settled in Liberia in 1906. *The New York Age,* April 27, 1905, November 30, 1905, February 26, 1906, September 20, 1906, January 3, 1907, July 11, 1907, September 16, 1909, January 22, 1914, January 29, 1914, April 2, 1914, July 9, 1914. William E. Bittle and Gilbert Geis, *The Longest Way Home: Chief Alfred C. Sam's Back to Africa Movement* (Detroit, 1964).

41. *The New York Age,* January 10, 1907, July 4, 1912.

42. *The New York Freeman,* February 28, 1885; Bulkley, "Race Prejudice," p. 90.

43. *New York Daily Tribune,* September 5, 22, 1900.

44. "Negro Exodus to Cities," *The New York Times,* May 28, 1903; Sutton E. Griggs, *Needs of the South* (Nashville, 1909), pp. 15, 28.

45. Tucker, "Negro Craftsmen," 550.

46. Paul, "A Group of Virginia Negroes," p. 35.

47. *Ibid.,* p. 31.

48. *The New York Age,* October 3, 1907; W. E. B. DuBois, "The Black North," *The New York Times,* December 15, 1901.

49. Langston Hughes, "New York," *Phylon,* XI (1950), 14.

50. R. R. Wright, Jr., "The Negro in Times of Industrial Unrest," *Charities,* XV (October 7, 1905), 69, 73; James Samuel Stemons, "The Industrial Color-Line in the North," *The Century Magazine,* LX (July 1900), 477–478; Mary White Ovington, "The Negro in the Trades Unions of New York," *The Annals,* XXVII (May 1906), 555–556.

51. Stanley M. Elkins has added great depth to our understanding of the personal psychological blight of the Peculiar Institution in his *Slavery* (Chicago, 1959).

52. W. E. B. DuBois, *The Souls of Black Folk* (New York, 1953), p. 68.

53. Edwin R. Embree, *Brown America* (New York, 1931), p. 37. "The Government by whom we were emancipated left us completely in the power of our former owners." Frederick Douglass, *Three Addresses on the Relations Subsisting between the White and Colored People of the United States* (Washington, D.C., 1886), p. 16. Also see Alrutheus Ambush Taylor, *The Negro in South Carolina During Reconstruction* (Washington, D.C., 1924), pp. 25, 55; Alrutheus Ambush Taylor, *The Negro in Reconstruction Virginia* (Washington, D.C., 1926), pp. 90–97.

54. W. E. B. DuBois, "The Negro Farmer," *Supplementary Analysis and Derivative Tables of the Twelfth Census* (Washington, D.C., 1906), *passim*.

55. *USIC*, X, 379, 820.

56. *Ibid.*, 428.

57. Haynes, *Negro at Work*, p. 30n.

58. J. S. Clarkson to J. E. Bruce, March 21, 1891. Bruce Manuscripts, Schomburg Collection.

59. George Edmund Haynes, "Conditions Among Negroes in the Cities," *The Annals*, XLIX (September 1913), 105–119.

60. *USIC*, xxi.

61. Philip A. Bruce, *The Plantation Negro as a Freeman: Observations on His Character, Condition, and Prospects in Virginia* (New York, 1889), p. 182.

62. John R. Rogers, *The Importance of Time as a Factor in the Solution of the Negro Problem* (New York, 1900?), p. 7; William Hannibal Thomas, *The American Negro: What He Was, What He Is, and What He May Become* (New York, 1901), p. 63.

63. John Ambrose Price, *The Negro: Past, Present and Future* (New York, 1907), pp. 101–103; Howard W. Odum, *Social and Mental Traits of the Negro: A Study in Race Traits, Tendencies, and Prospects* (New York, 1910), pp. 184ff; Thomas Nelson Page, "The Negro: The Southerner's Problem," *McClure's Magazine*, XXIII (May 1904), 100; *USIC*, X, 166–167.

64. Page, "The Negro," 100; Edgar Gardner Murphy, *The Task of The South* (n.p., 1903), pp. 29–34; Guion Griffis Johnson, "The Ideology of White Supremacy, 1876–1910," in Fletcher Melvin Green, ed., *Essays in Southern History* (Chapel Hill, 1949), 148, 154n., 156.

65. J. J. Watson, "Churches and Religious Conditions," *The Annals*, XLIX (September, 1913), 126. ". . . In the time of slavery the parents exercised a much stricter control over their children than they do now." *The Southern Workman*, XXIX (February 1900), 68.

66. *USIC*, X, 50; 504; 770; W. E. B. DuBois, *The Souls of Black Folk: Essays and Sketches* (New York, 1903), p. 310.

67. Frederick S. Hoffman, *Race Traits and Tendencies of the American Negro* (New York, 1896), p. 310.

68. William P. Calhoun, *The Caucasian and the Negro in the United States. They Must Separate. If Not, Then Extermination; A Proposed Solution: Colonization* (Columbia, S.C., 1902), pp. 139, 141–142.

69. Robert Wilson Shufeldt, *The Negro: A Menace to American Civilization* (Boston, 1907); Carlyle McKinley, *An Appeal to Pharaoh: The Negro Problem, and Its Radical Solution* (Columbia, S.C., 1907); Charles Carroll, *The Negro a Beast, or, In the Image of God* (St. Louis, Mo., 1900); William P. Pickett, *The Negro Problem: Abraham Lincoln's Solution* (New York, 1909).

70. Bert James Loewenberg, "Efforts of the South to Encourage Immigration, 1865–1900," *South Atlantic Quarterly*, XXXIII (October 1934), 363–385.

71. In 1907 the Attorney General of the United States ruled that states, but not individuals, could advertise for immigrants abroad and pay their passage to America without violating the Contract Labor Law. *The New York Age,* March 28, 1907, June 21, 1906, July 19, 1906, October 31, 1907.

72. C. Vann Woodward, *Origins of the New South, passim; The New York Age,* May 26, 1888.

73. Rowland T. Berthoff, "Southern Attitudes Toward Immigration, 1865–1914," *The Journal of Southern History,* XVII (August 1951), 328–360.

74. *USIC,* X, 382–383; 518.

75. *Raleigh Signal,* February 28, 1889, quoted in Frenise A. Logan, "The Movement of Negroes from North Carolina, 1876–1894," *The North Carolina Historical Review,* XXIII (January 1956), 54.

76. Price, *The Negro,* pp. 105–106.

77. DuBois, "Negro Farmer," pp. 523, 527, 532–533; Woofter, *Negro Migration, passim.*

78. Senator George F. Hoar to J. E. Bruce, February 25, 1895. Bruce Manuscripts, Schomburg Collection; "Italian Cotton vs. Negro Cotton in the Southern States," *The Colored American Magazine,* XIII (September 1907), 167.

79. Commissioner of Labor, *Labor Laws of the United States, with Decisions of Courts Relating Thereto,* in *Twenty-Second Annual Report* (Washington, D.C., 1908), *passim.*

80. Lafayette M. Hershaw, "Peonage," The American Negro Academy, *Occasional Paper, No. 15* (Washington, D.C., 1915), 10; Katherine Coman, "The Negro as a Peasant Farmer," *Quarterly Publication of the American Statistical Association,* IX (June 1904), 54; Thomas J. Edward, "The Tenant System and Some Changes Since Emancipation," *The Annals,* XLIX (September 1913), 38–46.

81. Jack Greenberg, *Race Relations and the American Law* (New York, 1960), p. 157. A Georgia plantation owner stated in an interview in 1903 that "the planters in the black belt will have to maintain their right to claim their contract labor, or else they will have to go out of business. . . ." Quoted in John R. Commons, *Races and Immigrants in America* (New York, 1920), p. 138. In *Bailey* vs. *State of Alabama,* the Supreme Court held such labor contracts in violation of the Thirteenth Amendment. Justice Hughes, delivering the opinion of the Court, concluded that the "words involuntary servitude have a 'larger meaning than slavery.' . . . The plain intention was to abolish slavery of whatever name and form . . . to make labor free, by prohibiting that control by which the personal service of one man is disposed or coerced for another's benefit. . . ." 219 *United States Reports,* 241.

82. *The Crisis,* XIII (December 1916), 89.

83. *USIC,* X, 429; *The New York Age,* May 11, June 8, 29, 1905; Logan, "The Movement of Negroes," 57–59.

84. *USIC,* X, 906–912.

85. *Ibid.,* 514; *The New York Age,* June 29, 1905. "Without the colored laborer," wrote Frederick Douglass, "the South would be a howling wilderness, given up to bats, owls, wolves, and bears." Douglass, *Three Addresses,* p. 13.

86. *Report of the New York City Commission on Congestion of Population* (New York, 1911), p. 11.

87. Benjamin H. Locke, "The Community Life of a Harlem Group of Negroes" (M.A. thesis, Columbia University, 1913), *passim.*

88. Ogburn, "The Richmond Negro," *passim;* Paul, "A Group of Virginia

Negroes," *passim;* R. R. Wright, Jr., "The Negro in Times of Industrial Unrest," 565; Clyde Vernon Kiser, *Sea Island to City: A Study of St. Helena Islanders in Harlem and Other Urban Centers* (New York, 1932), p. 219.

89. Ogburn, "The Richmond Negro," p. 47.

90. This is an exact copy of a typical labor contract. See Carl Kelsey, "Some Causes for Negro Emigration: The Men," *Charities,* XV (October 7, 1905), 16–17.

91. *USIC,* X, 428.

92. *Report of the New York Colored Mission, 1872* (New York, 1873), p. 8.

93. *The New York Age,* May 8, 1913.

94. Clyde, "Negro in New York City," p. 6; "Night Clubs," James Weldon Johnson Collection, Yale University.

95. *The Richmond Planet* carried regular advertisements for these companies. See, for example, February 23, 1895; Kelsey, "Some Causes for Negro Emigration," 17; *The New York Age,* September 11, 1913, February 5, 1914.

96. *The New York Globe,* July 7, 1883, October 18, 1884; *The New York Age,* August 17, December 28, 1905.

97. *The New York Age,* December 24, 1908, July 27, 1911.

98. "The Movement of Negroes from the Country to the City," *The Southern Workman,* XLII (April, 1913), 235.

99. DuBois, "The Black North," *The New York Times,* November 17, 1901; *The New York Age,* May 11, 1905.

100. Paul, "A Group of Virginia Negroes," p. 3.

101. The Reminiscences of Samuel J. Battle" (Oral History Research Office, Columbia University, 1960), p. 13.

102. Paul Laurence Dunbar, *The Sport of the Gods* (New York, 1902), pp. 112–113.

103. Folkways Records, Album No. FC7533.

104. Nellie M. Quander, "A Study of Insurance Among Negroes in the State of Virginia" (M.A. thesis, Columbia University, 1914), pp. 37 ff; "Some Efforts of American Negroes for their Own Social Betterment," *Atlanta University Publications, No. 3* (Atlanta, 1898), p. 19.

105. *The New York Age,* April 7, 1910.

106. Silas Xavier Floyd, *Life of Charles T. Walker, D.D.* (Nashville, 1902), pp. 105–106.

107. *The New York Age,* February 28, 1907.

108. "Dear Charlie—I find that the chitterlings went forward to you last week." Booker T. Washington to Charles W. Anderson, January 26, 1907. Washington Papers, Library of Congress, Box 35.

109. Box 18 in the J. G. Phelps Stokes Papers at Columbia University is full of requests for contributions from Negro institutions. Also see B. C. Caldwell, "The Work of the Jeanes and Slater Funds," *The Annals,* XLIX (September 1913), 173–176.

110. *The New York Freeman,* November 28, 1885; *The New York Age,* July 13, 1889, June 25, 1908, February 9, 1911.

111. Odette Harper, "Sketch of Pig Foot Mary" (WPA research paper, Schomburg Collection); *The New York Age,* November 12, 1927, July 20, 27, 1929.

112. *The New York Age,* February 13, 1913.

113. Mary McFadden, "Madame Walker" and Odette Harper, "Biographical Sketch of Madame C. J. Walker" (WPA research papers, Schomburg Col-

lection); *Baltimore Afro-American*, March 5, 1932. For pictures of the cabin in which Madame Walker was born and her villa in New York see *The Messenger*, VI (August, 1924), 255.

114. Biographical sketches of these and many other successful Negro migrants are scattered throughout the issues of *The New York Age*.

115. Reverend Dr. Adam Clayton Powell, Sr., *Against the Tide: An Autobiography* (New York, 1938).

116. Ray Stannard Baker, *Following the Color Line* (New York, 1908), *passim; The New York Age*, January 27, 1910.

NOTES TO CHAPTER 3

1. Linton Satterthwait, "The Color-Line in New Jersey," *The Arena*, XXV (April 1906), 394.

2. Joan Cohen, "The Social Conditions of the Negro in New York City, 1830–1865" (M.A. thesis, Columbia University, 1951), p. 38; Philmore L. Groisser, "The Free Negro in New York State, 1850–1860" (M.A. thesis, Columbia University, 1939), pp. 31–39; Dwight Lowell Dumond, *Antislavery: The Crusade for Freedom in America* (Ann Arbor, 1961), p. 300; Wilbur Young, "Plymouth Congregational Church" (WPA research paper, Schomburg Collection); *The Colored American*, June 3, 1837; Robert Ernst, *Immigrant Life in New York City, 1825–1863* (New York, 1949), p. 41; Charles Townsend Harris, *Memories of Manhattan in the Sixties and Seventies* (New York, 1928), p. 61.

3. Herman D. Bloch, "The New York Negro's Battle for Political Rights, 1777–1865," *International Review of Social History*, IX (1964), 65–80.

4. "Health and Physique of the Negro American," *Atlanta University Studies, No. 11* (Atlanta, 1906), p. 91; *The New York Age*, June 8, 1889, April 26, 1890, April 11, 1891; *The New York Globe*, February 9, 1884.

5. *The New York Freeman*, July 2, 1887.

6. The subject of Negro education in the North and in New York City is studied in great detail in Robert S. Dixon, "Education of the Negro in the City of New York, 1853–1900" (M.A. thesis, City College, 1935), and Leslie H. Fishel, Jr., "The North and the Negro, 1865–1900: A Study in Race Discrimination" (Ph.D. dissertation, Harvard University, 1954), pp. 183–248, 326–369, *passim*. The Fishel study is the most thorough history of race relations in the North in the late nineteenth century, and discusses all the specific points mentioned in this paragraph. It does not, however, emphasize the changing patterns of racial attitudes as I have attempted to do. Also see *The New York Age*, February 9, 1924, and June 27, 1925, for information on Miss Frazier.

7. *The New York Globe*, December 29, 1883; *The New York Freeman*, June 19, 1886, July 9, 1887; *The New York Age*, June 7, 1890.

8. Jacob A. Riis, *How the Other Half Lives: Studies Among the Poor* (London, 1891), p. 148.

9. *The New York Age*, January 4, 1900.

10. *The New York Globe*, June 30, August 25, September 1, 1883; *The New York Freeman*, July 25, 1885, July 16, September 3. 1887.

11. *The New York Globe*, July 28, 1883.

12. *The New York Freeman*, July 16, 1887.

13. W. E. B. DuBois, "The Black North," *The New York Times*, December 15, 1901. For an analysis of this attitude as a major theme in the Negro novel,

1890–1920, see Robert A. Bone, *The Negro Novel in America* (New Haven, 1958).

14. Benjamin Brawley, "The Negro Genius," *The Southern Workman*, XLIV (May 1915), 305–308.

15. The success of *The Clansman* and other of Dixon's works in the first two decades of the twentieth century must be set against the rise of racial antagonism in the North in these years. See *The Crisis*, LXII (January 1955), 37–38; Maxwell Bloomfield, "Dixon's *The Leopard's Spots:* A Study in Popular Racism," *American Quarterly*, XVI (Fall 1964), 387–401.

16. *The New York Age*, January 4, 1906.

17. *The Churchman*, L (September 20, 1884), 316.

18. *The Worker*, May 18, 1902.

19. Moses F. Sweester and Simeon Ford, *How to Know New York City* (New York, 1888), p. 11.

20. Dumond, *Antislavery*, p. 330.

21. *Harlem Local Reporter*, February 25, May 6, 1893; "Black Patti," in James Weldon Johnson Collection, Yale University.

22. *The New York Times*, October 4, 1900.

23. Diana N. Lockard, "The Negro on the Stage of the Nineteen Twenties" (M.A. thesis, Columbia University, 1960), chap. 1.

24. "Emma Harris" (WPA research paper, Schomburg Collection).

25. Mary White Ovington, *Half A Man: The Status of the Negro in New York* (New York, 1911), p. 135.

26. William L. Holler, "Bert Williams (Egbert Austin Williams), 1875–1922" (WPA research paper, Schomburg Collection), p. 3.

27. These plays and many others are collected in a special box of Negro vaudeville and minstrel shows at the Schomburg Collection, and in the extensive and magnificent Atkinson Collection at the University of Chicago.

28. Henry Collins Brown, *In the Golden Nineties* (New York, 1928), pp. 173–174; Howard W. Odum and Guy B. Johnson, *Negro Workaday Songs* (Chapel Hill, N.C., 1926), pp. 183–184.

29. George H. Coes, *Badly Sold: A Negro Act in Two Scenes* (Chicago, 1893).

30. F. E. Hiland, *Careless Cupid* (Boston, 1893), p. 5.

31. James Weldon Johnson, *Along This Way* (New York, 1933), pp. 152–153.

32. *The New York Age*, January 31, 1907; "Wealthy Negroes," *The New York Times*, July 14, 1895.

33. Johnson, *Along This Way, passim;* Holler, "Bert Williams," p. 8.

34. Johnson, *Along This Way*, p. 159. The game "Hit the Nigger" or "African Dodger"—in which vacationers threw baseballs at the head of a *real* person—was played in New York summer resorts until outlawed in 1917. *The Crisis*, X (July 1915), 114; *The New York Times*, October 2, 1916, May 3, 1917.

35. Lawrence Gelbert, "Bert Williams: Philosophical Tidbits Gleaned from His Songs and Stories" (WPA research paper, Schomburg Collection).

36. "We Wear the Mask," in *The Complete Poems of Paul Laurence Dunbar* (New York, 1921), p. 71.

37. W. E. B. DuBois, *The Souls of Black Folk: Essays and Sketches* (New York, 1953), p. 10.

38. "Raw Labor from the South," *The New York Times*, September 9, 1900.

39. There was a constant mockery of the so-called Negro aristocracy and

"400." See, for example, John Martin, "Dancing Through Two Centuries," Museum of the City of New York *Bulletin*, V (February 1942), 37.

40. Kelly Miller, "The Industrial Condition of the Negro in the North," *The Annals*, XXVII (May 1906), 543.

41. *The New York Freeman*, July 11, 1887.

42. A clipping of this review which appeared in *The Bookman*, XXIII (April 1906), was pasted on the back of an obituary of Dunbar in the Gumby Collection, Columbia University.

43. *The New York Age*, April 1, 1909.

44. Clyde Griffen, "An Urban Church in Ferment: The Episcopal Church in New York City, 1880–1900" (Ph.D. dissertation, Columbia University, 1960), p. 32.

45. *The New York Age*, April 17, 1913.

46. *The Crisis*, VIII (May 1914), 12.

47. *Ibid.*, IX (December 1914), 77–80.

48. *The New York Age*, April 9, June 21, 1906.

49. *Ibid.*, February 13, 1913. The depth of national racial hatred in the early twentieth century is clearly demonstrated in the longing and search for a "White Hope" to defeat Jack Johnson. Some of the anti-Negro legislation of these years, including those laws banning intermarriage, were partially stimulated by Johnson's second marriage to a white woman. See clippings under title "White Hope" in Gumby Collection, Columbia University. Florence Murray, editor, *The Negro Handbook, 1949* (New York, 1949), p. 350. The following, an article by Bill Corum in the *New York Journal American* at the time of Johnson's death in 1946, clearly demonstrates this racial antipathy: "Man alive, how I hated Jack Johnson in the Summer of 1910! Nor did I ever quite get over it. In recent years it became an aversion rather than a stronger feeling. But when he knocked out Jeffries at Reno I hated him. . . . I was 15 in a town of 4,000 people and until the Jeffries-Johnson fight . . . never heard of professional boxing." Clipping in Gumby Collection.

50. Ovington, *Half A Man*, p. 210. *The New York Age* and *The Crisis* carried dozens of articles and comments on this subject.

51. *The Crisis*, III (February 1912), 141.

52. *The New York Evening Journal*, December 12, 1910. Also see *The New York Times*, December 1, 1901; Mary White Ovington, "The Negro in the Trades Unions in New York," *The Annals*, XXVII (May 1906), 551–558; R. R. Wright, Jr., "The Negro in Times of Industrial Unrest," *Charities*, XV (October 7, 1905), 69–73; Mrs. Paul Laurence Dunbar, "Hope Deferred," *The Crisis*, VIII (September 1914), 238–242; Alma Herbst, *The Negro in the Slaughtering and Meat-Packing Industry in Chicago* (Boston and New York, 1932), pp. xviii–xix, 14–32, *passim; The New York Age*, June 13, 1907, August 19, 1909, January 20, 1910, November 30, 1911, June 6, 13, 1912, January 16, 1913.

53. Italicized in the original. Copy of act in Bruce Manuscripts, Schomburg Collection.

54. *The New York Age*, February 6, 1913.

55. Henry A. Spencer to John E. Bruce, March 22, 1910; Bruce to the Hon. Jesse S. Phillips, March 23, 1910. Bruce Manuscripts, Schomburg Collection.

56. Clippings from the *New York American*, September 30, 1904, in Stokes Manuscripts, Columbia University, Box 75.

57. Ovington, *Half A Man*, p. 76.

58. *Ibid.*, p. 34; *The New York Freeman,* July 18, 1885, January 16, 1886; *The New York Age,* January 31, 1907; "Certificate of Incorporation of the Society of the Sons of New York," November 28, 1891, in New York City Hall of Records.

59. See John H. Johnson, *A Place of Adventure: Essays and Sermons* (Greenwich, Conn., 1955), p. 10; "Boston, and Some Boston People," Bruce Manuscripts; W. E. B. DuBois, *The Philadelphia Negro: A Social Study* (Philadelphia, 1899), pp. 73n, 80; Roi Ottley, *The Lonely Warrior: The Life and Times of Robert S. Abbott* (Chicago, 1955), pp. 84–85; St. Clair Drake and Horace R. Cayton, *Black Metropolis: A Study of Negro Life in a Northern City* (New York, 1945), pp. 73–74, *passim.*

60. Charles Winslow Hall, "Racial Hatred," *The Colored American Magazine,* I (September 1900), 246; *The New York Age,* December 17, 1908, and *passim.*

61. *The New York Age,* June 22, 1905; Letter to the editor from Melvin J. Chisum, *The New York Times,* June 10, 1900.

62. DuBois, "The Black North," *The New York Times,* December 1, 1901.

63. *The New York Age,* April 6, 1905.

64. Langston Hughes, "High to Low," *The Midwest Journal,* I (Summer 1949), 26.

65. *The New York Freeman,* January 16, 1886; *The New York Age,* January 5, 1889, January 25, 1890, July 6, 1905, July 27, 1908.

66. *The New York Age,* May 14, 1908, July 7, 1910.

67. Miller, "Industrial Condition," 548; *The Boston Chronicle,* September 4, 1936. From 1900 to 1905 *The Southern Workman* printed an entire series of Miller's articles on this subject, and he continued to advocate a return to the farm until his death in 1939. See the excellent essay by Bernard Eisenberg, "Kelly Miller: The Negro Leader as Marginal Man," *Journal of Negro History,* XLV (July 1960), 182–187.

68. Paul Laurence Dunbar, *The Sport of the Gods* (New York, 1902), p. 213. The development of intraracial antagonism would be incomplete without mentioning the hostility that American Negroes, northern and southern, showed toward Negro immigrants from the West Indies. New York City was the largest urban center for foreign-born Negroes in the early twentieth century (12,851 in 1910). As this antagonism did not become a major theme in city history until the 1920's, I have saved discussion of it for Chapter 9.

69. John E. Bruce, "Practical Questions," Bruce Manuscripts, Schomburg Collection; *The Colored American Magazine,* XIII (July 1907), 68; "The Reminiscences of Samuel J. Battle" (Oral History Research Office, Columbia University, 1960), pp. 16–17; *The Crisis,* XII (August 1916), 166–167; *The New York Freeman,* May 15, 1886; *The New York Age,* May 25, 1905, October 5, 1916.

70. Florence E. Gibson, *The Attitudes of the New York Irish toward State and National Affairs, 1848–1892* (New York, 1951), p. 66; *The New York Age,* January 26, 1905; W. L. Bulkley, "Race Prejudice As Viewed from An Economic Standpoint," *Proceedings of the National Negro Conference, 1909* (New York, 1909?), 94.

71. This information and much that follows is derived from contemporary press reports.

72. Of the fifty Negro migrants studied by William Fielding Ogburn, all read the daily newspapers. "The Richmond Negro in New York City: His

Social Mind as Seen in His Pleasures" (M.A. thesis, Columbia University, 1909), p. 71.

73. The People vs. Arthur J. Harris, October 29, 1900. Transcript and summary of trial in New York City Magistrates Court.

74. *Ibid.*

75. *Ibid.; The World*, August 17, 1900.

76. *New York Daily Tribune*, August 17, 1900.

77. *Ibid.*, August 16, 1900.

78. Bernard J. York, Chairman of the Committee on Rules and Discipline, to Police Board, December 8, 1900 (Mayor Van Wyck Papers, Municipal Archives).

79. *New York Daily Tribune*, August 16, 1900.

80. *Ibid.*

81. *The New York Times*, August 16, 1900; *Autobiography of Dr. William Henry Johnson* (Albany, 1900), p. 148.

82. [Frank Moss], *Story of the Riot: Persecution of Negroes by Roughs and Policemen, in the City of New York, August, 1900* (New York, 1900), p. 5; Richard O'Connor, *Hell's Kitchen: The Roaring Days of New York's Wild West Side* (New York, 1958), p. 151.

83. *The New York Times*, August 20, 1900; Johnson, *Along This Way*, pp. 157–158.

84. *New York Daily Tribune*, August 16, 17, 1900.

85. Israel Ludlow to Bernard J. York, August 30, 1900 (Mayor Van Wyck Papers, Municipal Archives).

86. Bernard J. York to Police Board, December 8, 1900. *Ibid.*

87. *The World*, August 17, 1900.

88. Less than a month before the riot, the New York press had bitterly criticized the South for a race riot in New Orleans. Southerners now responded gleefully; stressed the universality of race hatred; made some comments about casting the first stone; and warned against the "young country negro" who flocks to the city to "lead a life of idleness." *Ibid.*, August 17, 18, 19, 1900.

89. *New York Daily Tribune*, August 19, 1900.

90. Clement Richardson, ed., *The National Cyclopedia of the Colored Race* (Montgomery, Alabama, 1919), I, 223; Mary White Ovington, *The Walls Came Tumbling Down* (New York, 1947), pp. 25–26.

91. *New York Daily Tribune*, August 27, 1900.

92. Some of the original postcards sent out by the Reverend Dr. Brooks may be found at the Schomburg Collection.

93. *New York Daily Tribune*, August 25, September 8, 1900; Israel Ludlow to Bernard J. York, President of Board of Police Commissioners, August 30, 1900 (Mayor Van Wyck Papers, Municipal Archives); Frank Moss to York, September 14, 1900, *ibid.*

94. "Notes of D. Macon Webster for a speech at protest meeting" (Miscellaneous Manuscripts, Schomburg Collection).

95. *The New York Times*, September 13, 1900.

96. J. G. Speed, "The Negro in New York: A Study of the Social and Industrial Condition of the Colored People in the Metropolis," *Harper's Weekly*, XLIV (December 22, 1900), 1249.

97. *New York Daily Tribune*, September 9, 1900.

98. John Hains vs. Herman A. Ohm, October 26, 1900; George L. Myers vs. John J. Cleary, October 26, 1900 (Mayor Van Wyck Papers, Municipal Archives).

99. Bernard J. York to Police Board, December 8, 1900 (Mayor Van Wyck Papers, Municipal Archives).

100. The People vs. Arthur J. Harris, October 29, 1900 (New York City Magistrates Court).

101. Harold W. Folletta, Acting Warden, Clinton Prison, to author, August 14, 1961.

102. Kelly Miller, "The American Negro as a Political Factor," *The Nineteenth Century*, LXVIII (August 1910), 297.

103. *Report of the Police Department of the City of New York* (New York, 1901), p. 10.

104. *The New York Times*, August 24, 1900.

NOTES TO CHAPTER 4

1. Historians have too often analyzed Progressivism primarily as a political movement. I define Progressivism as a national, broad-based movement—social, economic, industrial, medical, educational, religious, political, and so on. It was the *positive* national response to the shocking changes and inequities created by massive industrialization and unprecedented urbanization and the often-expressed awareness that American culture was being radically altered by them. The most enduring accomplishments of the Progressive movement, in my opinion, have been its social, industrial and economic reforms and these were most evident on the local, municipal and state levels. As any national reform movement in a democratic society would, it necessarily created issues which became influential in national political life. If one analyzes Progressivism only in its national political phase, however, it was often anti-Negro. Presidential candidates were sometimes willing to overlook the desires of a largely disfranchised group in hope of attracting white southern support. Theodore Roosevelt refused to seat southern Negro representatives at the 1912 Progressive convention in spite of protests by Jane Addams, Henry Moskowitz, Joel Spingarn and others. The segregationist and anti-Negro policies instituted during the Woodrow Wilson administrations are well-known. Progressivism as a political movement did therefore, as historians have pointed out, bypass the Negro. If, however, one includes social workers and industrial and municipal reformers in his definition of Progressivism, there was a serious, positive and hopeful interest expressed in Negro welfare by the Progressive movement. See Arthur S. Link, "The Negro as a Factor in the Campaign of 1912," *Journal of Negro History*, XXXII (January 1947), 81–99; Kathleen L. Wolgemuth, "Woodrow Wilson and Federal Segregation," *ibid.*, XLIV (January 1959), 158–173; Henry Blumenthal, "Woodrow Wilson and the Race Question," *ibid.*, XLVIII (January 1963), 1–21; Jane Addams, "The Progressive Party and the Negro," *The Crisis*, V (November 1912), 30–31.

2. *The New York Age*, November 3, 1910; "Night Clubs," James Weldon Johnson Collection.

3. A more thorough study of each of these cities would undoubtedly extend this list considerably.

4. W. E. B. DuBois, *The Souls of Black Folk: Essays and Sketches* (New York, 1953), p. 99.

5. *The New York Freeman*, May 23, June 6, 1885, January 9, February 13, April 3, 1886.

6. Augustus Taber, "New York Colored Mission: The Beginning of its Work," appended to the New York Colored Mission, *Twentieth Annual Report, 1885* (New York, 1886), p. 23.

7. *Report of the New York Colored Mission, 1904* (New York, 1905), p. 7.

8. *Report of the New York Colored Mission, 1880* (New York, 1881), p. 8.

9. "Certificate of Incorporation of the New York Colored Mission," August 3, 1871. New York City Hall of Records.

10. *Report on the New York Colored Mission, 1871* (New York, 1872), p. 3; and *Report, 1881* (New York, 1882), p. 8.

11. "The great ambition of the older people was to read the Bible before they died." Booker T. Washington, *Up from Slavery: An Autobiography* (New York, 1959), p. 21; *Report of the New York Colored Mission, 1893* (New York, 1894), pp. 13–15.

12. Mary White Ovington, "Beginnings of the N.A.A.C.P.," *The Crisis*, XXXII (June 1926), 76–77.

13. *New York Evening Post* as cited in *The New York Age*, July 6, 1905; Mary L. Lewis, "The White Rose Industrial Association," *The Messenger*, VII (April 1925), 158.

14. White Rose Industrial Association, *Annual Report for . . . 1911* (New York, 1912), p. 6.

15. See obituary in *The New York Age*, March 14, 1907; *The Crisis*, VII (December 1911), 51; Lassalle Best, "History of the White Rose Mission and Industrial Association" (WPA research paper, Schomburg Collection); Victoria Earle Matthews to Booker T. Washington, March 23, 1902. Washington Papers, Library of Congress, Box 1; August Meier, "Negro Racial Thought in the Age of Booker T. Washington, Circa 1880–1915" (Ph.D. dissertation, Columbia University, 1957), pp. 380–381.

16. Frances A. Kellor, "The Criminal Negro: A Sociological Study," *The Arena*, XXV (January–November 1901).

17. Frances A. Kellor, *Out of Work: A Study of Employment Agencies.* . . . (New York, 1904), p. vi.

18. For a detailed reply to Miss Kellor's charges see John N. Bogart to Mayor George B. McClellan, November 22, 1906, McClellan Papers, Municipal Archives. Also *Reports* of the Commissioner of Licenses and Bureau of Industries and Immigration; Kellor, "Report of the Research Department of the Woman's Municipal League," *Woman's Municipal League Bulletin*, IV (April 1906), 3–7.

19. *The New York Freeman*, May 16, 1885.

20. Agents "corral girls from the country districts." Kellor, *Out of Work*, pp. 73–74, 83, 97.

21. Louise DeKoven Bowen, *The Colored People of Chicago* (Chicago, 1913), n.p.

22. "Conditions Existing in the City of New York Prior to May 1st, 1904, Which Led to the Creation of this Office" (1909). Municipal Archives.

23. Frances A. Kellor, "Assisted Emigration from the South: The Women," *Charities*, XV (October 7, 1905), 12–13.

24. *Ibid.*, 14.

25. E. M. Rhodes, "The Protection of Girls Who Travel: A National Movement," *The Colored American Magazine*, XIII (August 1907), 114–115.

26. From September 1932 to February 1933, in twenty-four installments, Miss Ovington published her "Reminiscences" in *The Afro-American* of Baltimore. Most of the information for the following biographical sketch comes from there. *The Afro-American*, September 24, 1932.

27. *Ibid.*, September 17, 1932.

28. *Ibid.*, September 24, 1932.

29. *Idem.*

30. *Ibid.,* September 17, 1932; Mary White Ovington, *The Walls Came Tumbling Down* (New York, 1947), chap. 1; *The New York Age,* January 18, 1930.

31. *The Afro-American,* October 1, 1932; Mary White Ovington, *Half A Man: The Status of the Negro in New York* (New York, 1911), p. ix.

32. City and Suburban Homes Company, *Annual Report, 1904–1905* (New York, 1905), p. 11; *Annual Report, 1906–1907* (New York, 1907), pp. 7–8.

33. On Phipps as philanthropist see Moses Rischin, *The Promised City: New York's Jews, 1870–1914* (Cambridge, 1961), p. 109; and "Reminiscences of William H. Allen" (Oral History Research Office, Columbia University, 1950), pp. 57–58; *Real Estate Record and Builder's Guide,* LXXV (March 4, 1905), 460; "Model Tenements," *The Outlook,* LXXIX (February 11, 1905), 364–365.

34. Arthur Gary, "Sketch of the Constitution League of the United States" (WPA research paper, Schomburg Collection); Ruth Worthy, "A Negro in Our History: William Monroe Trotter, 1872–1934" (M.A. thesis, Columbia University, 1952), p. 91. On Milholland's role in the NAACP see *The Crisis,* XXXIII (February 1927), 181–182, XXXV (April 1928), 124, XXV (May 1928), 166.

35. "I feel as though now that the tenement is promised us things are going pretty well for a settlement in it. Mr. Phipps, I know, is interested." Mary White Ovington to Fred R. Moore, February 23, 1905. Washington Papers, Library of Congress, Box 29. *The Afro-American,* October 15, 1932; *Half A Man,* pp. 41–42; *The Walls Came Tumbling Down,* pp. 33–34.

36. William English Walling, "The Race War in the North," *The Independent,* LXV (September 3, 1908), 529–534; William English Walling, "The Founding of the NAACP," *The Crisis,* XXXVI (July 1929), 228.

37. *The Afro-American,* November 26, December 10, 1932; *Then and Now: NAACP, 1909–1959* (New York, 1959?); Mary White Ovington, *How the NAACP Began* (New York, 1914).

38. *The Crisis,* V (February 1913), 163–164.

39. Interview with Mrs. Richetta G. Wallace, November 3, 1961; Richetta G. Wallace to author, November 7, 1961.

40. Claude McKay, *A Long Way From Home* (New York, 1937), p. 113.

41. *The Afro-American,* September 10, 1932; "A Tribute to Miss Ovington," *The New York Age,* July 2, 1932; Oswald Garrison Villard, *Fighting Years: Memoirs of a Liberal Editor* (New York, 1939), pp. 191–198.

42. *The Afro-American,* February 25, 1933.

43. For a list of members of the CIICN see "Committee on the Industrial Improvement of the Negro in New York," a small booklet in the Stokes Manuscripts, Columbia University, Box 18; *The New York Age,* May 17, July 12, 1906.

44. *The New York Age,* July 12, 1906; Bulkley, "The School as a Social Center," *Charities,* XV (October 7, 1905), 76.

45. J. Wayne Wrightstone, Director of the New York City Board of Educational Research to author, February 7, 1962; *The Crisis,* II (October 1911), 236; James K. Owens, Syracuse University Archivist, to author, January 8, 1963; *Alumni Record and General Catalogue of Syracuse University* (Syracuse, 1911), III, 1546.

46. "A Slave Boy, Now a Professor," *Success,* April 8, 1899.

47. William Lewis Bulkley, "Race Prejudice as Viewed from an Economic

Standpoint," *Proceedings of the National Negro Conference, 1909* (New York, 1909?), pp. 92–93.

48. Interview with Henry S. Coshburn of Board of Education, February 23, 1962.

49. *The New York Age,* July 22, 1909.

50. Ralph Ellison, "William Lewis Bulkley" (WPA research paper, Schomburg Collection); *The New York Age,* March 22, 1924, September 3, 1933.

51. "I wish very much that you could see your way clear to attend the meetings of the Commission for Improving the Industrial Condition of the colored people in Greater New York. I am very much afraid that unless you do attend that Bulkley and his crowd will get hold of this important organization." Booker T. Washington to Charles W. Anderson, October 1, 1907. Washington Papers, Library of Congress, Box 37.

52. Charles W. Anderson to Booker T. Washington, April 3, 1909. Washington Papers, Library of Congress, Box 43; *The New York Age,* April 6, 1905.

53. *Ibid.,* November 5, 1914; Bulkley, "The School as a Social Center," 77.

54. *Ibid.,* October 31, 1907. "A Square Deal for New York Negroes," *The Outlook,* LXXXIII (June 23, 1906), 398–399.

55. William Lewis Bulkley to J. G. Phelps Stokes, November 14, 18, 1906. Stokes Manuscripts, Columbia University, Boxes 18 and 77.

56. Charles W. Anderson to Booker T. Washington, March 23, 1906. Washington Papers, Library of Congress, Box 2; William Lewis Bulkley, "The Industrial Condition of the Negro in New York City," *The Annals,* XXVII (May 1906), 595.

57. *The New York Age,* May 17, 1906.

58. "CIICN," Stokes Manuscripts; "Committee for Improving the Industrial Condition of Negroes in New York," *The Colored American Magazine,* XII (June 1907), 459–64; *The New York Age,* April 26, 1906.

59. William Jay Schieffelin to J. G. Phelps Stokes, May 24, 1906. Stokes Manuscripts, Columbia University, Box 18. On Schieffelin see "The Reminiscences of William Jay Schieffelin" (Oral History Research Office, Columbia University, 1949), and "Harmful Rush of Negroes to the North," *The New York Times Magazine,* VI (June 3, 1917).

60. From 1906 to 1911 *The New York Age* regularly printed articles on the CIICN and this information is largely derived from them.

61. *Ibid.,* October 19, 1911; *The Crisis,* VIII (September 1914), 243–46; *The Urban League: Its Story* (New York, 1939); Bulkley, "Race Prejudice," 97.

62. *The New York Age,* June 22, 1905.

63. *Ibid.,* June 26, 1913; *The Colored American Magazine,* XIII (September 1907), 211.

64. *The Horizon: A Journal of the Color Line,* V (November 1909), 1–2.

65. *The New York Age,* July 22, 1908.

NOTES TO CHAPTER 5

1. There is no legally definable modern community of Harlem. The first settlement was made in the area in 1636, and the town of New Harlaem created in 1658. The last Harlem colonial patent was made in 1686. Its boundaries ran roughly from present-day Seventy-fourth Street to One Hundred and Twenty-ninth Street, East River to Hudson River. Subsequent grants made

in the general area of New Harlaem in colonial times outside these boundaries were also often referred to as Harlem grants. Sometimes the name Harlem was used to designate all upper Manhattan. Harlem in the late nineteenth century was part of the Twelfth Ward, which included all Manhattan above Eighty-sixth Street. At the turn of the nineteenth century its residents generally defined the community as bordered by One Hundred and Tenth Street on the south, One Hundred and Fifty-fifth Street on the north, East River on the east, and present-day Morningside and St. Nicholas Avenues on the west, but were never rigid in applying this definition. The same holds true today. This absence of legally designated boundaries presents no significant difficulty for this study because after this chapter I shall use an ethnic definition—the specific sections within the general area of Harlem occupied by Negroes, and these can be traced in the greatest of detail. In the 1920's Negro Harlem was most often called Central Harlem or North Harlem.

2. James Riker, *Revised History of Harlem (City of New York): Its Origin and Early Annals* (New York, 1904), *passim.*

3. Col. Alonzo B. Caldwell, *A Lecture: The History of Harlem* (New York, 1882), pp. 20, 30–31.

4. *Deduction of the Harlaem Commons* (New York, 1872), pp. 28–29. For extensive genealogical data on Harlem descendants consult Riker, *Revised History,* pp. 426–814.

5. *The New York Times,* November 17, 1883.

6. Richard Webber, Jr., "Historical Sketch of Harlem," *Harlem Magazine,* I (October 1912), 17.

7. New York Public Library, *Book of Charters, Wills, Deeds and Other Official Documents* (New York, 1905), pp. 307–325; *Constitution of the Harlaem Library Formed by a Convention of the Inhabitants* (New York, 1817); William B. Silber, *A History of St. James Methodist Episcopal Church at Harlem, New York City, 1830–1880* (New York, 1882), p. 22; James Ford, *et al., Slums and Housing: With Special Reference to New York City* (Cambridge, Massachusetts, 1936), I, 324.

8. This information is from a nonpaginated collection of typewritten material at the New-York Historical Society entitled "Harlem Commons Syndicate."

9. Caldwell, *A Lecture,* pp. 12, 18–19.

10. *Harlem Magazine,* II (October 1913), 11–13.

11. Broadus Mitchell, *Alexander Hamilton: The National Adventure, 1788–1804* (New York, 1962), pp. 499–500; *Harlem Local Reporter,* May 10, 1893, July 9, 1904.

12. Caldwell, *A Lecture,* p. 24.

13. Riker, *Revised History,* pp. 191n., 256n., 398n., 474, 530n., 588–589.

14. "Old Timers' Tales of Harlem's Growth," *Harlem Magazine,* III (December 1914), 16.

15. Rev. Edgar Tilton, Jr., *The Reformed Low Dutch Church of Harlem: Historical Sketch* (New York, 1910), p. 11; The Collegiate Reformed Church of Harlem, *Two Hundred and Fiftieth Anniversary* (New York, 1910), p. 1.

16. Mitchell, *Alexander Hamilton,* p. 552.

17. "Harlem Commons Syndicate"; Riker, *Revised History,* pp. 488–489.

18. Riker, *Revised History,* p. 298.

19. "Harlem Commons Syndicate."

20. "The Fall of Shantytown," *Harlem Local Reporter,* March 5, 1890; "A Shanty Scene in Harlem," *ibid.,* August 13, 1892; Kate Holladay Claghorn, "The Foreign Immigrant in New York City," *Reports of the Industrial Com-*

mission on Immigration . . . and on Education (Washington, D.C., 1901), XV, 457.

21. "Old Timers' Tales of Harlem's Growth," *Harlem Magazine,* III (December 1914), 16–22; Michael C. O'Brien, "Memories of Hooker's Building," *ibid.,* IV (May 1916), 11, 17; *Harlem Local Reporter,* September 21, 1892.

22. Harlem Plains, the area that became Negro Harlem, is made of limestone which eroded more readily than the schist of Harlem Heights. For a general geological history of the area see Edward Hagaman Hall, "A Brief History of Morningside Park and Vicinity," American Scenic and Historic Preservation Society, *21st Annual Report* (Albany, 1916), 537–598; *History and Commerce of New York, 1891* (New York, 1892?) p. 82.

23. Caldwell, *A Lecture,* p. 27.

24. Charles H. Fuller, "Harlem—from 'Cradle Days' to Now," *Harlem Magazine,* XIV (October 1925), 6–7; Charles H. Haswell, *Reminiscences of New York by an Octogenarian, 1816–1860* (New York, 1896), p. 459.

25. *The Harlem Monthly Magazine,* I (April 1893), 1–2; James Grant Wilson, ed., *The Memorial History of the City of New York* (New York, 1893), III, 453.

26. Lloyd Morris, *Incredible New York: High Life and Low Life of the Last Hundred Years* (New York, 1951), pp. 95–96; Reginald Pelham Bolton, *$5,000,000 Speedway: A Useless Driveway* (n.p., n.d.); Charles Townsend Harris, *Memories of Manhattan in the Sixties and Seventies* (New York, 1928), p. 78; Herbert Manchester, *The Story of Harlem and the Empire City Savings Bank, 1889–1929* (New York, 1929), pp. 13, 16, 19.

27. *Harlem Magazine,* XVIII (May 1929), 15; Charles Henry White, "In Up-Town New York," *Harper's Monthly,* CXII (January 1906), 220–228.

28. New York and Harlem Railroad, *Act of Incorporation and Subsequent Acts, 1831–1863* (New York, 1864), pp. 3–4.

29. *Taintor's Route and City Guides, Harlem Route* (New York, 1867), p. 6.

30. Samuel M. Brown, "Harlem's Early Transit Facilities," *Harlem Magazine,* IV (September 1915), 11; Joseph Warren Greene, Jr., "New York City's First Railroad, The New York and Harlem, 1832 to 1867," *The New-York Historical Society Quarterly Bulletin,* IX (January 1926), 107–123.

31. Ella Bunner Graff, *Reminiscences of Old Harlem* (n.p., 1933), p. 5; Caldwell, *A Lecture,* p. 28.

32. A. J. Wall, "The Sylvan Steamboats on the East River, New York to Harlem," *The New-York Historical Society Bulletin,* VII (October 1924), 59–72.

33. I. N. Phelps Stokes, *The Iconography of Manhattan Island, 1498–1909* (New York, 1918), III, 808–831; Thomas Adams, Harold M. Lewis and Theodore T. McCroskey, *Population, Land Values and Government* (New York, 1929), pp. 51 ff; James Austin Stevens, *The Physical Evolution of New York City in a Hundred Years, 1807–1907* (n.p., n.d.); James L. Bahret, "Growth of New York and Suburbs Since 1790," *The Scientific Monthly* (November 1920), 404–418.

34. Walter Laidlaw, *Population of the City of New York, 1890–1930* (New York, 1932), p. 51.

35. Frederic A. Birmingham, *It Was Fun While It Lasted* (Philadelphia, 1960), p. 39.

36. *Harlem Magazine,* II (April 1914), 17–18; *Harlem Local Reporter,* May 28, 1892.

37. *History and Commerce of New York, 1891* (New York, 1892?), p. 90.

38. "Harlem Commons Syndicate"; *The Harlem Local: Twelfth Ward News,* January 4, 1873.

39. *Harlem Magazine,* V (December 1916), 13; Manchester, *The Story of Harlem,* p. 21.

40. "During several years after the discovery of Harlem (from the stations on the elevated railroad) its growth was phenomenal. . . ." *Harlem Local Reporter,* March 1, 1890.

41. *Harlem Magazine,* XVIII (May 1929), 14.

42. *Harlem Local Reporter,* March 5, 1890.

43. Wirt Howe, *New York At The Turn of the Century, 1899–1916* (Toronto, 1946), pp. 2–3; *Harlem Local Reporter,* March 25, 1891; "Last Rites on Billy Goats," *ibid.,* March 30, 1895.

44. *Harlem Magazine,* IV (November 1915), 13, XV (July 1926), 4.

45. O'Brien, "Memories of Hooker's Building," 17.

46. Berta Gilbert, "Morgenthau Reminisces About Harlem," *Harlem Magazine,* XX (May 1931), 4, 15–16; Record and Guide, *A History of Real Estate, Building, and Architecture in New York City During the last Quarter of a Century* (New York, 1898), pp. 94–95, 112; *Harlem Local Reporter,* January 2, 1895; *Harlem Life,* XV (October 28, 1899), XVI (February 3, 1900), 6; Vincent Sheean, *Oscar Hammerstein I: The Life and Exploits of an Impresario* (New York, 1956), pp. 40 ff.

47. *Harlem Local Reporter,* March 1, 1893.

48. *Ibid.,* March 1, 1890, July 4, 1894.

49. *Ibid.,* December 28, 1889; Newspaper clipping in "Harlem Commons Syndicate."

50. The operations of these Harlem claimants are preserved in a collection of their official transactions, reports of annual meetings, letters, genealogical charts and newspaper clippings in the "Harlem Commons Syndicate," New-York Historical Society. See also Walter H. Shupe, *First Annual Statement of the Harlem Commons Syndicate* (New York, 1884).

51. *Harlem Magazine,* XXI (August 1932), 9, 16.

52. Henry Pennington Toler, *Arise Take Thy Journey* (New York, 1903), p. 48; Carl Horton Pierce, *New Harlem Past and Present: The Story of an Amazing Civic Wrong Now At Last to be Righted* (New York, 1903).

53. Charles C. Baldwin, *Stanford White* (New York, 1931), pp. 194–195, 200; Birmingham, *It Was Fun While It Lasted,* p. 41; *Harlem Library Bulletin,* I (March 1903), n.p.; *Harlem Magazine,* II (September 1913), 25; Robert Coit Chapin, *The Standard of Living of Workingmen's Families in New York City* (New York, 1909), p. 85; *The Hammer and the Pen,* I (August 1898), 3–4.

54. *The New York Times,* November 21, 1920.

55. *Harlem Magazine,* XVI (June 1927), 4–5.

56. Sheean, *Oscar Hammerstein I,* pp. 42–46, 57, 66.

57. *Harlem Magazine,* I (June 1912), 29.

58. Birmingham, *It Was Fun While It Lasted,* p. 14.

59. *First Report of the Tenement House Commission of New York City* (New York, 1902), II, 103.

60. This is taken from a survey of biographical sketches that appeared regularly in *Harlem Magazine.*

61. *Harlem Local Reporter,* December 28, 1889. "An army of downtowners [are] making their residences in this delightful section." *Ibid.,* May 2, 1891.

62. *Harlem Magazine,* II (April 1914), 17–18.

63. *Harlem Local Reporter,* January 7, 1890; *135th Anniversary of the*

Battle of Harlem Heights: With a History and Ready Reference Directory of Harlem (New York, 1911).

64. Graff, *Reminiscences of Old Harlem*, p. 4.

65. *The Local Reporter*, January 6, 1883.

66. Interview with Max Bollt, February 9, 1962.

67. *Harlem Local Reporter*, May 10, 1893.

68. Harlem Presbyterian Church, *Church Bulletin* (April 17, 1908), n.p.

69. *New York Street Directory and Shoppers' Guide for 1898* (New York, 1898), p. 73.

70. *Harlem Local Reporter*, February 15, 1890, October 19, 1892, November 26, 1892.

71. Manchester, *The Story of Harlem*, pp. 24–25.

72. Respectively: *The Harlem Monthly Magazine, Harlem Life* and *Harlem Local Reporter*.

73. The Independence Day Association of Harlem, *Celebration*, 1886 (New York, 1887), 17; Harlem Wohlthätigkeits Verein, *Constitution* (New York, 1896); Harlem Independent Schützen Corps, *Golden Jubilee, 1880–1930* (New York, 1930); Konrad Bercovici, *Around the World in New York* (New York, 1924), 215; Harlem Regatta Association, *Official Programme* (New York, 1902); Harlem Democratic Club, *Constitution, By-Laws, Rules. . . .* (New York, 1889), 5; Harlem Republican Club, *By-Laws and List of Members* (New York, 1892); *Harlem Evening High School News*, November 1907; Harlem Board of Commerce, *Constitution and By-Laws* (New York, 1896).

74. *The Harlem Monthly Magazine*, I (April 1893), 2; *Harlem Magazine*, XXI (December 1932), 8.

75. *Harlem Local Reporter*, April 16, 1890.

NOTES TO CHAPTER 6

1. "The Reminiscences of Samuel J. Battle" (Oral History Research Office, Columbia University, 1960), p. 21; *The Harlem Local Reporter*, April 4, 1894.

2. *The Harlem Local Reporter*, March 1, 1893.

3. *Ibid.*, April 20, 1895.

4. *Ibid.*, August 2, 1893.

5. *The Sun's Guide to New York* (New York, 1892), p. 26.

6. William McAdoo, *Guarding A Great City* (New York, 1906), p. 91.

7. *The Harlem Local Reporter*, December 26, 1894. "A Walk in Harlem Brings Surprises," *The New York Times*, January 2, 1921.

8. *Ibid.*, July 18, 1894, August 4, 1894; *The Harlem Local Reporter and Bronx Chronicle*, January 1, 1898; Frances Blascoer, *Colored School Children in New York* (New York, 1915), p. 75.

9. *The Harlem Local Reporter*, September 1, 1894; *Harlem Magazine*, IV (June 1915), 9; *Uptown New York* (May–June 1934), 9.

10. *Ibid.*, September 21, 1892, March 1, 1893.

11. Frederic A. Birmingham, *It Was Fun While It Lasted* (Philadelphia, 1960), p. 39.

12. James Riker, *Revised History of Harlem (City of New York): Its Origin and Early Annals* (New York, 1904), p. 189.

13. *Ibid.*, p. 287; Rev. Edgar Tilton, Jr., *The Reformed Low Dutch Church of Harlem: Historical Sketch* (New York, 1910), p. 31; "Harlem Commons Syndicate," n.p.; Col. Alonzo B. Caldwell, *A Lecture: The History of Harlem* (New York, 1882), p. 23.

14. *The Daily Advertiser* [New York], January 15, 1791.

15. William B. Silber, *A History of St. James Methodist Episcopal Church at Harlem, New York City, 1830–1880* (New York, 1882).

16. Robert S. Dixon, "Education of the Negro in the City of New York, 1853–1900" (M.A. thesis, City College, 1935), pp. 13–14.

17. Jonathan Greenleaf, *A History of the Churches, of All Denominations, in the City of New York from the First Settlement to the Year 1846* (New York, 1846), p. 322.

18. *Ibid.*, p. 330.

19. Dixon, "Education of the Negro," pp. 14, 19, 25.

20. Ella Bunner Graff, *Reminiscences of Old Harlem* (n.p., 1933), p. 8.

21. *Ibid.*, p. 11.

22. *The Harlem Local Reporter*, December 8, 1894.

23. *Harlem Library Bulletin*, I (September 1902), 10.

24. Michael C. O'Brien, "Memories of Hooker's Building," *Harlem Magazine*, IV (May 1916), 17.

25. *The New York Age*, March 6, 1913.

26. *Ibid.*, September 20, 1890; "The Negro in New York," *The Sun*, January 30, 1901.

27. John P. Clyde, "The Negro in New York City" (M.A. thesis, Columbia University, 1899), pp. 3–4.

28. This information is derived from advertisements and personal notices which appeared in the Negro and white press in the 1880's and 1890's.

29. *The New York Age*, February 21, 28, 1891, January 26, 1895.

30. *The Harlem Local Reporter*, November 4, 1893; Jacob A. Riis, *The Battle With the Slum* (New York, 1902), pp. 110–111.

31. *The Harlem Local Reporter*, December 26, 1894; *The New York Times*, December 26, 1901.

32. *The New York Age*, October 20, 1888, April 20, 1889; *The New York Globe*, May 12, June 2, June 30, 1883.

33. *The Harlem Local Reporter*, October 31, 1891.

34. *The New York Age*, May 17, 1890, February 21, 1891.

35. I have compiled these statistics by locating the exact blocks delineated by the Tenement House Commission on the ward maps which the Commission published. The selection I made was limited to blocks with ten or more Negro families. The statistics omit nonfamily groups and are therefore no accurate guide to the exact number of Negroes in Harlem in 1902. They do, however, present a description of the distribution of Negroes in the general area. *First Report of the Tenement House Commission of New York City* (New York, 1902), II, 103, and maps.

36. *The Harlem Local Reporter*, April 12, 1893.

37. *Ibid.*, October 26, 1895, March 1, 1894.

38. The Harlem Relief Society of the City of New York, *First Annual Report, 1893* (New York, 1894), and *Second Annual Report, 1894* (New York, 1895). James Baldwin, who obviously speaks for a later generation, writes of the "bitter expectancy with which, in my childhood, we awaited winter: It is coming and will be hard; there is nothing anyone can do about it." "The Harlem Ghetto," in *Notes of a Native Son* (Boston, 1955), p. 57.

39. *The Harlem Local Reporter*, December 13, 1893.

40. *Ibid.*, February 25, 1893.

41. *Ibid.*, December 23, 1893.

42. The Harlem Relief Society, *Twenty-Second Annual Report, 1914* (New York, 1915), pp. 2–3, 13.

43. For a wonderful description of the Cake Walk see *The New York Age*, September 1, 1934. *The Harlem Local Reporter*, February 28, 1891, March 29, 1890; Jacob A. Riis, *How the Other Half Lives* (New York, 1890), p. 154.

44. Vincent Sheean, *Oscar Hammerstein I: The Life and Exploits of an Impresario* (New York, 1950), pp. 58–59, 63; *Harlem Life*, XV, (October 21, 1899), 3.

45. *The Harlem Local Reporter*, May 20, 1893, August 4, 1894.

46. *Real Estate Record and Builder's Guide*, LXXIII (January 16, 1904), 105, and LXXIII (June 4, 1904), 1306.

47. *Ibid.*, LXV (January 27, 1900), 141.

48. John Martin, *Rapid Transit: Its Effects on Rents and Living Conditions* (New York, 1909), p. 13; James L. Bahret, "Growth of New York and Suburbs Since 1790," *The Scientific Monthly* (November 1920), 412.

49. Walter Stabler, "Development of the West Side: A Review of Past and Present Phases," *Record and Guide*, LXX (August 2, 1902), 157.

50. ". . . More than ever before the market is dominated by expert professional operations." *Ibid.*, LXIX (January 10, 1903), 37.

51. *Ibid.*, LXXIII (March 26, 1904). ". . . much of the remaining vacant land on the Upper East Side and in Harlem has passed into the hands of building loan operators. . . ." *Ibid.*, LXXV (January 14, 1905), 58.

52. Abraham Cahan, *The Rise of David Levinsky* (New York, 1960), p. 464.

53. *Record and Guide*, LXX (September 6, 1902), 328.

54. Howard Marion Lesourd, "A Harlem Neighborhood" (M.A. thesis, Columbia University, 1913), p. 6; Eleanor L. Symonds, "Population Shifting in Manhattan" (M.A. thesis, Columbia University, 1924), pp. 3 ff.

55. James Speyer to J. G. Phelps Stokes, September 30, 1903. Stokes Manuscripts, Columbia University, Box 4.

56. Lillian D. Wald to J. G. Phelps Stokes, September 30, 1903, *ibid.*

57. "There is no one whose presence in the Harlem Federation I will value more than yours. . . ." Maurice H. Harris to Lillian D. Wald, December 7, 1906. Wald Manuscripts, New York Public Library; Sarah Sussman, "A Settlement Club" (M.A. thesis, Columbia University, 1918).

58. *The Harlem Local Reporter*, September 10, 1900; "Liber 150," p. 124 and "Liber 127," p. 359, New York City Hall of Records.

59. *Harlem Library Bulletin*, I (September 1902), 4–6, I (July 1903), n.p.; *The New York Times*, November 3, 1913, February 21, June 8, 1914.

60. *Record and Guide*, LXXII (October 3, 1903), 574; Cahan, *Rise of David Levinsky*, p. 191.

61. *The Harlem Local Reporter*, May 10, 1893; *Record and Guide*, LXXII (August 29, 1903), 373.

62. Elmer Rice, "A New York Childhood," *The New Yorker*, IV (September 22, 1928), 36–40.

63. Konrad Bercovici, "The Black Blocks of Manhattan," *Harper's Monthly Magazine*, CXLIX (October 1924), 615.

64. "The district north of 125th Street has suffered most severely from inaccessibility." *Record and Guide*, XLVII (January 10, 1891).

65. *The Harlem Local Reporter*, July 5, 1893.

66. *Ibid.*, July 13, 1895.

67. "There is every reason to believe that the rapid transit railway will have the effect of reserving the better part of Manhattan Island as far north as Harlem . . . for elevator flats, costly dwellings, and business buildings. . . ." *Record and Guide*, LXV (February 24, 1900), 317; LXXV (June 25, 1905),

370. "Harlemites are naturally more interested in rapid transit than any others in the city. . . ." *The Harlem Local Reporter,* January 25, 1893.

68. *Harlem Life,* XV (October 28, 1899), 3, XVI (February 13, 1900), 6.

69. See, for example, *New York Daily Tribune,* August 26, 1900.

70. *The New York Age,* June 11, 1914.

71. *Record and Guide,* LXXIV (October 1, 1904), 667.

72. "Interview with John E. Nail" (WPA Research Paper, Schomburg Collection).

73. *Record and Guide,* LXXIV (October 31, 1903), 775.

74. *Ibid.,* LXXV (January 14, 1905), 287; James Weldon Johnson, "The Making of Harlem," *Survey Graphic,* VI (March 1925), 635.

75. *The New York Age,* June 11, 1914.

NOTES TO CHAPTER 7

1. *Real Estate Record and Builders' Guide,* LXXV (January 14, 1905), 58.

2. John M. Royall in *The New York Age,* June 11, 1914; *Harlem Magazine,* III (October 1914), 24.

3. *The New York Age,* June 11, 1914.

4. Wilfred R. Bain, "Negro Real Estate Brokers" (WPA research paper, Schomburg Collection), p. 1.

5. Obituary in *The New York Age,* October 22, 1908.

6. Clement Richardson, editor, *The National Cyclopedia of the Colored Race* (Montgomery, Alabama, 1919), I, 258.

7. From letterhead on Payton's stationery. See Philip A. Payton, Jr., to Emmett J. Scott, August 3, 1906. Booker T. Washington Papers, Library of Congress, Box 4.

8. *The New York Age,* December 5, 1912; Booker T. Washington, *The Negro in Business* (Boston, 1907), pp. 197–205.

9. *Record and Guide,* LXXI (January 31, 1902), 316.

10. Washington, *The Negro in Business,* pp. 197–205.

11. See photograph in E. F. Dycoff, "A Negro City in New York," *The Outlook,* CVIII (December 23, 1914), 951.

12. Charles W. Anderson to Booker T. Washington, January 5, 1910. Washington Papers, Box 49.

13. When Booker T. Washington bought a controlling interest in the *Age* in 1907, Moore was made editor. August Meier, "Booker T. Washington and the Negro Press," *Journal of Negro History,* XXXVIII (January 1953), 67–90.

14. *The New York Age,* December 28, 1905.

15. Underlined in original. Philip A. Payton, Jr., to Emmett J. Scott, August 3, 1906. Washington Papers, Box 4.

16. *The New York Age,* November 15, 1906.

17. *Ibid.,* December 5, 1912.

18. Bain, "Negro Real Estate Brokers," p. 2; Richardson, *National Cyclopedia,* p. 258; Arthur J. Gary, "Housing and Sanitary Conditions of Negroes in Harlem" (WPA research paper, Schomburg Collection), p. 1.

19. Charles W. Anderson to Emmett J. Scott, April 1, 1910. Washington Papers, Box 49.

20. Philip A. Payton, Jr., to Emmett J. Scott, January 16, 1914. Washington Papers, Box 12.

21. "Certificate of Incorporation of the Afro-American Realty Company Filed and Recorded June 15, 1904." New York City Hall of Records.

22. Wilbur Young, "Sketch of James C. Thomas" (WPA research paper,

Schomburg Collection); *The New York Age,* April 21, 1910.

23. Reverend Dr. Adam Clayton Powell, Sr., *Against the Tide: An Autobiography* (New York, 1938).

24. Robert S. Dixon, "Education of the Negro in the City of New York, 1853–1900" (M.A. thesis, City College, 1935), p. 52.

25. "A Slave Boy Now a Professor," *Success,* April 8, 1899.

26. Young, "Sketch of James C. Thomas"; Washington, *The Negro in Business,* pp. 104–109.

27. Biographical sketch of Garner in *The New York Age,* September 21, 1905; W. E. B. DuBois, "The Segregated Negro World," *The World Tomorrow,* VI (May 1923), 136–138.

28. See stationery of Afro-American Realty Company with names of directors in Fred R. Moore to Emmett J. Scott, May 31, 1906. Washington Papers, Box 33.

29. The Afro-American Realty Company, *Prospectus* (New York, 1904), p. 7. Original in New York City Hall of Records.

30. E. F. Dycoff, "A Negro City in New York," 949–950; *The New York Age,* December 21, 1905; L. B. Bryan, "Negro Real Estate in New York" (WPA research paper, Schomburg Collection), pp. 2–3.

31. See *The New York Age* in 1905 and 1906 for advertisements.

32. *Prospectus,* pp. 3–7.

33. Fred R. Moore to Emmett J. Scott, December 27, 1905. Washington Papers, Box 29.

34. Fred R. Moore to Emmett J. Scott, September 21, 1905. *Ibid.,* Box 29.

35. This estimate, probably a conservative one, is derived from advertisements which appeared in the Negro press under Payton's name and scattered references in the Washington Papers.

36. Fred R. Moore to Emmett J. Scott, December 12, 1906. Washington Papers, Box 33.

37. Wilford H. Smith to Emmett J. Scott, May 8, 1906. *Ibid.,* Box 5.

38. Wilford H. Smith to Booker T. Washington, May 17, 1906. *Ibid.,* Box 5. Moore also thought of resigning with Smith and advised Scott to join them. Fred R. Moore to Emmett J. Scott, December 27, 1905. *Ibid.,* Box 29.

39. Charles J. Crowder vs. Afro-American Realty Company, a domestic corporation, and Philip A. Payton, Jr. Original in New York City Hall of Records.

40. Papers on Appeal from Order Vacating Order of Arrest. *Ibid.*

41. Crowder vs. Afro-American Realty Company, *passim; The New York Age,* January 31, February 7, 1907, November 19, 1908.

42. See Scott's prodding in Emmett J. Scott to Philip A. Payton, Jr., June 11, 1907; and Moore's reply, Fred R. Moore to Emmett J. Scott, no date. Washington Papers, Box 36.

43. Fred R. Moore to Emmett J. Scott, September 21, 1907. *Ibid.,* Box 36.

44. Underlined in original. Philip A. Payton, Jr., to Emmett J. Scott, August 3, 1906. *Ibid.,* Box 4.

45. Fred R. Moore to Emmett J. Scott, November 26, 1907. *Ibid.,* Box 36.

46. Melvin J. Chisum to Booker T. Washington, February 5, 1907. *Ibid.,* Box 6. Payton was interviewed during the course of the trial and declared: "The whole affair is a spite action brought against me by the former counsel of our company and several dissatisfied stockholders. . . ." *The New York Age,* January 31, February 7, 1907.

47. *The New York Age,* February 7, 1907.

48. Fred R. Moore to Emmett J. Scott, November 26, 1907. Washington Papers, Box 36.

49. *Ibid.*

50. Fred R. Moore to Emmett J. Scott, November 11, 1907. *Ibid.*, Box 36.

51. *Idem.* "I sincerely hope that a way out may be found. Payton can't borrow. . . ." Fred R. Moore to Booker T. Washington. *Ibid.*, Box 36.

52. Fred R. Moore to Emmett J. Scott, November 11, 1907; Booker T. Washington to Fred R. Moore, December 16, 1907. *Ibid.*, Box 36.

53. Fred E. Moore to Emmett J. Scott, November 26, 1907. *Ibid.*, Box 36.

54. Booker T. Washington to Fred R. Moore, December 16, 1907; Fred R. Moore to Booker T. Washington, December 23, 1907. *Ibid.*, Box 36.

55. The houses at 40, 42 and 44 West One Hundred and Thirty-fifth Street, the place where Payton and the Hudson Realty Company clashed in 1904, were advertised by a white corporation, Manheimer Brothers, in 1908. *The New York Age,* December 3, 1908.

56. "The company is allowed to lapse without one single word of explanation to the public or the stockholders. . . ." Draft of letter from Emmett J. Scott to Philip A. Payton, Jr., and Fred R. Moore, July 1908? Washington Papers, Box 41.

57. "Payton is out of the city. I shall take up your letter with him as soon as he returns—will see that a statement is issued if I have to do it myself. . . . Will send it to you as soon as prepared." Fred R. Moore to Emmett J. Scott, August 1, 1908. *Ibid.*, Box 41.

58. Fred R. Moore to Emmett J. Scott, October 19, 1908. *Ibid.*, Box 41.

59. *The New York Age,* July 30, 1908.

60. Richardson, *National Cyclopedia,* I, 258.

61. The houses that Payton controlled and their exact locations are derived from advertisements which appeared in *The New York Age* over a number of years.

NOTES TO CHAPTER 8

1. National League on Urban Conditions Among Negroes, *Housing Conditions Among Negroes in Harlem, New York City* (New York, 1915), p. 7. Hereafter cited as *Housing Conditions.*

2. Robert C. Weaver has pointed this out on a national scale in *The Negro Ghetto* (New York, 1948), *passim; The New York Times,* November 5, 1922.

3. The Independence Day Association of Harlem, *Celebration, 1886* (New York, 1887), p. 30.

4. At least five restrictive covenants were filed. See Section 7, Liber 127, pp. 365–368; Liber 128, pp. 145–150; Liber 151, pp. 134–146; Liber 152, pp. 297–301; Liber 159, pp. 7–15 at the New York City Hall of Records. The racial proviso in one agreement was also printed in *The Crisis,* IV (September 1912), 222.

5. *The New York Age,* June 8, December 4, 1911; *The Crisis,* III (January 1912), 99.

6. *Harlem Magazine,* II (February 1914), 21.

7. "Harlem Property Owners Discuss Negro Problem," *Harlem Home News,* April 7, 1911, July 31, August 28, 1913.

8. "Heart of Harlem Now Invaded by Negroes," "Harlem's Black Belt Is a Growing Menace," "Black Invaders Capture White Flat in 121st Street," *ibid.,* July 28, August 25, 1911, July 24, 1913.

9. *Ibid.,* June 2, June 23, August 25, September 22, 29, 1911.

10. *Ibid.,* April 7, 1911.

11. *Ibid.,* June 19, 1913; *The New York Times,* June 28, 1915; *Harlem Magazine,* II (February 1914), 24, II (April 1914), 25–28, II (August 1913),

17, 20, II (October 1913), 15, III (June 1914), 24; *The New York Age*, April 25, 1912.

12. *The New York Age*, October 3, 1912.

13. *Ibid.*, December 26, 1912, March 27, 1920; *Harlem Home News*, April 7, 1911.

14. *The New York Age*, June 11, 1914.

15. The theater was to be on One Hundred and Twenty-ninth Street and Lenox Avenue and the opponents argued that One Hundred and Thirtieth Street should be the permanent Negro-white dividing line. *The Crisis*, IX (February 1915), 12.

16. *The New York Age*, August 29, November 14, 1912, January 9, 1913.

17. *Ibid.*, August 14, 1913, August 20, 1921.

18. *Ibid.*, February 12, 1914.

19. *The New York Times* quoted in *The New York Age*, July 11, 1912; Section 7, Liber 184, p. 449; Richard J. Latimer, "History of St. James Presbyterian Church, New York City" (WPA research paper, Schomburg Collection); *The Crisis*, XXXIII (September 1927), 232.

20. *The New York Age*, February 6, 20, 1913, June 25, 1915, August 10, 1916, June 21, 1919, February 19, 1921; James Weldon Johnson, *Black Manhattan* (New York, 1930), p. 172.

21. ". . . Various parties have been purchasing different parcels of property in and about One hundred and thirty-seventh Street . . . and have leased or rented them to negro tenants for the purpose of compelling adjoining . . . owners to purchase the same to protect their holdings. . . ." Section 7, Liber 128, p. 145.

22. *Harlem Magazine*, III (July 1914), 24.

23. "Property Owners' Work Begun," *Harlem Magazine*, III (July 1914), 186.

24. Even Negro realtor John E. Nail advised whites against "panic selling": "If a Negro family gets in a house in your block . . . don't run away," he said. *The Crisis*, V (November 1912), 12.

25. *Housing Conditions*, pp. 13–14; *Harlem Magazine*, II (February 1914), 21; Meyer Jarmulowsky, "The Housing Problem of Negro Tenants from the Owner's Point of View," *The New York Age*, December 26, 1912.

26. Harlem Board of Commerce, *Harlem Survey* (New York, 1917?), p. 15.

27. Section 7, Liber 128, p. 146.

28. *The Crisis*, VII (February 1914), 175.

29. New York Urban League, "Twenty-Four Hundred Negro Families in Harlem: An Interpretation of the Living Conditions of Small Wage Earners" (typescript, Schomburg Collection, 1927), p. 7.

30. *The New York Age*, March 27, 1920.

31. George Edmund Haynes, "Conditions Among Negroes in the Cities," *The Annals*, XLIX (September 1913), 110; The President's Conference on Home Building and Home Ownership, *Report of the Committee on Negro Housing* (Washington, D.C., 1932), p. 25.

32. *The New York Age*, March 30, 1911.

33. *Ibid.*, November 22, 1906.

34. *Housing Conditions*, p. 8.

35. "Altogether, it is a healthful location." Seymour Paul, "A Group of Virginia Negroes in New York City" (M.A. thesis, Columbia University, 1912), pp. 20–21; *The New York Age*, June 27, 1912.

36. *Housing Conditions*, p. 16.

37. "The Negroes in Harlem . . . pay a much larger proportion of their income for rent than is paid by Negroes in . . . other cities. . . ." *Ibid.*, p. 17.

38. *Ibid.*, p. 29.

39. "Twenty-four Hundred Negro Families in Harlem," pp. 15–16.

40. Myrtle Evangeline Pollard, "Harlem As Is: The Negro Business and Economic Community. . . ." (M.A. thesis, City College, 1937), I, 172.

41. "Wealthy Negroes," *The New York Times*, July 14, 1895.

42. *The Messenger*, VI (August 1924), 255.

43. Ernest Jasper Hopper, "A Northern Negro Group" (M.A. thesis, Columbia University, 1912), pp. 40 ff.

44. *The New York Age*, May 12, 1934.

45. Robert Zachariah Johnstone, "The Negro in New York—His Social Attainments and Prospects" (M.A. thesis, Columbia University, 1911), p. 48.

46. "Eating places are springing up like mushrooms in Harlem." *The New York Age*, April 21, 1910, January 30, 1913.

47. Hopper, "A Northern Negro Group," pp. 17–18.

48. "Fifteen years ago a great stream of Negroes migrated from Chelsea to Harlem in search of better housing conditions." Charles William Nelson, "Social Activities of the Negro in Chelsea District, New York City" (M.A. thesis, Columbia University, 1921), pp. 4–7. "Downtown areas are being depleted of better classes." Reverend Ray Freeman Jenney, "A Sociological Study of a New York City Parish" (M.A. thesis, Columbia University, 1921), pp. 2–3. Norman L. Holmes, "Columbus Hill: The Story of a Negro Community," *Opportunity*, I (February 1923), 10–11; City and Suburban Homes Company, *Annual Report, 1930–1931* (New York, 1931), p. 8; Woofter, *Negro Problems in Cities* (New York, 1928), p. 101.

49. *The New York Age*, August 1, 1907, January 10, 1920; *The New York Times*, December 4, 1918.

50. George W. Hodges, *Touchstones of Methodism* (New York, 1947), pp. 50–62; *The New York Age*, March 30, 1911, February 6, March 17, 1923; *The New York Times*, March 17, 1923.

51. *The New York Age*, August 10, 1911.

52. Harold Cooke Phillips, "The Social Significance of Negro Churches in Harlem" (M.A. thesis, Columbia University, 1922), *passim*. By 1926 there were 140 Negro churches in Harlem. Ira De Augustine Reid, "Let Us Prey!" *Opportunity*, IV (September 1926), 274–278. In 1930, Harlem had 163 Negro churches. Greater New York Federation of Churches, *The Negro Churches of Manhattan* (New York, 1930), p. 19.

53. Lassalle Best, "Brief History of Seventh-Day Adventist Church Among Negroes in New York" (WPA research paper, Schomburg Collection), pp. 1–2; Ellen Terry, "Catholic Activities Among Negroes in New York City" (WPA research paper, Schomburg Collection), pp. 2–4; "The Reminiscences of Reverend George Barry Ford" (Oral History Research Office, Columbia University, 1956), pp. 2–3; *The New York Age*, November 3, 1910, June 13, October 12, 1912; *The Crisis*, IX (February 1915), 165.

54. Reverend Dr. Adam Clayton Powell, Sr., *Against the Tide: An Autobiography* (New York, 1938), pp. 67–70.

55. *The New York Age*, May 14, 1914.

56. *The New York Freeman*, April 17, 1886.

57. *The New York Age*, December 20, 1919, November 13, 1920.

58. *Ibid.*, March 30, 1911.

59. The Reverend Dr. Bishop's purchases can be traced, house-by-house and lot-by-lot, by checking the city's real estate records. See Section 7, Liber 124, p. 500; Liber 125, p. 470; Liber 127, pp. 15, 44; Liber 143, p. 410; Liber 154, p. 60; Liber 181, p. 487; Liber 184, p. 323.

60. Waring Cuney, "Notes From An Interview with Reverend Shelton Bishop" (WPA research paper, Schomburg Collection).

61. *Harlem Magazine*, II (February 1914), 24.

62. *The New York Age*, June 24, December 9, 1909, January 29, 1914.

63. "Million Dollar Deal," *The New York Age*, March 30, 1911, January 16, 1913; *The Crisis*, II (May 1911), 5.

64. Arthur Gary, "An Account of the Nail and Parker Business Enterprises"; Wilfred R. Bain, "Negro Real Estate Brokers"; Louis B. Bryan, "Brief History of the Chamber of Commerce" (WPA research papers, Schomburg Collection). For a picture of the business partners see *The New York Age*, March 30, 1911, February 10, 1916. "John E. Nail, *The Crisis*, XXIX (March 1925), 220–221; *The President's Conference*, p. 7 and *passim*.

65. Odetta Harper, "Interview with John E. Nail"; Waring Cuney, "Interview with Jerome B. Peterson: An Account of Wealthy Negroes, 1880–1890"; Richard J. Latimer, "History of Negro Saloons" (WPA research papers, Schomburg Collection); "John E. Nail Scrapbook," James Weldon Johnson Collection, Yale University.

66. This quotation is a paraphrase of an interview with John E. Nail in the 1930's. Pollard, "Harlem As Is," pp. 173–174. Also see description of Nail's bar in "Night Clubs," James Weldon Johnson Collection, Yale University.

67. *The New York Age*, February 10, 1916, January 4, 1917, March 15, 1947; "Nail Scrapbook," Johnson Collection, Yale University.

68. *Ibid.*, July 31, 1920; *Housing Conditions*, p. 12; Bureau of the Census, *Fifteenth Census, 1930: Population* (Washington, D.C., 1933), IV, 1130–1134; John E. Nail to James Weldon Johnson, July 9, 1914, Johnson Collection, Yale University.

69. *The Crisis*, XIV (September 1917), 260; *The New York Age*, July 12, 19, 1917. Payton's name was apparently a respected one at his death. Those who bought his interests called themselves the "Payton Apartments Corporation." See also John E. Nail to James Weldon Johnson, July 4, 1914. Johnson Collection, Yale University.

70. *Who's Who in Colored America* (New York, 1927), p. 199. When Terry returned to Virginia for visits he was showered with attention. "It seemed as if every other person I met had something to do with raising me," he said in a speech at Tuskegee. *The New York Age*, January 15, 1914, September 27, November 29, 1917, January 26, 1918. There are Terry letters in the Booker T. Washington Collection.

71. *The New York Age*, September 20, 1917, November 15, 29, December 6, 1919, February 28, March 13, April 3, 1920; Melvin J. Chisum to Booker T. Washington, September 10, 1906. Washington Papers, Library of Congress, Box 2; *The Crisis*, XXIX (March 1925), 220–221.

72. This information comes from items which appeared in *The Crisis* and *The New York Age* over the years. Also see Wilfred R. Bain, "Harlem Branch Y.M.C.A." and "West 137th St. Branch, Y.M.C.A." (WPA research papers, Schomburg Collection); Elbridge L. Adams, "The Negro Music School Settlement," *Southern Workman*, XLIV (March 1915), 161–165.

73. Frederick A. Birmingham, *It Was Fun While It Lasted* (Philadelphia, 1960), *passim*; *The New York Age*, July 20, 1911, January 30, 1926; *The New*

York Times, July 4, 1920, November 5, 1922; "Harlem's Astor Row for Colored Tenants," *ibid.,* November 21, 1920.

74. *Harlem Magazine,* I (April 1913), 22, II (August 1913), 17; "A Carnival and Pageant for Harlem," *ibid.,* III (August 1914), 16; *The New York Times,* November 5, 1922, April 23, 1924.

75. *Harlem Magazine,* XVI (June 1927), 4–5; *The New York Age,* October 4, 1930, June 9, 1934.

76. *Harlem Magazine,* XI (May 1921), XX (April 1931), 3–4; *The New York Age,* June 21, 1930, May 26, 1934.

77. Harlem Board of Commerce, *Harlem Survey* (New York, 1917?), pp. 1–3; *Harlem Magazine,* IV (December 1915), 14, VI (January 1917), 15–16; *The New York Times,* April 16, 1916, June 11, 1927.

78. *Harlem Magazine,* XIV (April 1925), 13, XXI (December 1932), 8; *Uptown New York,* XXII (January–February 1933), 10.

79. E. Franklin Frazier, "Negro Harlem: An Ecological Study," *The American Journal of Sociology,* XLIII (July 1937), 72–88; *The New York Age,* May 26, 1910, June 12, 1913; Reverend Dr. Alexander Walters, *My Life and Work* (New York, 1917), pp. 196–197.

NOTES TO CHAPTER 9

1. The Mayor's Commission on Conditions in Harlem, "The Negro in Harlem: A Report on Social and Economic Conditions Responsible for the Outbreak of March 19, 1935" (unpublished manuscript in La Guardia Papers, Municipal Archives), p. 53. This important study, prepared under the direction of E. Franklin Frazier, will hereafter be cited as "The Negro in Harlem."

2. "The Future Harlem," *The New York Age,* January 10, 1920.

3. John E. Nail to James Weldon Johnson, March 12, 1934, Johnson Collection, Yale University; "Harlem Conditions Called Deplorable," *The New York Times,* September 6, 1927.

4. "Let Them Come," "The New Exodus," *The New York Age,* March 3, 1923, October 16, 1920, September 14, 1929.

5. Bureau of the Census, *Fifteenth Census, 1930: Population* (Washington, D.C., 1933), II, 216–218; Walter Laidlaw, *Population of the City of New York, 1890–1930* (New York, 1932), p. 51.

6. Reverend Dr. Adam Clayton Powell, Sr., *Against the Tide: An Autobiography* (New York, 1938), pp. 70–71.

7. Bureau of the Census, *Fifteenth Census, 1930:* Population (Washington, D.C., 1933), II, 216–218. Note the difference in Chicago's migrant population. In order of greatest numbers Chicago Negroes came from Mississippi, Tennessee, Georgia, Alabama and Louisiana.

8. James Ford, *et al., Slums and Housing: With Special Reference to New York City* (Cambridge, Mass., 1936), II, 311–315.

9. *Ibid.,* p. 317; Bureau of the Census, *Negroes in the United States, 1920–1932* (Washington, D.C., 1935), p. 55.

10. Winfred B. Nathan, *Health Conditions in North Harlem, 1923–1927* (New York, 1932), pp. 13–14.

11. *Harlem Magazine,* XIX (June 1930), 8; Mayor's Commission on City Planning, *East Harlem Community Study* (typescript in New York Public Library, 1937), p. 16.

12. *Slums and Housing,* p. 370; Antonio T. Rivera to La Guardia, June 24, 1935, La Guardia Papers; "Harlem Puerto Ricans Unite to Prove Faith," *The*

New York Times, July 2, August 9, 16, 1926; *Opportunity,* IV (October 1926), 330.

13. *The New York Age,* August 27, 1927, March 31, 1928, January 11, 1930; *The New York Times,* October 19, 1924.

14. *Slums and Housing,* p. 314.

15. The attempt of Negroes to move into Washington Heights, Yonkers and Westchester was opposed in these sections as it had been in Harlem earlier. The Neighborhood Protective Association of Washington Heights urged landlords to sign racially restrictive covenants. Mortgage pressures from financial institutions closed down a Negro housing development in Yonkers. As a result of population pressure, however, another large ghetto was created in the Bedford-Stuyvesant section of Brooklyn in the 1920's. Of the 68,921 Negroes in Brooklyn in 1930, 47,616 lived in what is now called Bedford-Stuyvesant. "Negro Community Near Yonkers Abandoned," *The New York Age,* July 3, 1926, March 24, August 4, 1928, April 19, 26, 1930; *Slums and Housing,* p. 314. For a sketch of Brooklyn's Negro community see Ralph Foster Weld, *Brooklyn Is America* (New York, 1950), pp. 153–173.

16. The President's Conference on Home Building and Home Ownership, *Report of the Committee on Negro Housing* (Washington, D.C., 1931), p. 5.

17. Bureau of the Census, *Fifteenth Census, 1930: Population* (Washington, D.C., 1933), II, 70; Ira De Augustine Reid, *The Negro Immigrant* (New York, 1938), pp. 248–249; Barrington Dunbar, "Factors in the Cultural Background of the American Southern Negro and the British West Indian Negro that Condition their Adjustment in Harlem" (M.A. thesis, Columbia University, 1935), *foreword,* p. 4.

18. Reid, *The Negro Immigrant,* pp. 31–35; Reid, "Negro Immigration to the United States," *Social Forces,* XVI (March 1938), 411–417; W. A. Domingo, "Restricted West Indian Immigration and the American Negro," *Opportunity,* II (October 1924), 298–299.

19. W. A. Domingo, "Gift of the Black Tropics," in Alain Locke, ed., *The New Negro: An Interpretation* (New York, 1925), p. 343.

20. *The New York Age,* July 9, 1924, February 4, 1928; Harry Robinson, "The Negro Immigrant in New York" (WPA research paper, Schomburg Collection), p. 9.

21. Garrie Ward Moore, "A Study of a Group of West Indian Negroes in New York City" (M.A. thesis, Columbia University, 1923), pp. 19–20; Reid, *The Negro Immigrant,* pp. 126–128; *The New York Age,* February 28, 1931, July 29, 1933.

22. "The Negro in New York" (unpublished WPA manuscript, Schomburg Collection), pp. 25–27; Gardner N. Jones, "The Pilgrimage to Freedom" (WPA research paper, Schomburg Collection), p. 25.

23. Reid, *The Negro Immigrant,* p. 159.

24. *Ibid.,* p. 123; "Communists in Harlem," *The New York Age,* September 21, 1929, October 2, 9, 1926, December 24, 1927, January 21, May 12, December 8, 1928, September 21, 1929.

25. Domingo, "Gift of the Black Tropics," p. 347.

26. Robinson, "Negro Immigrant in New York," pp. 21–22; Moore, "West Indian Negroes in New York City," p. 26.

27. "The Reminiscences of George S. Schuyler" (Oral History Research Office, Columbia University, 1960), p. 73.

28. Robinson, "Negro Immigrant in New York," p. 9; "The Negro in New York," p. 25; Moore, "West Indian Negroes in New York City," p. 25; Reid,

The Negro Immigrant, p. 133; *The Messenger,* VII (September 1925), 326, 337–338; *The New York Age,* February 22, 1930; Baltimore *Afro-American,* January 9, 1932.

29. Moore, "West Indian Negroes in New York City," p. 5.

30. Dunbar, "Negro Adjustment in Harlem," pp. 14–25.

31. Reid, *The Negro Immigrant, passim.*

32. *Ibid.,* p. 125; Greater New York Federation of Churches, *Negro Churches in Manhattan* (New York, 1930).

33. Reid, *The Negro Immigrant,* p. 174; Moore, "West Indian Negroes in New York City," pp. 20–25; Dunbar, "Negro Adjustment in Harlem," chap. IV, pp. 22–23.

34. Roi Ottley, *'New World A-Coming': Inside Black America* (New York, 1943), pp. 47–48; Gardner Jones, "The Pilgrimage to Freedom" (WPA research paper, Schomburg Collection), p. 25; Beverly Smith, "Harlem—Negro City," *New York Herald Tribune,* February 14, 1930; Reid, *The Negro Immigrant,* p. 115; *The New York Age,* July 19, 1924, March 17, 1934; Dunbar, "Negro Adjustment in Harlem," chap. III, p. 4; Walter White, "The Paradox of Color," in Alain Locke, ed., *The New Negro: An Interpretation* (New York, 1925), p. 367.

35. *The New York Age,* March 3, 24, April 21, 1928; Domingo, "The Gift of the Black Tropics," p. 344–345; Reid, *The Negro Immigrant,* p. 235.

36. "Harlem Slums," *The Crisis,* XLVIII (December 1941), 378–381; *The New York Age,* January 22, 1927.

37. New York Urban League, "Twenty-four Hundred Negro Families in Harlem: An Interpretation of the Living Conditions of Small Wage Earners" (typescript, Schomburg Collection, 1927), pp. 16–18.

38. *Report of the Committee on Negro Housing,* p. 64.

39. "Appreciation" of prices "came [when owners] remained calm. . . ." T. J. Woofter, *et al., Negro Problems in Cities* (New York, 1928), p. 75. *The New York Times* printed dozens of articles on Harlem's new business prosperity.

40. "Harlem Real Estate Increasing in Value," *Harlem Magazine,* VIII (February 1920), 18b; "Unprecedented Demand for Harlem Real Estate," *ibid.,* X (November 1920), 6; "Revival of Speculative Activity on Harlem's Main Thoroughfare," *The New York Times,* January 18, 1920, July 24, 1921, June 10, 1923, February 13, 1927.

41. "Of all the gouging landlords in Harlem, the colored landlords and agents are the worst, according to the records of the Seventh District Municipal Court." "Race Landlord is Hardest on His Tenants," *The New York Age,* November 20, 1920, June 16, September 22, 1923, May 29, 1926.

42. "The Negro in Harlem," pp. 27–32; *The New York Age,* April 26, 1930.

43. Bureau of the Census, *Fourteenth Census, 1920:* Population (Washington, D.C., 1923), IV, 366–367, 1157–1179; *Fifteenth Census, 1930: Occupations* (Washington, D.C., 1933), 1130–1134; Helen B. Sayre, "Negro Women in Industry," *Opportunity,* II (August 1924), 242–244.

44. *Report of the Committee on Negro Housing,* p. 64; *Negro Problems in Cities,* p. 122.

45. "Twenty-four Hundred Negro Families in Harlem," p. 19; Sidney Axelrad, *Tenements and Tenants: A Study of 1104 Tenement Families* (New York, 1932), p. 15; New York Building and Land Utilization Committee, *Harlem Family Income Survey* (New York, 1935), p. 3; James H. Hubert,

"Harlem—Its Social Problems," *Hospital Social Service*, XXI (January 1930), 44.

46. *Report of the Committee on Negro Housing*, p. vii.

47. William Wilson to La Guardia, October 6, 1944, La Guardia Papers.

48. *Health Conditions in North Harlem*, pp. 16–17; *Fifteenth Census, 1930: Population* (Washington, D.C., 1933), II, 733–734; "The Negro in Harlem," p. 20.

49. ". . . The greatest need is the construction of model tenements. These should consist of one, two, three and four room apartments." "Modern Housing Needs," *The New York Age*, February 12, 1921, January 20, 1923, January 26, 1926, January 29, 1927; "The Negro in Harlem," p. 53; Eugene Kinckle Jones, "Negro Migration in New York State," *Opportunity*, IV (January 1926), 9.

50. Victor R. Daly, "The Housing Crisis in New York City," *The Crisis*, XXXI (December 1920), 61–62.

51. National Urban League, *Housing Conditions Among Negroes, New York City* (New York, 1915), *passim; Ford, et al., Slums and Housing*, p. 338.

52. "Very often it is found that there are two shifts." William Wilson to La Guardia, October 6, 1944, La Guardia Papers; *The New York Age*, March 12, 1921, February 26, 1927; "Along Rainbow Row," *The New York Times*, August 15, 1921, January 27, 1922; "Twenty-four Hundred Negro Families in Harlem," *passim;* Roscoe Conkling Bruce, "The Dunbar Apartment House: An Adventure in Community Building," *The Southern Workman*, LX (October 1931), 418.

53. *New York Herald Tribune*, February 12, 13, 1930.

54. "I promoted a weekly party, to get money to pay rent." "Boisterous rent parties, flooded with moonshine, are a quick and sure resource." "The Reminiscences of Benjamin McLaurin" (Oral History Research Office, Columbia University, 1960), p. 155; *The New York Age*, August 11, 1923, June 21, December 11, 1926; Clyde Vernon Kiser, *Sea Island to City* (New York, 1932), pp. 44–45.

55. Booker T. Washington, *Up from Slavery: An Autobiography* (New York 1959), pp. 122–123. Note the following statement of a recent study: "There are many cases in which migratory workers do not understand or properly use ordinary living facilities, such as toilets, showers, bedding, kitchen appliances, and garbage cans. The result has been unnecessary damage to property and needless expense for repairs." 87th Cong., 1st Sess., *Senate Report 1098* (1961), p. 8.

56. *The New York Age*, August 1, 1912, June 5, 1920, September 16, 1922, July 14, 1928; National Urban League, *Housing Conditions Among Negroes*, pp. 9–10; "The Negro in Harlem," p. 113; Eslanda Goode Robeson, *Paul Robeson: Negro* (London, 1930), p. 46.

57. Woofter, *et al., Negro Problems in Cities*, pp. 79, 84; "The Negro in Harlem," p. 53; Ernest W. Burgess, "Residential Segregation in American Cities," *The Annals*, CXL (November 1928), 105–115; Ford, *et al., Slums and Housing*, p. 749.

58. Owen R. Lovejoy, *The Negro Children of New York* (New York, 1932), p. 15.

59. *The New York Age*, October 28, 1922, January 17, 1925; *Housing Conditions Among Negroes, passim;* "Twenty-four Hundred Negro Families in Harlem," *passim*.

60. "I do not think I need to say that our problem of Harlem is one of the

most serious we have to face." Langdon W. Post (Chairman of New York City Housing Authority) to La Guardia, April 30, 1936, La Guardia Papers. "The Negro families of the West Harlem section have undoubtedly the most serious housing problem in the City." Ford, *et al., Slums and Housing*, p. 326. *The New York Times*, September 16, 1920, October 17, 23, 1921, April 22, 1922, January 17, June 13, 1925; *The New York Age*, February 28, August 8, 1925, January 9, 1926; "Preliminary Report on the Subject of Housing (1935)," La Guardia Papers.

61. "High Cost of Dying," *The New York Age*, February 25, 1928.

62. *Health Conditions in North Harlem, passim; The Negro Children of New York*, p. 22; "Fighting the Ravages of the White Plague Among New York's Negro Population," *Opportunity*, I (January 1923), 23–24; Dr. Louis R. Wright, "Cancer as It Affects Negroes," *ibid.*, VI (June 1928), 169–170, 187; Louis I. Dublin, "The Effect of Health Education on Negro Mortality," *Proceedings of the National Conference on Social·Work, 1924* (Chicago, 1924), 274–279. Hereafter cited as PNCSW.

63. ". . . Syphilitic infection is one of the most fruitful causes of still-births, miscarriages, and early death of infants." New York Association for Improving the Condition of the Poor, *Health Work for Mothers and Children in a Colored Community* (New York, 1924), p. 3; "The Negro's Health Progress During the Last Twenty-five Years," *Weekly Bulletin of the Department of Health*, XV (June 12, 1926), 93–96; *Fifteenth Census, 1930: Population* (Washington, D.C., 1933), II, 959; E. K. Jones, "The Negro's Struggle for Health," *PNCSW, 1923* (Chicago, 1923), 68–72.

64. Adapted from Godea J. Drolet and Louis Werner, "Vital Statistics in the Development of Neighborhood Health Centers in New York City," *Journal of Preventive Medicine*, VI (January 1932), 69.

65. In 1920, 30.3 per cent of white women in the city worked, and 57.9 per cent of colored women were employed. *Fourteenth Census, 1920: Population* (Washington, D.C., 1923), IV, 367. Robert Morse Woodbury, *Causal Factors in Infant Mortality* (Washington, D.C., 1925); L. T. Wright, "Factors Controlling Negro Health," *The Crisis*, XLII (September 1935), 264–265, 280, 284; Mildred Jane Watson, "Infant Mortality in New York City, White and Colored, 1929–1936" (M.A. thesis, Columbia University, 1938); Charles Herbert Garvin, "White Plague and Black Folk," *Opportunity*, VIII (August 1930), 232–235.

66. For "voodoo" and "devil worship" among West Indians see Reid, *The Negro Immigrant*, pp. 48–49, 136–138.

67. ". . . Many [are] bringing with them their simple faith in roots, herbs, home remedies, [and are] imposed upon by unscrupulous venders of worthless . . . remedies " Dr. Peter Marshall Murray, "Harlem's Health," *Hospital Social Service*, XXII (October 1930), 309–313; C. V. Roman, "The Negro's Psychology and His Health," *PNCSW, 1924* (Chicago, 1924), 270–274; *Opportunity*, IV (July 1926), 206–207; *The Crisis*, XLII (August 1935), 243; *The New York Age*, September 23, 1922, February 17, July 21, August 11, 25, 1923, January 6, April 5, 1924, February 21, March 14, 1925, January 18, July 23, 1927.

68. Note the striking similarities between the medical and healing superstitions of urban Negroes in the twentieth century and those of slaves in the early nineteenth century. The following is a description of slave superstition by an ex-slave: "There is much superstition among the slaves. Many of them believe in what they call 'conjuration,' tricking, and witchcraft; and some of

them pretend to understand the art, and say that by it they can prevent their masters from exercising their will over their slaves. Such are often applied to by others, to give them power to prevent their masters from flogging them. The remedy is most generally some kind of bitter root; they are directed to chew it and spit toward their masters. . . . At other times they prepare certain kinds of powders, to sprinkle their masters' dwellings." *Narrative of the Life and Adventures of Henry Bibb, An American Slave, Written by Himself* (New York, 1849), pp. 25–31.

69. Beverly Smith, "Harlem—Negro City," *New York Herald Tribune*, February 11, 1930; Ira De Augustine Reid, "Let Us Prey!" *Opportunity* IV (September 1926), 274–278; Reverend James H. Robinson, *Road Without Turning: An Autobiography* (New York, 1950), 231.

70. *The New York Age*, February 19, 1927; *The New York Times*, September 24, 1919.

71. Zora Neale Hurston, *Dust Tracks on a Road* (Philadelphia, 1942), pp. 279–280.

72. *The New York Age*, January 15, 1927, February 9, 1929, August 23, 1930, August 8, September 19, 1931, July 23, 1932, August 26, 1933, September 1, 1934.

73. "A Wide Open Harlem," *ibid.*, September 2, 1922.

74. Committee of Fourteen, *Annual Reports*, 1914–1930; *The Crisis*, XXXVI (November 1929), 417–418; *The Messenger*, VI (January 1924), 14.

75. Langston Hughes, "Young Prostitute," *The Crisis*, XXVI (August 1923), 162.

76. "Gambling is popular in Harlem, but the big shots of the racket are white." Fiorello La Guardia, "Harlem: Homelike and Hopeful" (unpublished manuscript, La Guardia Papers), p. 9; "A Summary of Vice Conditions in Harlem," Committee of Fourteen, *Annual Report for 1928* (New York, 1929), 31–34; *The New York Times*, February 13, 1922; *The New York Age*, February 28, 1925, May 18, 1929. Although whites seemed to control most of Harlem vice, Virgin Islander Casper Holstein—well-known as a philanthropist and café owner—was reputed to be a head of the numbers racket.

77. "Harlem—The Bettor," *The New York Age*, March 7, 1925, November 6, 20, 1926, June 4, 1927, June 23, 1928; *The New York Times*, June 12, 1922, March 11, 1927; "New York: Utopia Deferred," *The Messenger*, VII (October, November 1925), 344–349, 370.

78. *The New York Age*, September 16, 1922, April 21, 1923; *New York Herald Tribune*, February 13, 1930; *The Messenger*, VI (August 1924) 247, 262.

79. Lovejoy, *The Negro Children of New York*, p. 37; *New York Herald Tribune*, February 12, 1930; Joint Committee on Negro Child Study in New York City, *A Study of Delinquent and Neglected Negro Children Before the New York City Children's Court* (New York, 1927).

80. Jacob Theobald, "Some Facts About P.S. 89, Manhattan," *The New York Age*, January 17, 1920; "Report of Subcommittee on Education," La-Guardia Papers; "The Problem of Education and Recreation," *ibid.*; "The Negro in Harlem," p. 73; Lovejoy, *The Negro Children of New York*, p. 22; *The New York Age*, March 12, 1921.

81. "Results of the Crime and Delinquency Study," La Guardia Papers; *The New York Age*, January 6, February 17, June 23, 1923, June 12, 1926, December 3, 1927, July 28, 1928, January 4, 1930. A white Harlem policeman, at a later date, wrote the following: "Every one of [us] is made to feel like a soldier

in an army of occupation. He is engulfed by an atmosphere of antagonism." *The Crisis*, LII (January 1945), 16–17.

82. Lovejoy, *The Negro Children of New York*, p. 15; "The Negro in Harlem," p. 110; *The New York Age*, February 9, 1929; "The Reminiscences of George S. Schuyler" (Oral History Research Office, Columbia University, 1960), p. 232.

NOTES TO CHAPTER 10

1. Reverend Dr. Adam Clayton Powell, Sr., "The Church and Social Work," *Opportunity*, I (January 1923), 15.

2. Owen R. Lovejoy, *The Negro Children of New York* (New York, 1932), p. 29; Marion Forrester, "Young Folks Sit Up and Take Notice," *Opportunity*, XVI (January 1938), 23; Winfred B. Nathan, *Health Conditions in North Harlem, 1923–1927* (New York, 1932), p. 57.

3. Beverly Smith, "Harlem—Negro City," *New York Herald Tribune*, February 10, 12, 1930.

4. James H. Hubert, "Social Work in New York City," *Opportunity*, IV (March 1926), 102–103; National Urban League, *What You Need, Where to Find It, How to Use It* (New York, 1916).

5. *Opportunity*, I (January 1923), 32; *The New York Times*, June 22, 1920; *The New York Age*, July 2, 1921, July 22, 1922, March 31, 1923, March 27, 1926; *The Crisis*, XXXVI (February 1929), 52.

6. The New York Tuberculosis and Health Association had itself originated as a committee of the Charity Organization Society. Forrester B. Washington, "Health Work for Negro Children," *Proceedings of the National Conference on Social Work, 1925* (Chicago, 1925), 229–230; Henry O. Harding, "Health Opportunities in Harlem," *Opportunity*, IV (December 1926), 386–387.

7. Drs. Peyton F. Anderson and Jerome S. Peterson, "Warring Against Tuberculosis in Harlem," *The Crisis*, XLIV (November 1942), 356–357, 359, 366; *The New York Age*, July 21, 1923, October 1, 1927; *Opportunity*, V (December 1927), 379; Katherine Z. Wells, "Health Education in Harlem," *ibid.*, I (December 1923), 361–363.

8. Louis I. Dublin, "The Effect of Health Education on Negro Mortality," *Proceedings of the National Conference on Social Work, 1924* (Chicago, 1924), 274–279.

9. Peyton and Peterson, "Warring Against Tuberculosis in Harlem," *passim.;* James Ford, *et al.*, *Slums and Housing: With Special Reference to New York City* (Cambridge, Mass., 1936), pp. 334–335.

10. For early nineteenth century examples see Robert Ernst, *Immigrant Life in New York City, 1825–1863* (New York, 1949), *passim*.

11. George R. Arthur, *Life on the Negro Frontier* (New York, 1934), p. 14; Owen R. Lovejoy, *The Negro Children of New York* (New York, 1932), p. 31.

12. Peyton and Peterson, "Warring Against Tuberculosis in Harlem," 359.

13. Elise Johnson McDougald, "The School and its Relation to the Vocational Life of the Negro," *Proceedings of the National Conference of Social Work, 1923* (Chicago, 1923), 415–418; Nathan, *Health Conditions in North Harlem*, p. 11; McDougald, "The Task of Negro Womanhood," in Locke, *The New Negro* (New York, 1925), pp. 369–382.

14. *The New York Age*, September 4, 18, 1920, September 8, 1923, August 8, 1925, December 11, 1926, May 5, 1928; Frank R. Crosswaith, "The Trade

Union Committee for Organizing Negroes," *The Messenger*, VII (August 1925), 296–297, V (July 1923), 758, VII (July 1925), 261.

15. Daisy Cargile Reed, "For Harlem Negro Children," *Opportunity*, VI (August 1928), 246–247; *The New York Age*, May 7, 1927, June 30, 1928, March 28, 1931; *The Crisis*, XXXII (September 1926), 242–243.

16. "The New Philanthropy," *Opportunity*, VIII (January 1929), 5, IV (August 1926), 263; *The New York Age*, May 8, 15, 1926.

17. Ford, *et al.*, *Slums and Housing*, pp. 744–748.

18. Alfred Alexander, "The Housing of Harlem," *The Crisis*, XXXV (October 1928), 333–335, 351–353; Roscoe Conkling Bruce, "The Dunbar Apartment House: An Adventure in Community Building," *The Southern Workman*, LX (October 1931), 417–428.

19. *Architecture*, LIX (January 1929), 5–12; Ford, *et al.*, *Slums and Housing*, p. 745; *The Crisis*, XXXIV (December 1927), 340; Arthur J. Gary, "Interview with Roscoe Conkling Bruce" (WPA research paper, Schomburg Collection).

20. Roscoe Conkling Bruce, "The Idea of Cooperative Housing," in the President's Conference on Home Building and Home Ownership, *Report of the Committee on Negro Housing* (Washington, D.C., 1925), 245–248; *The Crisis*, XXXVI (February 1929), 53; *The New York Age*, January 26, 1929.

21. City and Suburban Homes Company, *First Annual Report, 1896–1897* (New York, 1897), p. 1.

22. T. J. Woofter, *et al.*, *Negro Problems in Cities* (New York, 1928), p. 164; "The Idea of Cooperative Housing," 246.

23. "The Dunbar National Bank," *The Crisis*, XXXV (November 1928), 370–371, 387; *The New York Age*, February 15, 1930.

24. "Mr. Rockefeller Quits Harlem," *The New York Age*, November 5, 1932, February 16, 1935, October 17, December 5, 1936, January 9, 1937, April 23, 30, May 28, 1938.

25. The Mayor's Commission on Conditions in Harlem, "The Negro in Harlem: A Report on Social and Economic Conditions Responsible for the Outbreak of March 19, 1935" (unpublished manuscript in La Guardia Papers, Municipal Archives), pp. 26, 65.

NOTES TO CHAPTER 11

1. *The New York Age*, September 4, 1913, March 27, 1917.

2. Samuel Michelson, "History of the Democratic Party in Harlem, 1916–1932" (WPA research paper, Schomburg Collection), p. 1; *The New York Times*, October 20, 1898, January 12, 1900.

3. *The New York Freeman*, July 3, 1886; Frances Blascoer, *Colored School Children in New York* (New York, 1915), p. 125.

4. *The New York Age*, November 12, 1887; *The New York Globe*, January 6, 20, 1883; Robert Zachariah Johnstone, "The Negro in New York—His Social Attainments and Prospects" (M.A. thesis, Columbia University, 1911), p. 37.

5. Anderson to Washington, November 14, 1914, Washington Papers, Box 75.

6. M. Rothman, "Chief Lee"; Mr. Robinson, "Biography of Edward (Chief) Lee" (WPA research papers, Schomburg Collection).

7. *The New York Age*, May 31, 1890.

8. *The New York Globe*, January 6, 1883.

9. *The Crisis*, XXII (October 1921), 264.

10. "The United Colored Democracy—A Resumé," *The New York State Contender*, October 11, 1929; Waring Cuney, "The United Colored Democracy" (WPA research paper, Schomburg Collection); *The New York Age*, March 16, 1929.

11. John L. Love, "The Potentiality of the Negro Vote, North and West," The American Negro Academy, *Occasional Paper, No. 11* (Washington, D.C., 1905), p. 66.

12. Negroes occasionally supported Democratic presidents in the late nineteenth century but no stable and regular party organization continued its existence beyond election time.

13. "List of New York Negroes Appointed or Elected to Public Office, 1900–1939"; James Gardner, "Brief History of Ferdinand Q. Morton of New York" (WPA research papers, Schomburg Collection); *The Crisis*, XI (February 1916), 167. There is a collection of newspaper clippings on Morton in the biographical files of the Schomburg Collection.

14. There is a folder of newspaper clippings on Anderson's life at the Schomburg Collection. Hereafter cited as "Clippings." Also see biographical sketch in *National Cyclopedia of the Colored Race* (Montgomery, Ala., 1919), I, 447.

15. "Clippings"; *The New York Age*, January 11, April 12, 1890, March 30, 1911.

16. James Weldon Johnson, *Along This Way* (New York, 1933), pp. 218–223.

17. Anderson to Washington, November 14, 1931, Box 64; Washington to Anderson, March 2, 1906, Box 2; Anderson to Washington, April 1, October 7, 1908, Box 38, Washington Papers.

18. "Clippings"; *The New York Age*, March 23, 1918; Colored Citizens of New York, *Testimonial for Charles W. Anderson* (New York, 1915), in James Weldon Johnson Memorial Collection, Yale University.

19. Anderson to Washington, January 30, 1908; Anderson to Scott, March 18, 1908, Washington Papers, Box 38.

20. "Anderson confirmed, heartiest congratulations." P. B. S. Pinchback to Washington, March 14, 1904, *ibid.*, Box 4.

21. Anderson to Washington, October 31, 1904, Box 1; May 27, October 21, 1907, Box 35; Anderson to Emmett J. Scott, October 23, 1915, Box 68; Scott to Anderson, December 7, 1915, *ibid.*, Box 9.

22. Washington to Anderson, July 22, 1904, Box 1; Anderson to Washington, May 27, October 21, November 19, 1907, Box 35; March 24, 1908, *ibid.*, Box 38.

23. Anderson to Washington, September 10, October 30, 1911, *ibid.*, Box 15.

24. Anderson to Scott, November 1, 1905, *ibid.*, Box 27.

25. Anderson to Washington or Scott, September 25, 27, 1905, Box 27; June 1, 1906, Box 2; February 9, 16, 21, July 25, 1907, Box 35; April 23, 1908, Box 38; July 17, 20, December 14, 1909, Box 43; January 11, July 7, August 1, November 4, 1910, Box 49; October 24, 1913, Box 64; Scott to Anderson, November 5, 1913, *ibid.*, Box 64.

26. "Our people throughout the country, who admire and respect you, and are looking to you, would be very greatly encouraged if you could see your way clear to appoint two or three of our representative colored men to re-

sponsible places. . . ." Washington to Whitman, August 24, 1915; Anderson to Washington, September 22, 1915, *ibid.*, Box 9.

27. Anderson to Washington, July 5, 1911, *ibid.*, Box 52. "The Reminiscences of Samuel J. Battle" (Oral History Research Office, Columbia University, 1960), pp. 38–39.

28. Anderson to Washington, March 17, 1915, Box 68; Anderson to Scott, July 31, 1915, Box 9; October 23, November 16, 1915, Box 68, Washington Papers. For a list of Wilson's removals in New York City see *The New York Age*, March 25, 1915.

29. W. E. B. DuBois to Oswald Garrison Villard, March 31, 1915, Johnson Collection.

30. Anderson to Scott, October 14, November 2, 1915, Box 9, Washington Papers.

31. "Clippings"; *The Crisis*, XIX (April 1920), 340; *Opportunity*, I (May 1923), 25; *The New York Age*, November 6, 1920, April 26, 1924, September 12, October 17, 1925; *The New York Times*, September 14, 1920. I have used the term "ward" in this chapter for stylistic reasons, although there were technically no wards in New York City.

32. *The New York Age*, April 10, July 4, 1920, May 31, April 7, 1923, September 19, 26, 1925; Anderson to Scott, October 14, 1915, Box 9, Washington Papers.

33. "Clippings"; Johnson, *Along This Way*, pp. 218–223; *The New York Age*, April 22, 1933, July 14, 1934, January 19, 1935, February 5, 19, 1938.

34. John Albert Morsell, "The Political Behavior of Negroes in New York City" (Ph.D. dissertation, Columbia University, 1951), p. 25. Unfortunately, much of this study of Negro politics is questionable because the author uses statistics for Harlem's Assembly Districts as a basis for analysis—and these AD's included many white voters.

35. *Ibid.*, pp. 32–35; *The New York Age*, November 9, 1889, October 3, 1910, June 14, 1930.

36. As Assembly District returns include white voters it is necessary to analyze election district statistics in order to obtain accurate information on Negro voting in the 1920's. Election districts usually cover one or two blocks —and their boundaries within the Assembly District are often changed. In the 1920's election districts in the Nineteenth and Twenty-first AD's were altered five or six times. It was not possible, therefore, to get a uniform set of returns from the *same* districts throughout the decade. I selected eight ED's from the center of the ghetto at each election (from slides of districts in the New York City Municipal Library), however, and these sections were *at least* 90 per cent Negro at all times. All the following returns, and those in the body of the chapter, are drawn from the *Official Canvass of Votes* published annually in *The City Record* and the *Annual Reports of the Board of Elections:*

NEGRO PRESIDENTIAL VOTE, IN PERCENTAGES, 1920–1936

	Republican	Democratic	Other
1920	97.6	2.4	—
1924	85.3	11.5	3.2
1928	70.8	29.2	—
1932	47.4	50.3	2.3
1936	14.4	84.6	1.0

37.   NEGRO GUBERNATORIAL VOTE, 1920–1932

	Republican	Democratic	Other
1920	62.2	37.8	—
1922	34.5	65.5	—
1924	63.7	36.3	—
1926	58.6	41.4	—
1928	68.8	31.2	—
1930	53.1	45.7	1.2
1932	42.3	55.7	2.0

38.   NEGRO MAYORALTY VOTE, 1921–1932

	Republican	Democratic	Other
1921	26.4	73.6	—
1925	52.9	46.1	—
1929	56.5	37.4	6.1
1932	42.4	55.5	2.1

39. James Weldon Johnson, "The Gentleman's Agreement and the Negro Vote," *The Crisis*, XXVIII (October 1924), 264.

40. Hylan to Joseph S. McLane, October 26, 1921; Hylan to George E. Taylor, July 27, 1925; *Daily Star*, July 12, 1921, all in Hylan Papers, Municipal Archives.

41. Morton to John F. Smith, secretary to mayor, March 26, 1924, January 12, 1925, Hylan Papers; "N.A.A.C.P. Efforts for Negroes in New York City Hospitals," memorandum in La Guardia Papers.

42. This information is derived from clippings, speeches and memoranda in the Hylan and Walker Papers. Hylan was apparently the first mayor to keep a separate file on Harlem and Negroes. Also see J. S. McLane to Hylan, October 25, 1921; Hylan to Hon. John M. Parker, December 23, 1922; John R. Shillady to Hylan, February 21, 1918; Hylan to James H. Hubert, no date; *The New York Times*, November 20, 1923, August 19, Septmeber 4, 1925; *The New York Age*, December 4, 1926, February 4, 1928.

43. "The Life Work of Edward Austin Johnson," *The Crisis*, XL (April 1933), 81.

44. *Who's Who in Colored America*, 1927 (New York, 1927), pp. 105–106; Johnson, *Light Ahead for the Negro* (New York, 1904), pp. 17–19, 80, 88, 118.

45. *The New York Age*, August 23, 1924.

46. *The New York Age*, September 7, 1929, June 14, 1930.

47. *General Laws of the State of New York, 1918* (New York, 1919), pp. 44–45, 319.

48. Arthur W. Little, *From Harlem to the Rhine: The Story of New York's Colored Volunteers* (New York, 1936); Emmett J. Scott, *Scott's Official History of the American Negro in the World War* (Chicago, 1919), chap. 15; Addie W. Hunton and Kathryn M. Johnson, *Two Colored Women with the American Expeditionary Forces* (Brooklyn, 1920), pp. 69–72; *The New York Age*, May 25, 1918, February 14, 1919, February 28, 1931.

49. *General Laws of New York, 1930* (New York, 1931), pp. 215–216; *Opportunity*, VIII (December 1930), 380; *The New York Times*, July 30,

1917; *The New York Age,* February 14, May 22, 1920, December 18, 1926, January 18, April 19, May 3, 17, September 27, 1930; Francis E. Rivers, "Negro Judges in Harlem," *The Crisis,* XXXVII (November 1930), 377, 393.

50. *Who's Who in Colored America, 1938–1940* (Brooklyn, 1940), p. 383; "Ferdinand Q. Morton," *The Crisis,* XXX (July 1925), 115–116; *The New York Times,* April 3, 1925; *The New York Age,* May 28, 1927, February 8, 22, August 2, October 11, 18, 25, 1930, March 16, April 6, 13, 1935, August 6, 1938; Harlem Committee on Political Facts, *Whom the Gods Would Destroy—They First Make Newspaper Managers!* (New York, 1933?), p. 2, in La Guardia Papers; Edgar T. Rouzeau, "Harlem Seeks Political Leadership," *The Crisis,* XLII (September 1935), 268, 274.

51. *The New York Age,* April 5, 1924, August 7, 14, September 25, October 9, 1926.

52. *Ibid.,* July 24, September 11, 1926, September 8, November 3, 1928, August 19, 1929.

53. Abraham Grenthal, "Grenthal Advocates Extension of Rent Laws," *Harlem Magazine,* XIV (December 1925), 11, 22; *The New York Age,* February 9, August 16, 1924, January 3, 10, 1925, March 27, 1926, February 26, April 9, 16, June 24, 1927.

54. Public letter of Moore to Grenthal, *The New York Age,* July 25, 1929, March 3, 24, 1928.

55. "Grenthal on His Political Deathbed," *Advance* in *ibid.,* August 17, 1929; "Why Grenthal Should Go," February 25, August 18, 1928, March 9, June 22, August 31, 1929.

56. *Ibid.,* June 22, July 6, August 24, 31, September 14, 21, 1929.

57. "The Reminiscences of Martin C. Ansorge" (Oral History Research Office, Columbia University, 1949), *passim;* "The Reminiscences of Samuel S. Koenig" (Oral History Research Office, Columbia University, 1950), *passim; Official Canvass of the Votes* for returns in congressional elections.

58. "Notes of D. Macon Webster for Speech at Protest Meeting" (manuscript in Schomburg Collection).

NOTES TO EPILOGUE

1. HARYOU, *Youth in the Ghetto: A Study of the Consequences of Powerlessness and a Blueprint for Change* (New York, 1964); Columbia University Bureau of Applied Social Research, *A Harlem Almanac* (New York, 1964).

2. *The New York Age,* January 1, 1927.

3. Carl Van Doren, "The Negro Renaissance," *The Century Magazine,* III (March 1926), 637.

4. Gilbert Seldes, "The Negro's Songs," *The Dial,* LXXX (March 1926), 247–251.

5. As the Garvey movement has been discussed at length and competently in a number of sources I have avoided any lengthy analysis of it here. See: E. David Cronin, *Black Moses: The Story of Marcus Garvey and the Universal Negro Improvement Association* (Madison, Wisc., 1955); E. U. Essien-Udom, *Black Nationalism: A Search for an Identity in America* (Chicago, 1962); Essien-Udom, "The Nationalist Movements of Harlem," *Freedomways,* III (Summer 1963), 335–342; Richard B. Moore, "Africa-Conscious Harlem," *ibid.,* 315–334.

6. Langston Hughes, *The Big Sea* (New York, 1940), p. 240.

7. *Ibid.,* p. 81.

8. "The Reminiscences of George S. Schuyler" (Oral History Research Office, Columbia University, 1960), p. 208.

9. Claude McKay, *A Long Way From Home* (New York, 1937), chap. XXVII, *passim,* and *Home to Harlem* (1927); "Harlem: Mecca of the New Negro," *The Survey,* LIII (March 1, 1925), 629–724; Alain Locke, ed., *The New Negro: An Interpretation* (New York, 1925).

10. Alain Locke and Lothrop Stoddard, "Should the Negro Be Encouraged to Cultural Equality?" *The Forum,* LXXVIII (October 1927), 508; Locke, "Enter the New Negro," *The Survey,* LIII (March 1, 1925), 631–634; Locke, "Negro Contributions to America," *The World Tomorrow,* XII (June 1929), 255–257.

11. *The New York Times,* January 26, 1925.

12. James Weldon Johnson to Carl Van Vechten, envelope dated March 6, 1927. James Weldon Johnson Collection of Negro Arts and Letters, Yale University.

13. Hughes, *The Big Sea,* p. 228.

14. Johnson to Van Vechten, envelope dated March 6, 1927. Johnson Collection.

15. See, for example, Robert W. Bagnall, "The Divine Right of Race," *The World Tomorrow,* VI (May 1923), 149; Herbert A. Miller, "Democracy and Diversity," *ibid.,* VII (June 1924), 190–191; Robert E. Park, *The Immigrant Press and Its Control* (New York, 1922); Horace M. Kallen, *Culture and Democracy in the United States: Studies in the Group Psychology of the American Peoples* (New York, 1924).

16. "The Reminiscences of Bruno Lasker" (Oral History Research Office, Columbia University, 1957), p. 242 and chap. IX.

17. *The Annals of the American Academy of Political and Social Science,* CXL (November 1928).

18. *The World Tomorrow,* VI (May 1923) and IX (April 1926).

19. Laurence Buermeyer, "The Negro Spirituals and American Art," *Opportunity,* IV (May 1926), 158–159, 167; Harry Alan Potamkin, "African Sculpture," *ibid.,* VI (May 1929), 139–140, 147; James Weldon Johnson to Carl Van Vechten, envelope dated February 16, 1931, Johnson Collection; A. M. Chirgwin, "The Vogue of the Negro Spiritual," *The Edinburgh Review,* CCXLVII (January 1928), 57–74; Darius Milhaud, "The Jazz Band and Negro Music," *The Living Age,* CCCXXIII (October 18, 1924), 169–173.

20. Langston Hughes, "The Negro Artist and the Racial Mountain," *The Nation,* CXXII (June 23, 1926), 693; Charles S. Johnson, "The Balance Sheet: Debits and Credits in Negro-White Relations," *The World Tomorrow,* XI (January 1928), 13–16; Ernest Boyd, "Readers and Writers," *The Independent,* CXVI (January 16, 1926), 77; George Jean Nathan, "The Wail of the Negro," *The American Mercury,* XVIII (September 1929), 114–116; Claude McKay to James Weldon Johnson, April 30, 1928, Johnson Collection.

21. "The New White Man," *The World Tomorrow,* X (March 1927), 124–125.

22. Rudolph Fisher, "The Caucasian Storms Harlem," *The American Mercury,* XI (May 1927), 396.

23. Eugene Gordon, "The Negro's Inhibitions," *The American Mercury,* XIII (February 1928), 159–165; Clement Wood, "Hosea Before the Rotary Club," *The World Tomorrow,* VIII (July 1925), 209–210; Herman Keyserling, "What the Negro Means to America," *The Atlantic Monthly,* CXLIV (October 1929), 444–447; Joseph Wood Krutch, "Black Ecstasy," *The Nation,*

CXXV (October 26, 1927), 456–458; George S. Schuyler, "Blessed Are the Sons of Ham," *ibid.*, CXXIV (March 23, 1927), 313–315; "Black Voices," *ibid.*, CXIX (September 17, 1924), 278.

24. George Chester Morse, "The Fictitious Negro," *The Outlook and Independent*, CLII (August 21, 1929), 648.

25. McKay, *A Long Way From Home*, p. 322.

26. Beverly Smith, "Harlem—Negro City," *New York Herald Tribune*, February 10, 1930.

27. "The Reminiscences of Carl Van Vechten" (Oral History Research Office, Columbia University, 1960), p. 196.

28. *The Crisis*, XXXIX (September 1932), 293; *The New York Age*, August 6, 1927. For a survey of Harlem cabarets see Archie Seale, "The Rise of Harlem as an Amusement Center," *The New York Age*, November 2, 1935; and obituary of Moe Gale, owner of the Savoy Ballroom, *The New York Times*, September 3, 1964.

29. "The Slumming Hostess," *The New York Age*, November 6, 1926.

30. "Giving Harlem a Bad Name," "Is Harlem to be a Chinatown?", "In the Negro Cabarets," "Nordic Invasion of Harlem," *ibid.*, September 5, 1922, October 27, 1923, July 23, August 6, 1927; Committee of Fourteen, *Annual Report for 1926* (New York, 1927), pp. 31–32; and *Annual Report for 1928* (New York, 1929), pp. 31–34.

31. "The Reminiscences of Carl Van Vechten," p. 205.

32. Carl Van Vechten, *Nigger Heaven* (New York, 1926), *passim.*

33. "The Negro in Art—A Symposium," *The Crisis*, XXXI (March 1926), 219–220; *ibid.*, XXXIV (September 1927), 248.

34. Chester T. Crowell, "The World's Largest Negro City," *The Saturday Evening Post*, CXCVIII (August 8, 1925), 9; "The Caucasian Storms Harlem," 398.

35. "I am to be hostess at the Dark Tower Sunday Night April 21st, and I thought probably you and your friends would like to be present. . . ." A'Lelia Walker to Max Ewing, April 18, 1929. Ewing Collection, Yale University. A'Lelia Walker was the daughter and heir of Madame C. J. Walker. Eric R. Walrond, "The Black City," *The Messenger*, VI (January 1924), 14; *The New York Age*, October 29, 1927.

36. Paul Oliver, *Bessie Smith* (New York, 1959), p. 45. Ermine Kahn, "Lenox Avenue—Saturday Night," *The World Tomorrow*, VIII (November 1925), 337.

37. *The New York Age*, November 27, 1926.

38. Hubert H. Harrison, "The Significance of Lulu Bell," *Opportunity*, IV (July 1926), 228–229: *The Crisis*, XXXII (May 1926), 34; "Black Harlem Dramatized," *The Literary Digest*, C (March 16, 1929), 21–24; James Weldon Johnson to Carl Van Vechten, envelope dated April 4, 1930, Johnson Collection.

39. Quoted in Diana N. Lockard, "The Negro on the Stage in the Nineteen Twenties" (M.A. thesis, Columbia University, 1960), p. 38.

40. "The Fictitious Negro," 649; Charles S. Johnson, "Public Opinion and the Negro," *Proceedings of National Conference in Social Work, 1923* (Chicago, 1924), 497–502.

41. The most glaring exception to this generalization is Langston Hughes.

42. "Harlem had been too long the nighttime playground of New York. . . ." Alain Locke, "La Guardia and Harlem," manuscript in La Guardia Papers. Locke, "Harlem: Dark Weather-Vane," *Survey Graphic*, XXV (Au-

NOTES TO *THE ENDURING GHETTO*

1. As there is relatively little published data on antebellum Negro life in New York City I have included some comparative material from Philadelphia in these years.

2. Florence M. Cromien, *Negroes in the City of New York: Their Number and Proportion in Relation to the Total Population, 1790–1960* (New York, n.d.); *Census of the State of New York for 1875* (Albany, 1877), p. 29.

3. Gilbert Osofsky, *Harlem: The Making of a Ghetto* (New York, 1966), *passim*.

4. *A Statistical Inquiry into the Condition of the People of Colour of the City and Districts of Philadelphia* (Philadelphia, 1849), p. 37. Early nineteenth-century writers assumed that all-Negro neighborhoods were the dominant pattern in the North. Such folk designations as "Stagg Town," "Little Africa" and "Nigger Hill" referred respectively to New York's, Boston's and Cincinnati's black sections in the Jacksonian period. Leon F. Litwack, *North of Slavery: The Negro in the Free States, 1790–1860* (Chicago, 1961), pp. 168–170.

5. *A Statistical Inquiry*, pp. 5–8; Pennsylvania Society for Promoting the Abolition of Slavery, *The Present State and Condition of the Free People of Color of the City of Philadelphia* (Philadelphia, 1838), pp. 3–6.

6. Rhoda G. Freeman, "The Free Negro in New York City in the Era Before the Civil War" (Ph.D. dissertation, Columbia University, 1966), p. 440; *Census of the State of New York for 1875* (Albany, 1877), pp. 116–119; *Eleventh Census, 1890; Population* (Washington, D.C., 1894), I, 564.

7. Robert C. Weaver, *The Negro Ghetto* (New York, 1948), pp. 4–6.

8. *Report of the Committee of Merchants for the Relief of the Colored People, Suffering from the Late Riots in the City of New York* (New York, 1863), *passim*; Osofsky, *Harlem*, pp. 46–52.

9. Charles Dickens, *American Notes for General Circulation* (London, 1850), pp. 61–63.

10. James Ford, *et al.*, *Slums and Housing: With Special Reference to New York City* (Cambridge, Mass., 1936), II, 673; New York *Daily Tribune*, June 5, 1850; Robert Ernst, *Immigrant Life in New York City, 1825–1863* (New York, 1949), p. 39.

11. *Report of the Committee of Merchants for the Relief of the Colored People*, pp. 7, 22.

12. *A Statistical Inquiry*, pp. 37–38.

13. The Federation of Churches and Christian Workers in New York City, *Second Sociological Canvass* (New York, 1897), p. 85; *The New York Freeman*, March 7, 1885.

14. Reid, "Twenty-four Hundred Negro Families in Harlem: An Interpretation of the Living Conditions of Small Wage-Earners" (typescript, Schomburg

Collection, 1927); Frazier, "The Negro in Harlem: A Report on Social and Economic Conditions Responsible for the Outbreak of March 19, 1935" (typescript, La Guardia Papers).

15. Joan Gordon, *The Poor of Harlem: Social Functioning of the Underclass* (New York, 1965), p. 142. On the harmful psychological implications of inadequate housing for present ghetto residents see *ibid., pp.* 33–48, and the unpublished study, "A Report of Attitudes of Negroes in Various Cities" (summer, 1966), prepared for the Senate Subcommittee on Executive Reorganization.

16. Michael Harrington popularized the findings of the United States Civil Rights Commission. The commission concluded that the entire American population could fit into three New York City boroughs if its density were equal to some of Harlem's worst blocks. Harrington, *The Other America: Poverty in the United States* (New York, 1962), p. 62.

17. James Freeman Clarke, "Condition of the Free Colored People of the United States," *The Christian Examiner,* LXI (March, 1859), p. 258.

18. See, for example, William Wells Brown, *The Black Man: His Antecedents, His Genius, and His Achievements* (Boston, 1863); and Martin Robison Delany, *The Condition, Elevation and Destiny of the Colored People of the United States* (Philadelphia, 1852).

19. Charles H. Wesley, *Negro Labor in the United States, 1850–1925* (New York, 1927), pp. 29–68, 142.

20. *Census of the State of New York for 1855* (Albany, 1857), pp. 8 and *passim.;* Ernst, *Immigrant Life,* pp. 214–217; Franklin B. Hough, *Statistics of the Population of the City and County of New York . . .* (New York, 1866), p. 240; Leon F. Litwack, *North of Slavery: The Negro in the Free States, 1790–1860* (Chicago, 1961), pp. 153–186.

21. *Report of the Committee of Merchants for the Relief of the Colored People,* p. 7; Pennsylvania Society, *The Present State and Condition,* p. 21.

22. Samuel Ringgold Ward, *Autobiography of A Fugitive Negro: His Anti-Slavery Labours in the United States, Canada, and England* (London, 1855), pp. 29–30. "Less than two-thirds of those [Negroes] who have trades follow them. A few of the remainder pursue other avocations from choice, but the greater number are compelled to abandon their trades on account of the unrelenting prejudice against their color." Benjamin C. Bacon, *Statistics of the Colored Population of Philadelphia* (Philadelphia, 1859), p. 15. When a register of Negro craftsmen was compiled in 1838 it was considered necessary to mark the names of those *presently* following their trades with asterisks. *Register of Trades of the Colored People in the City of Philadelphia* (Philadelphia, 1838).

23. Nathan Glazer and Daniel Patrick Moynihan, *Beyond the Melting Pot* (Cambridge, Mass., 1963), p. 230; Arthur M. Ross and Herbert Hill, eds., *Employment, Race and Poverty* (New York, 1967), pp. 40–47.

24. Osofsky, *Harlem, passim;* Kenneth Clark, *Dark Ghetto* (New York, 1965), pp. 34–41, 55–62; Harlem Youth Opportunities Unlimited, *Youth in the Ghetto* (New York, 1964), pp. 245–290; Glazer and Moynihan, *Beyond the Melting Pot,* pp. 29–44.

25. Charles C. Andrews, *The History of the New-York African Free-Schools from their Establishment in 1787 . . .* (New York, 1830), p. 56.

26. *The Liberator,* June 23, 1854.

27. Florence E. Gibson, *The Attitudes of the New York Irish Toward State and National Affairs, 1848–1892* (New York, 1951), p. 66; *The New York Age,*

January 26, 1905; W. L. Bulkley, "Race Prejudice As Viewed from an Economic Standpoint," *Proceedings of the National Negro Conference*, 1909 (New York, 1909), 94.

28. "Black-White," *Newsweek*, LXVIII (August 22, 1966); William Brink and Louis Harris, *Black and White: A Study of U.S. Racial Attitudes Today* (New York, 1967), p. 136.

29. Quoted in Charles M. Wiltse, ed., *David Walker's Appeal . . . to the Coloured Citizens of the World* (New York, 1965), p. 57.

30. James McCune Smith, "The German Invasion," *Anglo-African Magazine*, I (February, 1859), 50.

31. *The Liberator*, November 10, 1854.

32. Quoted in Freeman, "The Free Negro in New York City," p. 131.

33. Quoted in Benjamin Quarles, *Frederick Douglass* (Washington, D.C., 1948), p. 217.

34. *Malcolm X Speaks* (New York, 1965), pp. 25–26.

35. See, for example, the changing responses to poll-taker samples since the 1930's presented in Mildred Schwartz, *Trends in White Attitudes Toward Negroes* (Chicago, 1967).

36. Frazier, "The Negro in Harlem," pp. 27–32.

37. Andrews, *New-York African Free-Schools*, pp. 85–103.

38. *Ibid.*, pp. 57–58; *A Statistical Inquiry*, p. 22. The American Moral Reform Society, the Black Garrisonian organization in Philadelphia, repeatedly spoke of the problem of black children who didn't attend school because of inadequate clothing, and also of their struggles to raise some money to outfit such youngsters. *Pennsylvania Freeman*.

39. Andrews, *New-York African Free-Schools*, p. 117.

40. "A Word to Our People," *Anglo-African Magazine*, I (September, 1859), 293. "What Are We Doing?," *The Mirror of Liberty*, I (July, 1838), 4.

41. 'When we call to mind, that . . . there are at least 1200 children between the ages of 5 and 20, of whom no account is received, the greater part of whom are probably growing up in idle and vicious habits; it is clear that this is one of the most painful facts brought to light by this inquiry." *A Statistical Inquiry*, p. 22. See also Andrews, *New-York African Free-Schools*, pp. 113–127; Bacon, *Statistics of the Colored Population*, pp. 8–12; Pennsylvania Society, *The Present State and Condition*, p. 19.

42. Charles B. Ray, "Communication from the New York Society for the Promotion of Education Among Colored Children," *Anglo-African Magazine*, I (July, 1859), pp. 222–224. "The managers of the different Anti-Slavery Societies in this city will permit us to suggest whether they might not employ a portion of their time and influence . . . in doing something for the cause of education among those of the despised caste." David Ruggles, "African Free Schools in the City of New York," *The Mirror of Liberty*, I (January, 1839), 32–33.

43. Andrews, *New-York African Free-Schools*, pp. 117–118. The emphasis is Andrews'.

44. *Proceedings of the New England Anti-Slavery Convention: Held in Boston*, May 24, 25, 26, 1836 (Boston, 1836), pp. 48–49. "The colored people are almost altogether deprived of the opportunity of bringing up their children to mechanical employments, to commercial business, or other more lucrative occupations, whereby so many of our white laborers are enabled to rise above the drudgery in which they commence their . . . life." Pennsylvania Society, *The Present State and Condition*, p. 12.

45. M. H. Freeman, "The Educational Wants of the Free Colored Population," *Anglo-African Magazine*, I (April, 1859), 116.

46. Bulkley, "The School as a Social Center," *Charities*, IV (October 7, 1905), 76.

47. Frances Blascoer, *Colored School Children in New York* (New York, 1915), p. 18.

48. New York State, *Second Report of the New York State Temporary Commission on the Condition of the Colored Urban Population* (Albany, 1939), p. 108.

49. *The Autobiography of Malcolm X* (New York, 1966), p. 36.

50. *Youth in the Ghetto*, pp. 161–244.

51. James Bryant Conant, *Slums and Suburbs: A Commentary on Schools in Metropolitan Areas* (New York, 1961), p. 18.

52. The phrase is by Elliott Shapiro, a former Harlem educator. See Nat Hentoff, *Our Children Are Dying* (New York, 1966).

53. Clark, *Dark Ghetto, passim.*

Index

Gilbert Osofsky taught American history at the University of Illinois, Chicago, before his death in 1974. He was among the first historians to recognize the usefulness of folkloristic sources in writing the history of peoples who have left no written record, an approach that informed his book *Puttin' on Ole Massa*. He also wrote *The Burden of Race*.

ELEPHANT PAPERBACKS

American History and American Studies
Stephen Vincent Benét, *John Brown's Body*, EL10
Henry W. Berger, ed., *A William Appleman Williams Reader*, EL126
Andrew Bergman, *We're in the Money*, EL124
Paul Boyer, ed., *Reagan as President*, EL117
Robert V. Bruce, *1877: Year of Violence*, EL102
George Dangerfield, *The Era of Good Feelings*, EL110
Clarence Darrow, *Verdicts Out of Court*, EL2
Floyd Dell, *Intellectual Vagabondage*, EL13
Elisha P. Douglass, *Rebels and Democrats*, EL108
Theodore Draper, *The Roots of American Communism*, EL105
Joseph Epstein, *Ambition*, EL7
Lloyd C. Gardner, *Spheres of Influence*, EL131
Paul W. Glad, *McKinley, Bryan, and the People*, EL119
Daniel Horowitz, *The Morality of Spending*, EL122
Kenneth T. Jackson, *The Ku Klux Klan in the City, 1915–1930*, EL123
Edward Chase Kirkland, *Dream and Thought in the Business Community,*
    1860–1900, EL114
Herbert S Klein, *Slavery in the Americas*, EL103
Aileen S. Kraditor, *Means and Ends in American Abolitionism*, EL111
Leonard W. Levy, *Jefferson and Civil Liberties: The Darker Side*, EL107
Seymour J. Mandelbaum, *Boss Tweed's New York*, EL112
Thomas J. McCormick, *China Market*, EL115
Walter Millis, *The Martial Spirit*, EL104
Nicolaus Mills, ed., *Culture in an Age of Money*, EL302
Nicolaus Mills, *Like a Holy Crusade*, EL129
Roderick Nash, *The Nervous Generation*, EL113
William L. O'Neill, ed., *Echoes of Revolt: The Masses, 1911–1917*, EL5
Gilbert Osofsky, *Harlem: The Making of a Ghetto*, EL133
Edward Pessen, *Losing Our Souls*, EL132
Glenn Porter and Harold C. Livesay, *Merchants and Manufacturers*, EL106
John Prados, *Presidents' Secret Wars*, EL134
Edward Reynolds, *Stand the Storm*, EL128
Edward A. Shils, *The Torment of Secrecy*, EL303
Geoffrey S. Smith, *To Save a Nation*, EL125
Bernard Sternsher, ed., *Hitting Home: The Great Depression in Town and*
    Country, EL109
Athan Theoharis, *From the Secret Files of J. Edgar Hoover*, EL127
Nicholas von Hoffman, *We Are the People Our Parents Warned Us Against,*
    EL301
Norman Ware, *The Industrial Worker, 1840–1860*, EL116
Tom Wicker, *JFK and LBJ: The Influence of Personality upon Politics*, EL120
Robert H. Wiebe, *Businessmen and Reform*, EL101
T. Harry Williams, *McClellan, Sherman and Grant*, EL121
Miles Wolff, *Lunch at the 5 & 10*, EL118
Randall B. Woods and Howard Jones, *Dawning of the Cold War*, EL130

ELEPHANT PAPERBACKS

Literature and Letters

Stephen Vincent Benét, *John Brown's Body*, EL10
Isaiah Berlin, *The Hedgehog and the Fox*, EL21
Robert Brustein, *Dumbocracy in America*, EL421
Anthony Burgess, *Shakespeare*, EL27
Philip Callow, *Son and Lover: The Young D. H. Lawrence*, EL14
James Gould Cozzens, *Castaway*, EL6
James Gould Cozzens, *Men and Brethren*, EL3
Clarence Darrow, *Verdicts Out of Court*, EL2
Floyd Dell, *Intellectual Vagabondage*, EL13
Theodore Dreiser, *Best Short Stories*, EL1
Joseph Epstein, *Ambition*, EL7
André Gide, *Madeleine*, EL8
Gerald Graff, *Literature Against Itself*, EL35
John Gross, *The Rise and Fall of the Man of Letters*, EL18
Irving Howe, *William Faulkner*, EL15
Aldous Huxley, *After Many a Summer Dies the Swan*, EL20
Aldous Huxley, *Ape and Essence*, EL19
Aldous Huxley, *Collected Short Stories*, EL17
Sinclair Lewis, *Selected Short Stories*, EL9
William L. O'Neill, ed., *Echoes of Revolt: The Masses, 1911–1917*, EL5
Budd Schulberg, *The Harder They Fall*, EL36
Ramón J. Sender, *Seven Red Sundays*, EL11
Peter Shaw, *Recovering American Literature*, EL34
Wilfrid Sheed, *Office Politics*, EL4
Tess Slesinger, *On Being Told That Her Second Husband Has Taken His First
    Lover, and Other Stories*, EL12
B. Traven, *The Bridge in the Jungle*, EL28
B. Traven, *The Carreta*, EL25
B. Traven, *The Cotton-Pickers*, EL32
B. Traven, *General from the Jungle*, EL33
B. Traven, *Government*, EL23
B. Traven, *March to the Montería*, EL26
B. Traven, *The Night Visitor and Other Stories*, EL24
B. Traven, *The Rebellion of the Hanged*, EL29
Anthony Trollope, *Trollope the Traveller*, EL31
Rex Warner, *The Aerodrome*, EL22
Thomas Wolfe, *The Hills Beyond*, EL16

ELEPHANT PAPERBACKS

European and World History
Mark Frankland, *The Patriots' Revolution*, EL201
Lloyd C. Gardner, *Spheres of Influence*, EL131
Gertrude Himmelfarb, *Darwin and the Darwinian Revolution*, EL207
Gertrude Himmelfarb, *Victorian Minds*, EL205
Thomas A. Idinopulos, *Jerusalem*, EL204
Ronnie S. Landau, *The Nazi Holocaust*, EL203
Clive Ponting, *1940: Myth and Reality*, EL202
Scott Shane, *Dismantling Utopia*, EL206

Theatre and Drama
Robert Brustein, *Dumbocracy in America*, EL421
Robert Brustein, *Reimagining American Theatre*, EL410
Robert Brustein, *The Theatre of Revolt*, EL407
Irina and Igor Levin, *Working on the Play and the Role*, EL411
Plays for Performance:
  Aristophanes, *Lysistrata*, EL405
  Pierre Augustin de Beaumarchais, *The Marriage of Figaro*, EL418
  Anton Chekhov, *The Cherry Orchard*, EL420
  Anton Chekhov, *The Seagull*, EL407
  Euripides, *The Bacchae*, EL419
  Euripides, *Iphigenia in Aulis*, EL423
  Euripides, *Iphigenia Among the Taurians*, EL424
  Georges Feydeau, *Paradise Hotel*, EL403
  Henrik Ibsen, *Ghosts*, EL401
  Henrik Ibsen, *Hedda Gabler*, EL413
  Henrik Ibsen, *The Master Builder*, EL417
  Henrik Ibsen, *When We Dead Awaken*, EL408
  Heinrich von Kleist, *The Prince of Homburg*, EL402
  Christopher Marlowe, *Doctor Faustus*, EL404
  The Mysteries: Creation, EL412
  The Mysteries: The Passion, EL414
  Sophocles, *Electra*, EL415
  August Strindberg, *The Father*, EL406
  August Strindberg, *Miss Julie*, EL422